Frommer's®

Japanese Phrasebook & Culture Guide

1st Edition

WILEY
Wiley Publishing, Inc.

Published by:

Wiley Publishing, Inc.
111 River St.
Hoboken, NJ 07030-5774

FM:

ISBN-13: 978-0-470-22858-6

Editor: Jennifer Polland
Japanese Editor: Yoji Yamaguchi & Tomoko Yamaguchi
Series Editor: Maureen Clarke
Travel Tips & Culture Guide: Chester Dawson & Miyuke Dawson
Illustrations: Maciek Albrecht
Photo Editor: Richard H. Fox

Translation, Copyediting, Proofreading, Production, and Layout by:
Lingo Systems, 15115 SW Sequoia Pkwy, Ste 200, Portland, OR 97224

For information on our other products and services or to obtain technical support, please contact our Customer Care Department within the U.S. at 800/762-2974, outside the U.S. at 317/572-3993 or fax 317/572-4002.
Wiley also publishes its books in a variety of electronic formats. Some content that appears in print may not be available in electronic formats.

Manufactured in the United States of America

5 4 3 2 1

Contents

An Invitation to the Reader

In researching this book, we discovered many wonderful saying and terms useful to travelers in Japanese. We're sure you'll find others. Please tell us about them so we can share them with your fellow travelers in upcoming editions. If you were disappointed by any aspect of this book, we'd like to know that, too. Please write to:

Frommer's Japanese Phrasebook & Culture Guide, 1st Edition
Wiley Publishing, Inc.
111 River St. • Hoboken, NJ 07030-5774

An Additional Note

The packer, editors and publisher cannot be held responsible for the experience of readers while traveling. Your safety is important to us, however, so we encourage you to stay alert and aware of your surroundings. Keep a close eye on cameras, purses, and wallets, all favorite targets of thieves and pickpockets.

Frommers.com

Now that you have the language for a great trip, visit our website at **www.frommers.com** for travel information on more than 3,600 destinations. With features updated regularly, we give you instant access to the most current trip-planning information available. At Frommers.com, you'll also find the best prices on airfares, accommodations, and car rentals—and you can even book travel online through our travel booking partners. At Frommers.com, you'll also find:

- Online updates to our most popular guidebooks
- Vacation sweepstakes and contest giveaways
- Newsletter highlighting the hottest travel trends
- Online travel message boards with featured travel discussions

INTRODUCTION: HOW TO USE THIS BOOK

More than 120 million people in Japan are native speakers of Japanese. Many more speak it as a second language. Japanese is a cosmopolitan tongue, heavily influenced by Chinese and receptive to foreign "loan" words (see page 18). Conversely, many Japanese words have entered the English language lexicon, in the worlds of technology, art, food, and more.

Although more and more Japanese—especially younger people and people in larger cities—can speak at least some English, most locals will appreciate your attempt, no matter how limited, to speak their language. Being able to communicate in this rich and historic tongue will prove both challenging and rewarding, and it will also help you to make new friends.

Our intention is not to teach you Japanese; a class or audio program is better for that. Our aim is to provide a portable travel tool that's easy to use on the spot. The problem with most phrasebooks is that you practically have to memorize the contents before you know where to look for a term you need pronto. This phrasebook is designed for fingertip referencing, so you can whip it out and find the words you need fast.

Part of this book organizes terms by chapters, like the sections in a Frommer's guide—getting a room, getting a good meal, etc. Within those divisions, we tried to organize phrases intuitively, according to how frequently most readers would be likely to use them. The most unique feature, however, is the two-way PhraseFinder dictionary in the back, which lists words as well as phrases organized by keyword. Say a taxi driver hands you ¥500 instead of ¥1,000. Look up "change" in the dictionary and discover how to say: "Sorry, but this isn't the correct change."

To make best use of the content, we recommend that you spend some time flipping through it before you depart for your trip. Familiarize yourself with the order of the chapters. Read through the pronunciations section in chapter one and practice pronouncing random phrases throughout the book. Try looking up a few phrases in the phrasebook section as well as in the dictionary. This way, you'll be able to locate phrases faster and speak them more clearly when you need them.

What will make this book most practical? What will make it easiest to use? These are the questions we asked ourselves repeatedly as we assembled these travel terms. Our immediate goal was to create a phrasebook as indispensable as your passport. Our far-ranging goal, of course, is to enrich your experience of travel. And with that, we wish you ***Ganbatte kudasai!*** (Have a great trip!)

CHAPTER ONE

SURVIVAL JAPANESE

If you tire of toting around this phrasebook, tear out this chapter. You should be able to navigate your destination with only the terms found in the next 32 pages.

BASIC GREETINGS

For a full list of greetings, see p114.

Hello.	こんにちは。 *kon nichi wa.*
How are you?	お元気ですか？ *ogenki desu ka.*
I'm fine, thanks.	元気です、どうもありがとう。 *genki desu, dōmo arigatō.*
And you?	あなたもお元気ですか？ *anata mo ogenki desu ka.*
My name is ____.	____と申します。 *____ to mōshimasu.*
And yours?	あなたのお名前は？ *anata no onamae wa.*
It's a pleasure to meet you.	あなたにお会いできて嬉しいです。 *anata ni oai dekite ureshii desu.*
Please.	どうぞ。 *dōzo.*
Thank you.	どうもありがとう。 *dōmo arigatō.*
Yes.	はい。 *hai.*
No.	いいえ。 *iie.*
Okay.	オッケイ。 *okkei.*

No problem.	いいですよ。 *ii desu yo.*
I'm sorry, I don't understand.	すみませんが、わかりません。 *sumi masen ga, wakari masen.*
Would you speak slower please?	もう少しゆっくり話していただけませんか？ *mō sukoshi yukkuri hanashite itadake masen ka.*
Would you speak louder please?	もう少し大きな声で話していただけませんか？ *mō sukoshi ōkina koe de hanashite itadake masen ka.*
Do you speak English?	英語を話しますか？ *eigo o hanashi masu ka.*
Do you speak any other languages?	他の国の言葉も話しますか？ *hoka no kuni no kotoba mo hanashi masu ka.*
I speak ____ better than Japanese.	日本語よりも____の方が うまく話せます。 *nihongo yori mo ____ no hō ga umaku hanase masu.*
Would you please repeat that?	もう一度繰り返していただけますか？ *mō ichido kuri kaeshite itadake masu ka.*
Would you point that out in this dictionary?	この辞書でそれを指していただけませんか？ *kono jisho de sore o sashite itadake masen ka.*

THE KEY QUESTIONS

With the right hand gestures, you can get a lot of mileage from the following list of single-word questions and answers.

Who?	誰？ *dare.*
What?	何？ *nani.*

When?	いつ? *itsu.*
Where?	どこ? *doko.*
To where?	どこへ? *doko e.*
Why?	なぜ? *naze.*
How?	どう? *dō.*
Which?	どれ? *dore.*
How many? / How much?	いくつ / いくら、どれくらい? *ikutsu/ ikura, dorekurai*

THE ANSWERS: WHO

For full coverage of pronouns, see p23.

I	私 *watashi*
you	あなた *anata*
him	彼 *kare*
her	彼女 *kanojo*
us	私たち *watashi tachi*
them	彼ら *karera*

THE ANSWERS: WHEN

For full coverage of time-related terms, see p13.

now	今 *ima*
later	後 *ato*

in a minute	すぐ *sugu*
today	今日 *kyō*
tomorrow	明日 *ashita*
yesterday	昨日 *kinō*
in a week	1週間後に *isshū kango ni*
next week	来週 *raishū*
last week	先週 *senshū*
next month	来月 *raigetsu*
At ____	____に *ni*
ten o'clock this morning.	今朝の10時 *kesa no jū ji*
two o'clock this afternoon.	今日の午後2時 *kyō no gogo ni ji*
seven o'clock this evening.	今晩7時 *konban shichi ji*

For full coverage of numbers, see p6.

THE ANSWERS: WHERE

here	ここ *koko*
there	そこ *soko*
near	近い *chikai*
closer	もっと近い *motto chikai*

closest	一番近い *ichiban chikai*
far	遠い *tōi*
farther	もっと遠い *motto tōi*
farthest	一番遠い *ichiban tōi*
across from	の向かい *no mukai*
next to	の隣 *no tonari*
behind	の後ろ *no ushiro*
straight ahead	ここをまっすぐ *koko o massugu*
left	左 *hidari*
right	右 *migi*
up	上 *ue*
down	下 *shita*
lower	もっと低い *motto hikui*
higher	もっと高い *motto takai*
forward	前 *mae*
back	後ろ *ushiro*
around	周り *mawari*

across the street	この道の向こう側 *kono michi no mukō gawa*
down the street	この道(の先) *kono michi (no saki)*
on the corner	角に *kado ni*
kitty-corner	斜め向かい *naname mukai*
____ blocks from here	ここから____目の角 *koko kara ____ me no kado*

For a full list of numbers used for blocks, see the section "Generic Inanimate Objects" on p. 11.

THE ANSWERS: WHICH

this one	これ *kore*
that (that one, close by)	それ *sore*
(that one, in the distance)	あれ *are*
these	これら *korera*
those (those there, close by)	それら *sorera*

NUMBERS & COUNTING

one	一 *ichi*	six	六 *roku*
two	二 *ni*	seven	七 *shichi/nana*
three	三 *san*	eight	八 *hachi*
four	四 *shi/yo/yon*	nine	九 *kyū*
five	五 *go*	ten	十 *jū*

eleven	十一 *jū ichi*	thirty	三十 *san jū*
twelve	十二 *jū ni*	forty	四十 *yon jū*
thirteen	十三 *jū san*	fifty	五十 *go jū*
fourteen	十四 *jū shi*	sixty	六十 *roku jū*
fifteen	十五 *jū go*	seventy	七十 *nana jū*
sixteen	十六 *jū roku*	eighty	八十 *hachi jū*
seventeen	十七 *jū shichi/jū nana*	ninety	九十 *kyū jū*
eighteen	十八 *jū hachi*	one hundred	百 *hyaku*
nineteen	十九 *jū kyū*	two hundred	二百 *ni hyaku*
twenty	二十 *ni jū*	one thousand	千 *sen*
twenty-one	二十一 *ni jū ichi*		

COUNTERS

When counting objects, you need to use a counter. In English you simply put a number before the item you wish to count and pluralize it; for example, one car, two cars, etc. In Japanese, which has no plural form, you instead use a separate counter word that varies depending on the type of thing you wish to count. The item being counted comes first, followed by the number, which is in turn followed by the counter word. The counters vary according to the type, shape, or size of each item. The pronunciation of either the number or the counter will vary in some instances. Note that the numbers four (*shi*), seven (*shichi*) and nine (*kyu*) can also be *yon*, *nana*, and *ku* when counting objects.

PEOPLE

one person	一人 *hitori*
two people	二人 *futari*
three people	三人 *sannin*
four people	四人 *yonin*
five people	五人 *gonin*
six people	六人 *rokunin*
seven people	七人 *shichinin / nananin*
eight people	八人 *hachinin*
nine people	九人 *kyūnin or kunin*
ten people	十人 *jyūnin*

MECHANICAL OBJECTS

one mechanical object	一台 *ichidai*
two mechanical objects	二台 *nidai*
three mechanical objects	三台 *sandai*
four mechanical objects	四台 *yondai*
five mechanical objects	五台 *godai*
six mechanical objects	六台 *rokudai*
seven mechanical objects	七台 *nanadai*

eight mechanical objects	八台 *hachidai*
nine mechanical objects	九台 *kyūdai*
ten mechanical objects	十台 *jyūdai*

FLAT OBJECTS

one flat object	一枚 *ichimai*
two flat objects	二枚 *nimai*
three flat objects	三枚 *sanmai*
four flat objects	四枚 *yonmai*
five flat objects	五枚 *gomai*
six flat objects	六枚 *rokumai*
seven flat objects	七枚 *nanamai*
eight flat objects	八枚 *hachimai*
nine flat objects	九枚 *kyūmai*
ten flat objects	十枚 *jyūmai*

SMALL ANIMALS

one small animal	一匹 *ippiki*
two small animals	二匹 *nihiki*
three small animals	三匹 *sanbiki*

four small animals	四匹 *yonhiki*
five small animals	五匹 *gohiki*
six small animals	六匹 *roppiki*
seven small animals	七匹 *nanahiki*
eight small animals	八匹 *happiki*
nine small animals	九匹 *kyūhiki*
ten small animals	十匹 *jyuppiki*

CYLINDRICAL OBJECTS

one cylindrical object	一本 *ippon*
two cylindrical objects	二本 *nihon*
three cylindrical objects	三本 *sanbon*
four cylindrical objects	四本 *yonhon*
five cylindrical objects	五本 *gohon*
six cylindrical objects	六本 *roppon*
seven cylindrical objects	七本 *nanahon*
eight cylindrical objects	八本 *hachihon/happon*
nine cylindrical objects	九本 *kyūhon*
ten cylindrical objects	十本 *jyuppon*

GENERIC INANIMATE OBJECTS

one object	一つ *hitotsu*
two objects	二つ *futatsu*
three objects	三つ *mittsu*
four objects	四つ *yottsu*
five objects	五つ *itsutsu*
six objects	六つ *muttsu*
seven objects	七つ *nanatsu*
eight objects	八つ *yattsu*
nine objects	九つ *kokonotsu*
ten objects	十 *tō*

MEASUREMENTS

Measurements will usually be metric, though you may need a few American measurement terms.

inch	インチ *inchi*
foot	フット *futto*
mile	マイル *mairu*
millimeter	ミリメートル *miri mētoru*
centimeter	センチメートル *senchi mētoru*
meter	メートル *mētoru*

A Little Tip

Double consonants in Japanese are *kk, ss, tt* and *pp.* They are pronounced as a single consonant preceded by a short pause. For example:

bikkuri *(bee-(k)-koo-ree)*
zasshi *(zah-(s)-shee)*
matte! *(mah-(t)-teh!)*
ippai *(ee-(p)-pah-ee)*

kilometer	キロメートル *kiro mētoru*
hectare	ヘクタール *hekutāru*
squared	平方形の *hēhōkei no*
short	短い *mijikai*
long	長い *nagai*

VOLUME

milliliters	ミリリットル *miri rittoru*
liter	リットル *rittoru*
kilo	キロ *kiro*
ounce	オンス *onsu*
cup	カップ *kappu*
pint	パイント *painto*
quart	クォート *kuōto*

gallon	ガロン *garon*

QUANTITY

some	いくつか(の) / いくらか(の) *ikutsuka (no) / ikuraka (no)*
none	少しもない、全くない *sukoshi mo nai, mattaku nai*
all	すべて / すべての *subete/subete no*
many / much	沢山の *takusan no*
a little bit (can be used for quantity or for time)	少し *sukoshi*
dozen	ダース *dāsu*

SIZE

small	小さい *chiisai*
the smallest (literally "the most small")	もっとも小さい *mottomo chiisai*
medium	中位の *chū kurai no*
big	大きい *ōkii*
fat	太った *futotta*
wide	広い *hiroi*
narrow	狭い *semai*

TIME

Time in Japanese is referred to, literally, by the hour. What time is it? translates literally as "What hour is it?"

For full coverage of number terms, see p6.

HOURS OF THE DAY

What time is it?	今何時ですか? *ima nan ji desu ka.*
At what time?	何時に? *nan ji ni.*
For how long?	どのくらい? *dono kurai.*
It's one o'clock.	1時です。 *ichi ji desu.*
It's two o'clock.	2時です。 *ni ji desu.*
It's two thirty.	2時半(2時30分)です。 *ni ji han (ni ji san juppun) desu.*
It's two fifteen.	2時15分です。 *ni ji jū go fun desu.*
It's a quarter to three.	2時45分です。 *ni ji yon jū go fun desu.*
It's noon.	正午です。 *shōgo desu.*
It's midnight.	真夜中です。 *mayonaka desu.*
It's early.	早いです。 *hayai desu.*
It's late.	遅いです。 *osoi desu.*
in the morning	午前 *gozen*
in the afternoon	午後 *gogo*
at night	夜 *yoru*
dawn	夜明け *yo ake*

A.M.	午前 *gozen*
P.M.	午後 *gogo*

DAYS OF THE WEEK

Sunday	日曜日 *nichi yō bi*
Monday	月曜日 *getsu yō bi*
Tuesday	火曜日 *ka yō bi*
Wednesday	水曜日 *sui yō bi*
Thursday	木曜日 *moku yō bi*
Friday	金曜日 *kin yō bi*
Saturday	土曜日 *do yō bi*
today	今日 *kyō*
tomorrow	明日 *ashita*
yesterday	昨日 *kinō*
the day before yesterday	おととい *ototoi*
one week	一週間 *isshū kan*
next week	来週 *raishū*
last week	先週 *senshū*

DAYS OF THE MONTH

When saying or writing the date in Japanese, the month always precedes the day.

1	1日	*tsuitachi*
2	2日	*futsuka*
3	3日	*mikka*
4	4日	*yokka*
5	5日	*itsuka*
6	6日	*muika*
7	7日	*nanoka*
8	8日	*yōka*
9	9日	*kokonoka*
10	10日	*tōka*
11	11日	*jūichi nichi*
12	12日	*jūni nichi*
13	13日	*jūsan nichi*
14	14日	*jūyokka*
15	15日	*jūgonichi*
16	16日	*jūroku nichi*
17	17日	*jūshichi nichi*
18	18日	*jūhachi nichi*
19	19日	*jūku nichi*
20	20日	*hatsuka*
21	21日	*nijūichi nichi*
22	22日	*nijūni nichi*
23	23日	*nijūsan nichi*
24	24日	*nijūyokka*
25	25日	*nijūgo nichi*
26	26日	*nijūroku nichi*
27	27日	*nijūshichi nichi*
28	28日	*nijūhachi nichi*
29	29日	*nijūku nichi*
30	30日	*sanjū nichi*
31	31日	*sanjūichi nichi*

MONTHS OF THE YEAR

January	一月 *ichi gatsu*
February	二月 *ni gatsu*
March	三月 *san gatsu*
April	四月 *shi gatsu*
May	五月 *go gatsu*
June	六月 *roku gatsu*
July	七月 *shichi gatsu*
August	八月 *hachi gatsu*
September	九月 *ku gatsu*
October	十月 *jū gatsu*
November	十一月 *jū ichi gatsu*
December	十二月 *jū ni gatsu*

SEASONS OF THE YEAR

spring	春 *haru*
summer	夏 *natsu*
autumn	秋 *aki*
winter	冬 *fuyu*

"JAPLISH"

Gairaigo is not to be confused with what is often known as 'Japlish,' or badly misused English that is sometimes incomprehensible and often hilarious. While the prevalence of Japlish is decreasing as English is more widely used in Japan, it is still not unusual to encounter signs warning you to "Take care of your feet" (i.e., watch your step) or department store specials on "flying pans."

Another form of Japlish is English words that are used strictly for their sound or even visual appearance as text, without regard for their literal meanings. This is a common practice among packagers and manufacturers. A popular soft drink bears the name Poccari Sweat; presumably, it does not reveal anything about the ingredients.

Gairaigo (Japanese Loan Words)

Gairaigo refers to Japanese terms that originated from words in foreign languages, mostly English. Though similar in pronunciation to the words of origin, their relationships to the original meanings are sometimes obscure. Here are some examples.

aisu (アイス) : i.e., 'ice'; ice cream, ice pop
baikingu (バイキング): i.e., 'Viking'; buffet, smorgasbord
bebiikaa (ベビーカー): i.e., 'baby car'; stroller, carriage
depāto (デパート): i.e., 'department'; department store
eakon (エアコン): i.e., 'air con'; air conditioning
furiidaiyaru (フリーダイヤル): i.e., 'free dial'; toll-free call
igirisu (イギリス): i.e., Inglez in Portuguese; Englishperson; the UK
kasutera (カステラ): i.e., castela in Dutch; sponge cake
saabisu (サービス): i.e., 'service'; gratis, free-of-charge
sumaato (スマート): i.e., 'smart' (British); slender, svelte
tabako (タバコ): i.e., 'tobacco'; cigarette

JAPANESE GRAMMAR BASICS

Compared to Western languages, little is known about the origins of Japanese or its connections to other tongues. The most popular theory places it in the family that includes Turkish, Mongolian, and Korean. Another theory links it to Polynesian and other languages in the South Pacific. In its present form, Japanese consists of native words as well as loan words from Chinese and Western languages such as English, Portuguese, and German (see page 18).

PRONUNCIATION

Most Japanese syllables consist of either a single vowel, or a consonant + a vowel.

Vowels are either short or long. The sound does not change, only the length of the syllable. However, a short or long vowel can change the meaning of a word entirely. For instance, *shujin* (husband) vs. *shūjin* (prisoner).

PRONUNCIATION GUIDE

Vowels

a:	ah like the a in father; hana *(hah-nah)*
ā:	elongated a (aah); okāsan *(oh-kaah-sahn)*
i:	ee like the ee in feed; migi *(mee-ghee)*
ī:	elongated i (eee); kīroi *(keee-ro-ee)*
u:	oo like the u in blue; sugu *(soo-ghoo)*
ū:	elongated u (ooo); kūkan *(kooo-kah-n)*
e:	eh like the e in bed; te *(teh)*
ē:	elongated e (eeh); dēta *(deeh-tah)*
o:	oh like the o in rose; omoi *(oh-moh-ee)*
ō:	elongated o (ooh); ōkii *(ooh-kee-ee)*

Vowel Combinations

ai:	kaidan *(kah-ee-dah-n)*
ae:	mae *(mah-eh)*
ao:	aoba *(ah-oh-bah)*
au:	kau *(kah-oo)*
ue:	tsukue *(tsoo-koo-eh)*

oi: oi *(oh-ee)*
oe: koe *(koh-eh)*

Consonants

k: as in English, like the k in kick; kekkon *(keh-k-koh-n)*
g: as in English, like the g in gum; genkan *(geh-n-kah-n)*
s: as in English, like the s in see; sara *(sah-rah)*
j: as in English, like the j in jump; jikan *(jee-kah-n)*
z: as in English, like the z in zoo; zubon *(zoo-boh-n)*
t: as in English, like the t in time; takai *(tah-kah-ee)*
d: as in English, like the d in dog; daikon *(dah-ee-koh-n)*
n: as in English, like the n in name, or at the end of a word, run; naka *(nah-kah)*, hon *(hoh-n)*
h: as in English, like the h in home; hashi *(hah-shee)*
b: as in English, like the b in baby; ban *(bah-n)*
p: as in English, like the p in pepper; pan *(pah-n)*
f: softer than English f and closer to h, like hf; fūsen *(hfoo-seh-n)*
m: as in English, like the m in man; manzoku *(mah-n-zoh-koo)*
y: as in English, like the consonant y in yes; yama *(yah-mah)*
r: closer to English l than r; tap the roof of your palate with your tongue; raku *(rah-koo)*
w: as in English, like the w in woman; wakai *(wah-kah-ee)*

Consonant Combinations

ky: ki *(kee)* + ya *(yah)*, yu *(yoo)* or yo *(yoh)*, pronounced almost simultaneously; kyaku *(kee-yah-koo)*, Kyōto *(kee-yooh-toh)*, kyūkei *(kee-yooo-keh-ee)*
sh: as in English, like sh in she; shabu-shabu *(shah-boo shah-boo)*
ch: as in English, like the ch in cherry; chōcho *(chooh choh)*
tsu: like ts at the end of hats in English, followed by u, although the u is nearly silent when it is followed by a consonant; tsukuru *(ts(oo)-koo-roo)*

ry: this is possibly the most difficult sound for non-native speakers to pronounce; ri *(ree)* + ya *(yah)*, yu *(yoo)* or yo *(yoh)*, pronounced almost simultaneously, remembering the r is closer to the English l; ryaku *(ree-yah-koo)*, ryūkō *(ree-yooo-kooh)*; ryōri *(ree-yooh-ree)*

WORD PRONUNCIATION

Japanese has no accented syllables, unlike English, which has accented and unaccented syllables (e.g., Is THIS the FACE that LAUNCHED a THOUsand SHIPS?). In spoken Japanese, all syllables receive the same level of stress. Some commonly mispronounced Japanese words or names

	Incorrect	Correct
karate	*kah-RAH-tee*	*kah-rah-teh*
sashimi	*sah-SHEE-mee*	*sah-shee-mee*
sayōnara	*SAH-yoh-NAH-rah*	*sah-yooh-nah-rah*
sukiyaki	*SOO-kee-YAH-kee*	*soo-kee-yah-kee*
Toyota	*toh-YOH-tah*	*toh-yoh-tah*

SENTENCE CONSTRUCTION

The basic sentence construction in English is:

subject – verb – object
i.e. I read a book.

In Japanese, the basic sentence structure is:

subject – object – verb
i.e. Watashi wa hon o yomimashita.

The position of subject and object can alternate (Hon o watashi wa yomimashita), but the verb always goes at the end of the sentence.

Subjects and objects are distinguished in the sentence by particles, or case markers, which follow them.

Particles

wa / ga (no English equivalent) subject **wah / gah**

Watashi wa ringo o tabemashita.
I ate an apple.
Watashi ga ringo o tabemashita.
It is I who ate the apple.

o (no English equivalent) direct object **oh**

Jane wa hon o kaimashita.
Jane bought a book.

Particles also specify such things as to, from, when and where an event is taking place.

de (in, by, with, at) how, where, in what **deh** circumstance

Te de sētā o araimashita
I washed the sweater by hand.
Mary wa doitsu de kenkyū shite imasu
Mary is doing research in Germany.
Watashi wa mainichi basu de kayotteimasu.
I commute by bus everyday.

e (to, toward) direction toward **eh**

Otōsan wa nyū yōku e ikimasu ka?
Is your father going to New York?

ka (or) or **kah**

Kurīmu ka sato wa ikaga desu ka?
Would you like cream or sugar?

kara (from) starting point **kah-rah**

Kare wa bosuton kara unten shitekimashita.
He drove from Boston.

made (up to, until) destination, end point **mah-deh**

Kuji kara goji made shigoto o shimasu
I work from nine until five.

ni (to, on, at) target; direction; when **nee**

Okāsan ni hana o agemashita.

I gave my mother flowers.

Watashitachi wa furansu ni ryokō ni ikimasu.

We are traveling to France.

Asa rokuji ni okiru yotei desu.

I plan to get up at six o'clock.

to (and) and **toh**

Onīsan to Onēsan wa hawai ni sunde imasu.

My older brother and older sister live in Hawaii.

PERSONAL PRONOUNS

I, me	**watashi**	**wah-tah-shee**
I, me	**boku** (male, informal)	**boh-koo**
I, me	**atashi** (female, informal)	**ah-tah-shee**
we, us	**watashitachi**	**wah-tah-shee-tah-chee**
you (sing.)	**anata**	**ah-nah-tah**
you (pl.)	**anatatachi**	**ah-nah-tah-tah-chee**
he, him	**kare**	**kah-reh**
she, her	**kanojo**	**kah-noh-joh**
they, them	**karera**	**kah-reh-rah**

Anata (you) is rarely used and can sound presumptuous and unnatural in the wrong context. For second-person direct address (you familiar), the safest bet is to use a proper name (either given or surname, depending on your relationship to that person) + *san*. With small children, *san* becomes *chan* or *kun* (see page 25). Or, if you are asking a question, you can drop the pronoun altogether and use just the interrogative verb form:

e.g., *Anata ga kimasu ka? Kimasu ka?*

Are you coming?

POSSESSIVE PRONOUNS

I becomes my, he becomes his and she becomes hers, etc., by adding the particle no (noh) after the pronoun.

I (**watashi**)	my (**watashi no**)	**watashi no kaban** (my bag)
he (**kare**)	his (**kare no**)	**kare no tokei** (his watch)
she (**kanojo**)	her (**kanojo no**)	**kanojo no kuruma** (her car)
we (**watashitachi**)	our (**watashitachi no**)	**watashitachi no resutoran** (our restaurant)
they (**karera**)	their (**karera no**)	**karera no ie** (their home)

A Little Tip

Japanese people introduce themselves with the surname first, followed by the given name (e.g., Watanabe Ken, instead of Ken Watanabe). However, it isn't necessary for non-Japanese to follow suit (e.g., "I'm Smith John"), as most people understand the difference in Japanese and Western conventions.

FORMS OF ADDRESS

As in English, the way you address another person in Japanese depends on your relationship, the context, and your relative social status. But for the most part, the question in English is whether to use a person's first name or last, in Japanese it is a bit more intricate. The honorific title is a suffix that is attached to a person's name (either given or surname).

Title	Appropriate for
-chan *(chah-n)*	young children; used with given name
-kun *(koo-n)*	boys' given name, 'subordinate' males
-sama *(sah-mah)*	after superior's, VIP's or customer's surname; also used in letters
-san *(sah-n)*	the most common and safest option, especially when meeting someone for the first time; can be used with either the given name or surname

As mentioned on page 23, the use of *anata* is not advisable in most situations. To politely address people whose names you do not know, you can use titles based on age and gender. See introductions on page 101.

AGE- & GENDER-BASED FORMS OF ADDRESS

bōya *(booh-yah)* young boy
o-bocchan *(oh-boh-t-chah-n)* young boy
ojō-san *(oh-jooh-sah-n)* young girl
onī-san *(oh-neee-sah-n)* young man; lit. 'big brother'
onē-san *(oh-neeh-sah-n)* young woman; lit. 'big sister'
oji-san *(oh-jee-sah-n)* middle-aged man; lit. 'uncle'
oba-san *(oh-bah-sah-n)* middle-aged woman; lit. 'aunt'
ojī-san *(oh-jeee-sah-n)* elderly man; lit. 'grandfather'
obā-san *(oh-baah-sah-n)* elderly woman; lit. 'grandmother'

PROFESSIONAL TITLES

buchō *(boo-chooh)* department manager
kachō *(kah-chooh)* section chief; manager
kōchō *(kooh-chooh)* school principal
sensei *(seh-n-seh-ee)* teacher, professor; also, doctor
shachō *(shah-chooh)* company president
tenchō *(teh-n-chooh)* store manager

VERBS

Unlike verbs in other languages, Japanese verbs are not conjugated according to person, gender, or number. Whether the subject is I, he, she, or they, the verb to walk is always *aruku*. Verbs are conjugated to show tense, negation, and level of completion or duration, as well as the status of the speaker or subject. In informal situations with family or friends, the plain, or dictionary, form of a verb is appropriate. In more formal settings, the polite, or *–masu*, form is called for.

Verbs consist of what is called a stem form, plus an ending. They are categorized according to the endings of their plain forms. The stem form does not change, except in the case of irregular verbs. They are conjugated by changing the endings, or adding a suffix.

'U' Verbs

These are verbs that end with 'u,' or [stem form] + u. They are conjugated by dropping the u and changing the syllable that immediately precedes it.

HANASU: 'to speak'

Plain present	**hanasu**	**hah-nah-soo**
Plain past	**hanashita**	**hah-nah-shee-tah**
Plain present negative	**hanasanai**	**hah-nah-sah-nah-ee**
Plain past negative	**hanasanakatta**	**hah-nah-sah-nah-kah-t-tah**
Polite present affirmative	**hanashimasu**	**hah-nah-shee-mah-soo**
Polite past affirmative	**hanashimashita**	**hah-nah-shee-mah-shee-tah**
Polite present negative	**hanashimasen**	**hah-nah-shee-mah-seh-n**
Polite past negative	**hanashimasen deshita**	**hah-nah-shee-mah-seh-n deh-shee-tah**

KIKU: to hear, listen

Plain present	kiku	kee-koo
Plain past	kiita	kee-ee-tah
Plain present negative	kikanai	kee-kah-nah-ee
Plain past negative	kikanakatta	kee-kah-nah-kah-t-tah
Polite present affirmative	kikimasu	kee-kee-mah-soo
Polite past affirmative	kikimashita	kee-kee-mah-shee-tah
Polite present negative	kikimasen	kee-kee-mah-seh-n
Polite past negative	kikimasen deshita	kee-kee-mah-seh-n deh-shee-tah

'Ru' Verbs

These are verbs that end with '*ru*', or [stem form] + *ru*. They are conjugated by dropping the *ru*.

TABERU: 'to eat'

Plain present	taberu	tah-beh-roo
Plain past	tabeta	tah-beh-tah
Plain present negative	tabenai	tah-beh-nah-ee
Plain past negative	tabenakatta	tah-beh-nah-kah-t-tah
Polite present affirmative	tabemasu	tah-beh-mah-soo
Polite past affirmative	tabemashita	tah-beh-mah-shee-tah
Polite present negative	tabemasen	tah-beh-mah-seh-n
Polite past negative	tabemasen deshita	tah-beh-mah-seh-n deh-shee-tah

MIRU: 'to see'

Plain present	**miru**	**mee-roo**
Plain past	**mita**	**mee-tah**
Plain present negative	**minai**	**mee-nah-ee**
Plain past negative	**minakatta**	**mee-nah-kah-t-tah**
Polite present affirmative	**mimasu**	**mee-mah-soo**
Polite past affirmative	**mimashita**	**mee-mah-shee-tah**
Polite present negative	**mimasen**	**mee-mah-seh-n**
Polite past negative	**mimasen deshita**	**mee-mah-seh-n deh-shee-tah**

IRREGULAR VERBS

These are verbs whose stem and ending change in conjugation.

SURU: 'to do'

Plain present	**suru**	**soo-roo**
Plain past	**shita**	**shee-tah**
Plain present negative	**shinai**	**shee-nah-ee**
Plain past negative	**shinakatta**	**shee-nah-kah-t-tah**
Polite present affirmative	**shimasu**	**shee-mah-soo**
Polite past affirmative	**shimashita**	**shee-mah-shee-tah**
Polite present negative	**shimasen**	**shee-mah-seh-n**
Polite past negative	**shimasen deshita**	**shee-mah-seh-n deh-shee-tah**

KURU: 'to come'

Plain present	kuru	koo-roo
Plain past	kita	kee-tah
Plain present negative	konai	koh-nah-ee
Plain past negative	konakatta	koh-nah-kah-t-tah
Polite present affirmative	kimasu	kee-mah-soo
Polite past affirmative	kimashita	kee-mah-shee-tah
Polite present negative	kimasen	kee-mah-seh-n
Polite past negative	kimasen deshita	kee-mah-seh-n deh-shee-tah

Te (or de) Form

By itself, this verb form is used as an informal request. It is commonly combined with other verbs or suffixes. To denote either past or present, the second, or auxillary, verb is conjugated.

U Verbs

OYOGU **oyoide** *(oh-yoh-ee-deh)* Swim.
KAKU **kaite** *(kah-ee-teh)* Write it.

Ru Verbs

OKIRU **okite** *(oh-kee-teh)* Wake up.
NERU **nete** *(neh-teh)* Go to sleep.

Irregular Verbs

SURU **shite** *(shee-teh)* Do.
KURU **kite** *(kee-teh)* Come.

Te + IMASU: present progression; "to be doing"

Densha o matte imasu.	I am waiting for a train.
Terebi o mite imasu.	He is watching TV.
Kaban o sagashite imasu.	She is looking for her bag.

Te + KUDASAI: Please (do something); polite request

Namae o kaite kudasai	Please write your name.
Hayaku okite kudasai.	Please wake up early.
Yoku benkyō shite kudasai.	Please study well.

Te + AGEMASU: to do something for someone else; a favor to someone else.

Musume ni puresento o katte agemasu.
I will buy my daughter a present.
Gohan o tsukutte agemashita.
I made dinner (for them).
Akachan no furo o junbi shite agemasu.
I will draw the baby's bath.

Note: The *te agemasu* can sound patronizing unless it's used in a proper way. For instance, to say "I bought my daughter a present", *katte agemasu* is OK, but if it is your mother, you would not use the te-agemasu form. Instead, you would simply say *Haha ni purezento o kaimashita.* (I bought my mother a present.) It should be used very carefully when speaking to someone senior or superior to you, or even among equals. It is best to avoid using it whenever in doubt.

Te + MORAU: someone doing something for you; a favor received

Kare ni kuruma o aratte moraimasu.
He is going to wash my car.
Kanojo ni doa o akete moraimashita.
She opened the door for me.
Haha ni shukudai o mite moratte imasu.
My mother is checking my homework.

DESU: to be

The word *desu* is a combination of the particle *de*, the verb *aru* (to exist) and the polite ending *masu*. It is used to express condition or identity, and like all verbs, appears at the end of a sentence.

Plain present	da	dah
Plain past	datta	dah-t-tah
Plain present negative	ja nai	jah-nah-ee
Plain past negative	ja nakatta	jah-nah-kah-t-tah
Polite present affirmative	desu	deh-soo
Polite past affirmative	deshita	deh-shee-tah
Polite present negative	de wa arimasen	deh-wah-ah-ree-mah-seh-n
Polite past negative	de wa arimasen deshita	deh-wah-ah-ree-mah-seh-n deh-shee-tah

ADJECTIVES

In Japanese the adjective appears either before the noun it is modifying, or at the end of the sentence preceding the word desu in conjugated form. For instance,

Sore wa takai tokei desu.
That's an expensive watch.
Sono tokei wa takai desu.
The watch is expensive.

There are two types of adjectives—the *I* adjectives, which are adjectives that end in i, and the *na* adjectives, which are combined with the suffix *–na* when modifying a noun (e.g., *jōzu na hito*, a skilled person). One exception is the word *kirei*, which means pretty or neat. Although it ends with the letter *i*, it is conjugated as a *na* adjective.

I-Adjective
warui: 'bad'

Plain present	warui	wah-roo-ee
Plain past	warukatta	wah-roo-kah-t-tah
Plain present negative	warukunai	wah-roo-koo-nah-ee
Plain past negative	warukunakatta	wah-roo-koo-nah-kah-t-tah
Polite present affirmative	warui desu	wah-roo-ee deh-soo
Polite past affirmative	warukatta desu	wah-roo-kah-t-tah deh-soo
Polite present negative	waruku arimasen	wah-roo-koo ah-ree-mah-seh-n
Polite past negative	waruku arimasen deshita	wah-roo-koo ah-ree-mah-seh-n deh-shee-tah

Na-Adjective
damena: 'failed'

Plain present	dame na	dah-meh nah
Plain past	dame datta	dah-meh dah-t-tah
Plain present negative	dame janai	dah-meh jah nah-ee
Plain past negative	dame janakatta	dah-meh jah nah-kah-t-tah
Polite present affirmative	dame desu	dah-meh deh-soo
Polite past affirmative	dame deshita	dah-meh deh-shee-tah
Polite present negative	dame de wa arimasen	dah-meh deh-wah ah-ree-mah-seh-n
Polite past negative	dame de wa arimasen deshita	dah-meh deh-wah ah-ree-mah-seh-n deh-shee-tah

IF YOU HAVE...1–2 DAYS

Tokyo, the cultural, economic, and political center of Japan, is arguably the best single stop for a short stay in Japan. The city's main hubs follow the circuitous course of the Yamanote train line of Japan Railways (JR). Following the Yamanote line clockwise, **Ueno** and nearby **Asakusa** are at roughly 12 o'clock, **Ginza (Yurakucho)** and **Shiodome** at 3 o'clock, **Shinagawa** at 6 o'clock, and **Shinjuku** and **Shibuya** at 9 o'clock.

Stroll through the impressive collection of Japanese art at the **Tokyo National Museum** in Ueno and then jump on the Ginza subway line to Asakusa Station, where you will find remnants of old Edo (the city's feudal era name) in the incense-perfumed precincts around **Sensoji**, Tokyo's oldest and liveliest temple. Just across the Sumida River is **Ryogoku**, where you can catch a sumo match during one of the seasonal tournaments.

Window-shopping in Ginza, home to some of the world's priciest real estate, wouldn't be complete without checking out tony department stores such as **Mitsukoshi** and **Matsuya**. Also stop in at the **Mikimoto** flagship store to see some of Japan's finest cultured pearls. Just down the street, under the elevated tracks near Yurakucho Station, you can order a chilled mug of draft beer and snack on charbroiled chicken skewers at one of the side-by-side yakitori-ya. Head the other way down Harumi street and you'll find both the baroque Japanese **Kabuki-za theater** and, further still, the **Tsukiji open air fresh fish market**. Arrive before noon to sample the world's best—and freshest—sushi. A few minutes walk to the south of Ginza is the Shiodome district, where a dozen of Tokyo's tallest and newest skyscrapers (many topped by restaurants with killer views of **Tokyo Bay's Rainbow Bridge**) shoot up out of the ground like concrete bamboo. That austere landscape is comfortably juxtaposed with tranquil gardens just a few blocks away inside the 300-year old **Hama Rikyu park**, once the duck-hunting grounds for the feudal Tokugawa shogunate and now an oasis from the mad scramble of 21st-century Tokyo.

Shinagawa is a major commuter hub with train lines connecting to the wealthy southern suburbs and **Yokohama**. Hop in a taxi for a quick ride to the **Hara Museum of Contemporary Art** or transfer onto the JR Keihin-Tohoku Line for a 30-minute ride to Yokohama and a relaxing dinner in that city's well-regarded Chinatown (**Chukagai**).

Shibuya and Shinjuku are the fun-loving sisters of modern Tokyo, where you'll find the most vibrant youth culture and nightlife. Right outside of Shibuya Station (take the Hachiko exit) is a mind-boggling sea of pedestrians known as the ***Hyakumon-iin kosaten*** ("million man intersection"). Once you've checked out the latest styles for hipsters in Shibuya's trendy boutiques, ride the train one stop to Harajuku—a tschotsky-filled Mecca for teenagers from all over Japan. No stop in Harujuku is complete without a visit to the nearby heavily pine-forested grounds of **Meiji Jingu**, one of Tokyo's most important shrines and the center of New Year's festivities.

Shinjuku is home to some of the swankest department stores in the city, such as **Istean**, **Odakyu** and **Takashimaya**. For sweeping views of the city and mountains beyond (including **Mt. Fuji**, weather permitting), head to the observation room on the 45th floor of the **Tokyo Metropolitan Government building** (*To-cho*).

IF YOU HAVE…3–5 DAYS

In addition to the "must-do" itinerary above, try to take in a uniquely Japanese professional baseball game at **Tokyo Dome**. Who knows? You might see the next Ichiro Suzuki or Hideki Matsui in action. Traditional theater such as boisterous *kabuki* or solemn *noh* is another option for culture buffs. If a favorite musical act is in town, you may be able to catch a concert live at the famed **Budokan** stadium—or at one of Tokyo's many world class jazz clubs. **Tokyo Midtown**, a much-hyped shopping and restaurant complex built on the former Defense Ministry headquarters in central Tokyo's foreigner-friendly Roppongi district, is a hot spot for trendy Tokyo-ites; it just opened in 2007. Those with more than three days to spare should consider a side trip to Japan's old feudal capital of Kamakura, just 30 miles outside of Tokyo, to see the **Great Buddha** (Daibutsu) at **Kotokuin Temple**; the JR Yokosuka line gets you here from Shinagawa. Or journey via the oddly named Odakyu Romance Car from Shinjuku to the natural hot spring resort of **Hakone**, about 60 miles from Tokyo, in the foothills of Mt. Fuji. The fourth or fifth day would be well worth spending in **Kyoto** or **Osaka** by taking one of the bullet trains (*shinkansen*) that depart from Tokyo about every 30 minutes.

IF YOU HAVE...7–10 DAYS

Be sure to spend time in **Kyoto** at the popular **Kiyomizu** temple surrounded by cherry trees, the solid gold-leaf-covered **Kinkakuji** temple, and the austere zen rock garden of **Ryoanji** temple. In the **Gion** district, you might spy an apprentice (*maiko*) running errands among the geisha houses. Don't forget to explore the wooded hills, lesser temples, handicraft shops and traditional restaurants of the city's quieter **Higashiyama-ku** district.

In **Osaka**, Japan's second largest and arguably most commerce-oriented city, you'll find all the requisite department stores and busy streetscapes of modern urban Japan. But the highlight—outside of majestic **Osaka Castle**, perhaps—is the food. Local specialties include *oshi-zushi* (pressed square-shaped sushi), *okonomiyaki* (pancake topped with pork, egg and cabbage) and *takoyaki* (ping-pong-ball-sized dumplings with octopus chunks). If time permits, take a trip inland to see the "other" Japan, where green rice patties, bamboo groves and soaring mountains dominate the landscape. Some options include a visit to the stunningly well-preserved feudal castle in central Japan's mountain-ringed city of **Matsumoto**, a stroll through the famed **Kenrokuen** gardens in the historic city of **Kanazawa** on the Japan Sea, or a night in one of the Spartan temples of **Mt. Koya** on the **Kii Peninsula**.

Those with a more adventurous streak may want to spend a day climbing Mt. Fuji, hiking the **Nakasendo** trail in the Japan Alps, or bicycling the 50-mile **Shimanami Kaido** route between **Shikoku** and **Hiroshima** prefecture along the **Seto Inland Sea**. During winter months, try a combination ski trip-hot spring tour by taking an express train to **Echigo-Yuzawa** or **Shiga-Kogen** in the Japan Alps. A flight to the city of **Sapporo** on Japan's northernmost island of **Hokkaido** puts you in easy reach of the **Niseko** or **Rusutsu** ski resorts (no need to pack down jackets or equipment—you can rent right on the slopes). For more information on these and other trips, consult the *Frommer's Japan* guidebook.

However long your visit to Japan, you are sure to develop an appreciation of the Japanese art of hospitality. *Yokoso*—welcome to Japan.

CHAPTER TWO

GETTING THERE & GETTING AROUND

This section deals with every form of transportation. Whether you've just reached your destination by plane or you're renting a car to tour the countryside, you'll find the phrases you need in the next 27 pages.

AT THE AIRPORT

I am looking for ____	____はどこですか。 *____ wa doko desu ka.*
a porter.	ポーター *pōtā*
the check-in counter.	チェックイン カウンター *chekku in kauntā*
the ticket counter.	チケット カウンター *chiketto kauntā*
arrivals.	到着ロビー *tōchaku robī*
departures.	出発ロビー *shuppatsu robī*
gate number ____.	____番ゲート *____ban gēto*

For full coverage of numbers, see p6.

the waiting area.	待合室 *machiai shitsu*
the men's restroom.	男性用トイレ *dansei yō toire*
the women's restroom.	女性用トイレ *josei yō toire*
the police station.	警察の派出所 *keisatsu no hashutsusho*
a security guard.	警備員 *keibi in*

the smoking area.	喫煙所 *kitsuen jo*
the information booth.	案内窓口 *annai madoguchi*
a public telephone.	公衆電話 *kōshū denwa*
an ATM.	ATM 機 *ATM ki*
baggage claim.	手荷物引き渡し所 *tenimotsu hikiwatashi jo*
a luggage cart.	荷物運搬カート *nimotsu unpan kāto*
a currency exchange.	外貨両替所 *gaika ryōgae jo*
a café.	喫茶店 *kissaten*
a restaurant.	レストラン *resutoran*
a bar.	バー *bā*
a bookstore or newsstand.	本屋か新聞雑誌売り場 *hon ya ka shinbun zasshi uriba*
a duty-free shop.	免税店 *menzei ten*
Is there Internet access here?	ここにはインターネットに接続できるところがありますか? *koko niwa intānetto ni setsuzoku dekiru tokoro ga arimasu ka.*
I'd like to page someone.	呼び出し放送をしていただけますか。 *yobidashi hōsō o shite itadake masu ka.*
Do you accept credit cards?	クレジットカードは使えますか? *kurejitto kādo wa tsukae masu ka*

CHECKING IN

I would like a one-way ticket to ____.	____行きの片道航空券を買いたいのですが。 *____ yuki no katamichi kōkūken o kaitai no desuga.*
I would like a round trip ticket to ____.	____行きの往復航空券を買いたいのですが。 *____ yuki no ōfuku kōkūken o kaitai no desuga.*
How much are the tickets?	その航空券の値段はいくらですか？ *sono kōkūken no nedan wa ikura desu ka .*
Do you have anything less expensive?	もう少し安いのはありませんか？ *mō sukoshi yasui nowa arimasen ka.*
How long is the flight?	飛行時間はどのくらいですか？ *hikō jikan wa dono kurai desu ka.*

For full coverage of number terms, see p6.

For full coverage of time, see p13.

What time does flight ____ leave?	____便は何時に出発しますか？ *____ bin wa nanji ni shuppatsu shimasu ka.*
What time does flight ____ arrive?	____便は何時に到着しますか？ *____ bin wa nanji ni tōchaku shimasu ka.*
Do I have a connecting flight?	接続便はありますか？ *setsuzoku bin wa arimasu ka.*
Do I need to change planes?	飛行機を乗り換える必要がありますか？ *hikōki o norikaeru hitsuyō ga arimasu ka.*
My flight leaves at __:__.	私のフライトは__:__に出発します。 *watashi no furaito wa __:__ ni shuppatsu shimasu.*

For full coverage of numbers, see p6.

Common Airport Signs

到着	Arrivals
出発	Departures
ターミナル	Terminal
ゲート	Gate
チケット取扱い	Ticketing
税関	Customs
手荷物引き渡し所	Baggage Claim
押す	Push
引く	Pull
禁煙	No Smoking
入口	Entrance
出口	Exit
男性用	Men's
女性用	Women's
シャトルバス	Shuttle Buses
タクシー	Taxis

What time will the flight arrive?
その便は何時に到着しますか?
sono bin wa nanji ni tōchaku shimasu ka.

Is the flight on time?
その便は定刻通りに出発しますか?
sono bin wa teikoku dōri ni shuppatsu shimasu ka.

Is the flight delayed?
その便は予定より遅れていますか?
sono bin wa yotei yori okurete imasu ka.

From which terminal is flight ____ leaving?
____便の出発ターミナルはどれですか?
____ bin no shuppatsu tāminaru wa dore desu ka.

From which gate is flight ____ leaving?	____便の出発ゲートは何番ですか？ *____bin no shuppatsu gēto wa nan ban desu ka.*
How much time do I need for check-in?	チェックインの手続きにどのくらい時間がかかりますか？ *chekku in no tetsuzuki ni dono kurai jikan ga kakarimasu ka.*
Is there an express check-in line?	特別優先チェックインカウンターはありますか？ *tokubetsu yūsen chekku in kauntā wa arimasu ka.*
Is there electronic check-in?	自動チェックイン機はありますか？ *jidō chekku in ki wa arimasu ka.*

Seat Preferences

I would like ____ ticket(s) in ____	____の航空券を____枚ください。 *____ no kōkūken o ____ mai kudasai.*
first class.	ファースト クラス *fāsuto kurasu*
business class.	ビジネス クラス *bijinesu kurasu*
economy class.	エコノミー クラス *ekonomī kurasu*
I would like ____	____がいいのですが。 *____ ga ii no desuga.*
Please don't give me ____	____以外のものをください。 *____ igai no mono o kudasai.*
a window seat.	窓側の座席 *mado gawa no zaseki*
an aisle seat.	通路側の座席 *tsūro gawa no zaseki*
an emergency exit row seat.	非常用出口に一番近い座席 *hijōyō deguchi ni ichiban chikai zaseki*

a bulkhead seat.	仕切り壁前の座席 *shiki kabe mae no zaseki*
a seat by the restroom.	トイレ近くの座席 *toire chikaku no zaseki*
a seat near the front.	前方の座席 *zenpō no zaseki*
a seat near the middle.	中央部の座席 *chūōbu no zaseki*
a seat near the back.	後方の座席 *kōhō no zaseki*
Is there a meal on the flight?	機内食は出ますか？ *kinaishoku wa demasu ka.*
I'd like to order ____	____をください。 ____ *o kudasai.*
a vegetarian meal.	ベジタリアン料理 *bejitarian ryōri*
I am traveling to ____.	____に旅行に行きます。 ____ *ni ryokō ni ikimasu.*
I am coming from ____.	____から来ます。 ____ *kara kimasu.*
I arrived from ____.	____から到着しました。 ____ *kara tōchaku shimashita.*

For full coverage of country terms, see English / Japanese dictionary.

I'd like to change / cancel / confirm my reservation.	予約の変更 / 取り消し / 確認をしたいのですが。 *yoyaku no henkō / torikeshi / kakunin o shitai no desuga.*
I have ____ bags to check.	預ける荷物は ____ 個あります。 *azukeru nimotsu wa ____ ko arimasu.*

For full coverage of numbers, see p6.

Passengers with Special Needs

Is that wheelchair accessible?	車椅子で入れますか？ *kurumaisu de haire masu ka.*
May I have a wheelchair / walker please?	車椅子か歩行器をお借りできますか？ *kurumaisu ka hokō ki o okari dekimasu ka.*
I need some assistance boarding.	搭乗するのを 手伝っていただきたいのですが。 *tōjō suru no o tetsudatte itadakitai no desuga.*
I need to bring my service dog.	介護犬を連れて行く必要があります。 *kaigo ken o tsurete iku hitsuyō ga arimasu.*
Do you have services for the hearing impaired?	聴覚障害者のためのサービスはありますか？ *chōkaku shōgaisha no tame no sābisu wa arimasu ka.*
Do you have services for the visually impaired?	視覚障害者のためのサービスはありますか？ *shikaku shōgaisha no tame no sābisu wa arimasu ka.*

Trouble at Check-In

How long is the delay?	どのくらい遅れていますか？ *donokurai okurete imasu ka.*
My flight was late.	飛行機の出発が遅れました。 *hikōki no shuppatsu ga okure mashita.*
I missed my flight.	飛行機に乗り遅れました。 *hikōki ni nori okure mashita.*
When is the next flight?	次の便はいつ出発しますか？ *tsugi no bin wa itsu shuppatsu shimasu ka.*

May I have a meal voucher? 食事利用券をいただけますか。
shokuji riyō ken o itadake masu ka.

May I have a room voucher? 客室利用券をいただけますか。
kyakushitsu riyō ken o itadake masu ka.

AT CUSTOMS / SECURITY CHECKPOINTS

I'm traveling with a group. 団体で旅行しています。
dantai de ryokō shite imasu.

I'm on my own. 個人で旅行しています。
kojin de ryokō shite imasu.

I'm traveling on business. 仕事で来ています。
shigoto de kite imasu.

I'm on vacation. 休暇中です。
kyūka chū desu.

I have nothing to declare. 申告するものはありません。
shinkoku suru mono wa arimasen.

I would like to declare ____. ____を申告します。
____ o shinkoku shimasu.

I have some liquor. お酒を買いました。
osake o kai mashita.

I have some cigars. タバコを買いました。
tabako o kai mashita.

They are gifts. これらはもらい物です。
kore wa morai mono desu.

They are for personal use. 個人用です。
kojin yō desu.

That is my medicine. それは私の薬です。
sore wa watashi no kusuri desu.

I have my prescription. 処方薬を持っています。
shohōyaku o motte imasu.

My children are traveling on the same passport. 子供たちもこのパスポートで旅行しています。
kodomotachi mo kono pasupōto de ryokō shite imasu.

I'd like a male / female officer to conduct the search.	検査するのは男性 / 女性の係員にしていただきたいです。 *kensa suru nowa dansei / josei no kakari in ni shite itadaki tai desu.*

Trouble at Security

Help me. I've lost ____	____を失くしてしまったのですが、探すのを手伝っていただけませんか。 *____ o nakushite shimatta no desuga, sagasu no o tetsudatte itadake masen ka.*
my passport.	私のパスポート *watashi no pasupōto*
my boarding pass.	私の搭乗券 *watashi no tōjōken*

Listen Up: Security Lingo

靴を脱いでください。 *kutsu o nuide kudasai.*	Please remove your shoes.
上着 / セーターを脱いでください。 *uwagi / sētā o nuide kudasai.*	Remove your jacket / sweater.
身に付けている貴金属をはずしてください。 *mi ni tsukete iru kikinzoku o hazushite kudasai.*	Remove your jewelry.
カバンをベルトコンベヤーに載せてください。 *kaban o beruto konbeyā ni nosete kudasai.*	Place your bags on the conveyor belt.
横に移動してください。 *yoko ni idō shite kudasai.*	Step to the side.
手で身体検査を行います。 *te de shintai kensa o okonai masu.*	We have to do a hand search.

my identification.	私の身分証明書 *watashi no mibun shōmei sho*
my wallet.	私の財布 *watashi no saifu*
my purse.	私のハンドバッグ *watashi no hando baggu*
Someone stole my purse / wallet!	誰かに財布を盗まれました! *dareka ni saifu o nusumare mashita.*

IN-FLIGHT

It's unlikely you'll need much Japanese on the plane, but these phrases will help if a bilingual flight attendant is unavailable or if you need to talk to a Japanese-speaking neighbor.

I think that's my seat.	それは私の席だと思いますが。 *sore wa watashi no seki dato omoi masuga.*
May I have ____ ?	____をいただけますか? ____ *o itadake masu ka.*
water	水 *mizu*
sparkling water	炭酸水 *tansan sui*
orange juice	オレンジ ジュース *orenji jūsu*
soda	ソーダ *sōda*
diet soda	ダイエット ソーダ *daietto sōda*
a beer	ビール *bīru*
wine	ワイン *wain*

For a complete list of drinks, see p91.

a pillow	枕 *makura*
a blanket	毛布 *mōfu*
a hand wipe	お絞り *oshibori*
headphones	ヘッドホーン *heddo hōn*
a magazine or newspaper	雑誌か新聞 *zasshi ka shinbun*
When will the meal be served?	食事はいつ出ますか? *shokuji wa itsu demasu ka.*
How long until we land?	あとどれくらいで着きますか? *ato dore kurai de tsuki masu ka.*
May I move to another seat?	別の席に移ってもいいですか? *betsu no seki ni utsuttemo iidesu ka.*
How do I turn the light on / off?	どうやって点灯 / 消灯しますか。 *dōyatte tentō / shōtō shimasu ka.*

Trouble In-Flight

These headphones are broken.	このヘッドホーンは壊れています。 *kono heddo hōn wa kowarete imasu.*
I spilled.	私がこぼしました。 *watashi ga koboshi mashita.*
My child spilled.	私の子供がこぼしました。 *watashi no kodomo ga koboshi mashita.*
My child is sick.	子供の具合が悪いのですが。 *kodomo no guai ga waruino desuga.*
I need an airsickness bag.	飛行機酔いの袋をいただけますか。 *hikōki yoi no fukuro o itadeke masuka.*

I smell something strange. 変なにおいがします。
henna nioi ga shimasu.

That passenger is behaving suspiciously. あの乗客の様子が変です。
ano jōkyaku no yōsu ga hen desu.

BAGGAGE CLAIM

Where is baggage claim for flight ____? ____便の手荷物引き渡し所はどこですか?
____ bin no tenimotsu hikiwatashi jo wa doko desu ka.

Would you please help with my bags? 荷物を手伝っていただけませんか?
nimotsu o tetsudatte itadake masen ka.

I am missing ____ bags. 荷物が ____ つ見つかりません。
nimotsu ga ____ tsu mitsukari masen.

For a full list of numbers used for bags, see the section "Generic Inanimate Objects on p.11

My bag is ____ 私の荷物 ____
watashi no nimotsu ____

lost. が失くなりました。
ga nakunari mashita.

damaged. が損傷しました。
ga sonshō shi mashita.

stolen. が盗まれました。
ga nusumare mashita.

a suitcase. はスーツケースです。
wa sūtsukēsu desu.

a briefcase. はブリーフケースです。
wa burīfukēsu desu.

a carry-on. は機内持込み用です。
wa kinai mochikomi yō desu.

a suit bag. はスーツバッグです。
wa sūtsubaggu desu.

a trunk. はトランクです。
wa toranku desu.

golf clubs. はゴルフクラブです。
wa gorufu kurabu desu.

For full coverage of color terms, see English / Japanese Dictionary.

hard. は硬いです。
wa katai desu.

made out of ____ ____製です。
____ sei desu.

canvas. キャンバス地
kyanbasu ji

vinyl. ビニール
binīru

leather. 皮
kawa

hard plastic. 硬いプラスチック
katai purasuchikku

aluminum. アルミニウム
aruminiumu

RENTING A VEHICLE

Is there a car rental agency in the airport? 空港内にレンタカー会社はありますか?
kūkō nai ni rentakā gaisha wa arimasu ka.

I have a reservation. 予約してあります。
yoyaku shite arimasu.

Vehicle Preferences

I would like to rent ____ ____を借りたいのですが。
____ o karitai no desuga.

an economy car. エコノミー車
ekonomī sha

a midsize car. 中型車
chūgata sha

a sedan.	セダン *sedan*
a convertible.	オープンカー *ōpun kā*
a van.	バン *ban*
a sports car.	スポーツカー *supōtsu kā*
a 4-wheel-drive vehicle.	4輪駆動車 *yon rin kudō sha*
a motorcycle.	バイク *baiku*
a scooter.	スクーター *sukūtā*
Do you have one with ____?	____が付いているのはありますか? ____ *ga tsuite iru nowa arimasu ka.*
air conditioning	エアコン *eakon*
a sunroof	サンルーフ *san rūfu*
a CD player	CDプレーヤー *CD purēyā*
satellite radio	衛星ラジオ *eisei rajio*
satellite tracking	衛星追跡システム *eisei tsuiseki shisutemu*
an onboard map	地図 *chizu*
a DVD player	DVDプレーヤー *DVD purēyā*
child seat	チャイルドシート *chairudo shīto*
Do you have a ____?	____はありますか? ____ *wa arimasu ka.*

smaller car	もっと小さい車 *motto chiisai kuruma*
bigger car	もっと大きい車 *motto ōkii kuruma*
cheaper car	もっと安い車 *motto yasui kuruma*
Do you have a non-smoking car?	禁煙車はありますか? *kinen sha wa arimasu ka.*
I need an automatic transmission.	オートマチック車が欲しいのですが。 *ōtomachikku sha ga hoshii no desuga.*
A standard transmission is okay.	マニュアル車でもいいです。 *manyuaru sha demo ii desu.*
May I have an upgrade?	アップグレードできますか? *appu gurēdo dekimasu ka.*

Money Matters

What's the daily / weekly / monthly rate?	日/週/月単位の料金はいくらですか? *nichi/shū/tsuki tan i no ryōkin wa ikura desu ka.*
How much is insurance?	保険はいくらかかりますか? *hoken wa ikura kakari masu ka.*
Are there other fees?	その他にもかかる料金はありますか? *sono hoka nimo kakaru ryōkin wa arimasu ka.*
Is there a weekend rate?	週末料金はありますか? *shūmatsu ryōkin wa arimasu ka.*

Technical Questions

What kind of fuel does it take?	使用燃料の種類は何ですか? *shiyō nenryō no shurui wa nan desu ka.*

Do you have the manual in English?	英語のマニュアルはありますか? *eigo no manyuaru wa arimasu ka.*
Do you have a booklet in English with the local traffic laws?	この地方の交通規則が英語版はありますか? *kono chihō no kōtsū kisoku ga eigoban wa arimasu ka.*

Technical Issues

Fill it up with ____	____で満タンにしてください。 *kono chihō no kōtsū kisoku ga ____ de mantan ni shite kudasai.*
Regular	レギュラー・ガソリン *regyurā gasorin*
Diesel	ディーゼル *dīzeru*
Unleaded	無鉛ガソリン *muen gasorin*
The ____ doesn't work.	____が機能しません。 *____ga kinō shimasen.*

See diagram on p53 for car parts.

It is already dented.	すでに凹みがあります。 *sudeni hekomi ga arimasu.*
It is scratched.	傷があります。 *kizu ga arimasu.*
The windshield is cracked.	フロントガラスにヒビが入っています。 *furonto garasu ni hibi ga haitte imasu.*
The tires look low.	タイヤの空気圧が低いようです。 *taiya no kūkiatsu ga hikui yō desu.*
It has a flat tire.	タイヤがパンクしています。 *taiya ga panku shite imasu.*
Whom do I call for service?	サービスを頼むには誰に電話をかければよいですか? *sābisu o tanomu niwa dare ni denwa o kakereba yoi desuka.*
It won't start.	エンジンがかかりません。 *enjin ga kakari masen.*

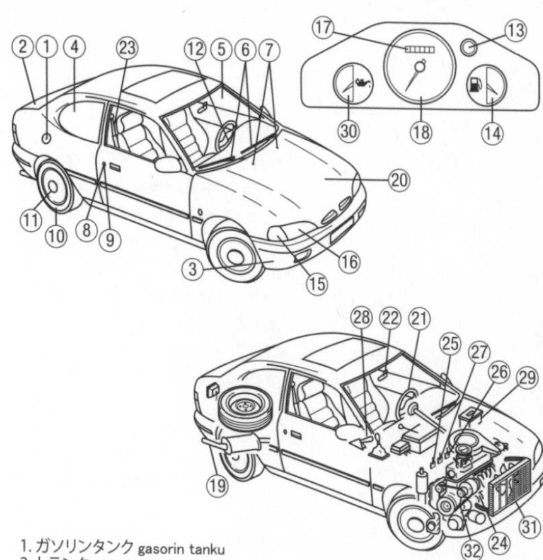

1. ガソリンタンク gasorin tanku
2. トランク toranku
3. バンパー banpā
4. 窓 mado
5. フロントガラス furonto garasu
6. ワイパー waipā
7. フロントガラス ウォッシャー furonto garasu wosshā
8. ドア doa
9. ロック rokku
10. タイヤ taiya
11. ホイールキャップ hoīru kyappu
12. ハンドル handoru
13. 非常灯 hijō tō
14. 燃料メーター nenryō mētā
15. ウィンカー winkā
16. ヘッドライト heddo raito
17. 走行距離計 sōkō kyori kei
18. 速度計 sokudo kei
19. マフラー mafurā
20. ボンネット bon netto
21. ハンドル handoru
22. バックミラー bakku mirā
23. シートベルト shīto beruto
24. エンジン enjin
25. アクセル akuseru
26. クラッチ kuracchi
27. ブレーキ burēki
28. サイドブレーキ saido burēki
29. バッテリー batterī
30. オイルゲージ oiru gēji
31. ラジエーター rajiētā
32. ファン ベルト fan beruto

It's out of gas.	ガソリンが入っていません。 *gasorin ga haitte imasen.*
The Check Engine light is on.	エンジンのチェックランプが点灯しています。 *enjin no chekku ranpu ga tentō shite imasu.*
The oil light is on.	オイル ランプが点灯しています。 *oiru ranpu ga tentō shite imasu.*
The brake light is on.	ブレーキ ランプが点灯しています。 *burēki ranpu ga tentō shite imasu.*
It runs rough.	走る時激しく振動します。 *hashiru toki hageshiku shindō shimasu.*
The car is over-heating.	車がオーバーヒートしています。 *kuruma ga ōbāhīto shite imasu.*

Asking for Directions

Excuse me, please.	ちょっとすみませんが。 *chotto sumimasen ga.*
How do I get to ____?	____への行き方を教えていただけますか。 *____eno ikikata o oshiete itadake masu ka.*
Go straight.	まっすぐ行きます。 *massugu iki masu.*
Turn left.	左に曲がります。 *hidari ni magari masu.*
Continue right.	そのまま右に進みます。 *sonomama migi ni susumi masu.*
It's on the right.	右側にあります。 *migi gawa ni arimasu.*
Can you show me on the map?	地図で示していただけませんか？ *chizu de shimeshite itadake masen ka.*
How far is it from here?	ここからどれくらいの距離がありますか？ *kokokara dore kurai no kyori ga arimasu ka.*

Is this the right road for ____?	____へ行きたいのですがこの道で合っていますか? *____ e ikitai no desu ga kono michi de atte imasu ka.*
I've lost my way.	道に迷ってしまいました。 *michi ni mayotte shimai mashita.*
Would you repeat that?	もう一度言っていただけませんか? *mō ichido itte itadake masen ka.*
Thanks for your help.	どうもありがとうございました。 *dōmo arigatō gozai mashita.*

For full coverage of direction-related terms, see p4.

Sorry, Officer

What is the speed limit?	制限速度は何キロですか? *seigen sokudo wa nan kiro desu ka.*
I wasn't going that fast.	それほどスピードは出していませんでした。 *sorehodo supīdo wa dashite imasen deshita.*
How much is the fine?	罰金はいくらですか? *bakkin wa ikura desu ka.*

Road Signs

制限速度	Speed Limit
停止	Stop
道を譲る	Yield
危険	Danger
行き止まり	No Exit
一方通行	One Way
進入禁止	Do Not Enter
道路閉鎖中	Road Closed
有料	Toll
現金のみ	Cash Only
駐車禁止	No Parking
駐車料金	Parking Fee
車庫	Parking Garage

Where do I pay the fine?	罰金はどこで払えばよいですか？ *bakkin wa doko de haraeba yoi desu ka.*
Do I have to go to court?	裁判所に行かなければなりませんか？ *saibansho ni ikanakereba narimasen ka.*
I had an accident.	事故に遭いました。 *jiko ni ai mashita.*
The other driver hit me.	相手の運転手が私にぶつかりました。 *aite no untenshu ga watashi ni butsukari mashita.*
I'm at fault.	私に落ち度があります。 *watashi ni ochido ga arimasu.*

BY TAXI

Where is the taxi stand?	タクシー乗り場はどこにありますか？ *takushī noriba wa doko ni arimasu ka.*

Listen Up: Taxi Lingo

乗ってく下さい！ *notte kudasai.*	Get in!
荷物はそこに置いてください。私がやります。 *nimotsu wa soko ni oite kudasai. watashi ga yarimasu.*	Leave your luggage. I got it.
何人乗りますか？ *nan nin norimasu ka.*	How many passengers?
お急ぎですか？ *oisogi desu ka.*	Are you in a hurry?

Is there a limo / bus / van for my hotel?	ホテルまで行ってくれるリムジンバス / バス / バンはありますか？ *hotel made itte kureru rimujin basu/ basu / ban wa arimasuka.*
I need to get to ____.	____に行きたいのですが。 *____ ni ikitai no desuga.*
How much will that cost?	料金はいくらくらいかかりますか？ *ryōkin wa ikura kurai kakari masu ka.*
How long will it take?	どのくらい時間がかかりますか？ *dono kurai jikan ga kakari masu ka.*
Can you take me / us to the train / bus station?	駅 / バス停までお願いします。 *eki / basutei made onegai shimasu.*
I am in a hurry.	ちょっと急いでいるんです。 *chotto isoide iru n desu.*
Slow down.	速度を落としてください。 *sokudo o otoshite kudasai.*
Am I close enough to walk?	ここからだと歩いていけますか？ *kokokara dato aruite ikemasu ka.*
Let me out here.	ここで降ろしてください。 *koko de oroshtie kudasai.*
That's not the correct change.	おつりが間違っています。 *otsuri ga machigatte imasu.*

BY TRAIN

How do I get to the train station?	駅へはどう行きますか。 *eki ewa dō iki masu ka.*
Would you take me to the train station?	駅までお願いします。 *eki made onegai shimasu.*
How long is the trip to ____?	____まではどのくらいかかりますか？ *____ made wa dono kurai kakari masu ka.*
When is the next train?	次の電車はいつ来ますか？ *tsugi no densha wa itsu kimasu ka.*
Do you have a schedule / timetable?	時刻表はありますか？ *jikoku hyo wa arimasu ka.*

Do I have to change trains?	電車を乗り換える必要がありますか？ *densha o norikaeru hitsuyō ga arimasu ka.*
a one-way ticket	片道切符 *katamichi kippu*
a round-trip ticket	往復切符 *ōfuku kippu*
Which platform does it leave from?	何番線から発車しますか？ *nan ban sen kara hassha shimasu ka.*
Is there a bar car?	ビュッフェはありますか？ *byuffe wa arimasu ka.*
Is there a dining car?	食堂車はありますか？ *shokudō sha wa arimasu ka.*
Which car is my seat in?	私の座席は何号車にありますか？ *watashi no zaseki wa nangōsha ni arimasu ka.*
Is this seat taken?	この席は空いていますか？ *kono seki wa aite imasu ka.*
Where is the next stop?	次の停車駅はどこですか？ *tsugi no teisha eki wa doko desu ka.*
How many stops to ____?	____までは停車駅が何個ありますか？ ____ *made wa teisha eki ga nan ko arimasu ka.*
What's the train number and destination?	電車の番号と行き先は何ですか？ *densha no bangō to ikisaki wa nan desu ka.*

BY BUS

How do I get to the bus station?
バス停に行く道を教えていただけませんか。
basutei ni iku michi o oshiete itadake masen ka.

Would you take me to the bus station?
バス停まで連れて行っていただけませんか？
basutei made tsurete itte itadake masen ka.

May I have a bus schedule?
バスの時刻表をもらえますか？
basu no jikokuhyō o moraemasu ka.

Which bus goes to ____?
____行きのバスはどれですか？
____ yuki no basu wa dore desuka.

Where does it leave from?
それはどこから発車しますか？
sore wa doko kara hassha shimasu ka.

How long does the bus take?
このバスでどのくらいかかりますか？
kono basu de dono kurai kakari masu ka.

How much is it?
それはいくらですか？
sore wa ikura desu ka.

Is there an express bus?
特急バスはありますか？
tokkyū basu wa arimasu ka.

Does it make local stops?
各停留所に停車しますか？
kaku teiryūjo ni teisha shimasu ka.

Does it run at night?
夜間も運行しますか？
yakan mo unkō shimasu ka.

When does the next bus leave?	次のバスはいつ 発車しますか？ *tsugi no basu wa itsu hassha shimasu ka.*
a one-way ticket	片道切符 *katamichi kippu*
a round-trip ticket	往復切符 *ōfuku kippu*
How long will the bus be stopped?	このバスはどのくらいの時間停車しますか？ *kono basu wa dono kurai no jikan teisha shimasu ka.*
Is there an air conditioned bus?	冷房のあるバスはありますか？ *reibō no aru basu wa arimasu ka.*
Is this seat taken?	この席は空いていますか？ *kono seki wa aite imassu ka.*
Where is the next stop?	次の停留所はどこですか？ *tsugi no teiryūjo wa doko desu ka.*
Please tell me when we reach ____.	____に着いたら教えていただけますか。 *____ ni itsuitara oshiete itadake masu ka.*
Let me off here.	ここで降ろしてください。 *koko de oroshite kudasai.*

BY BOAT OR SHIP

Would you take me to the port?	港までお願いします。 *minato made onegai shimasu.*
When does the ship sail?	この船はいつ出航しますか？ *kono fune wa itsu shukkō shimasu ka.*
How long is the trip?	目的地まではどのくらいかかりますか？ *mokutekichi made wa dono kurai kakari masu ka.*
Where are the life preservers?	救命用具はどこにありますか？ *kyūmei yōgu wa doko ni arimasu ka.*

I would like a private cabin.	船室は個室にしてください。 *senshitsu wa koshitsu ni shite kudasai.*
Is the trip rough?	航行中揺れますか？ *kōkōchū yuremasu ka.*
I feel seasick.	船酔いしたみたいです。 *funayoi shita mitai desu.*
I need some seasick pills.	船酔いに効く薬がほしいのですが。 *funayoi ni kiku kusuri ga hoshii no desuga.*
Where is the bathroom?	トイレはどこですか？ *toire wa doko desu ka.*
Does the ship have a casino?	船内にカジノはありますか？ *sennai ni kajino wa arimasu ka.*
Will the ship stop at ports along the way?	途中で停まる港はありますか？ *tochū de tomaru minato wa arimasu ka.*

BY SUBWAY

Where's the subway station?	地下鉄の駅 はどこにありますか？ *chikatetsu no eki wa doko ni arimasu ka.*
Where can I buy a ticket?	切符はどこで買えますか？ *kippu wa doko de kaemasu ka.*
Could I have a map of the subway?	地下鉄の地図をいただけますか？ *chikatetsu no chizu o itadake masu ka.*
Which line should I take for ____?	____へ行くにはどの線に乗ればいいですか？ *____ e iku niwa dono sen ni noreba ii desu ka.*
Is this the right line for ____?	____へ行きたいのですがこの線でいいですか？ *____ e ikitai no desuga kono sen de ii desu ka.*

Which stop is it for ____?	____へ行くにはどの駅で降りればいいですか？ *____ e iku niwa dono eki de orireba ii desu ka.*
How many stops is it to ____?	____まで停車駅は何個ありますか？ *____ made teisha eki wa nan ko arimasu ka.*
Is the next stop ____?	次の駅は____ですか？ *tsugi no eki wa ____ desu ka.*
Where are we?	ここはどこですか？ *koko wa doko desu ka.*

SUBWAY TICKETS

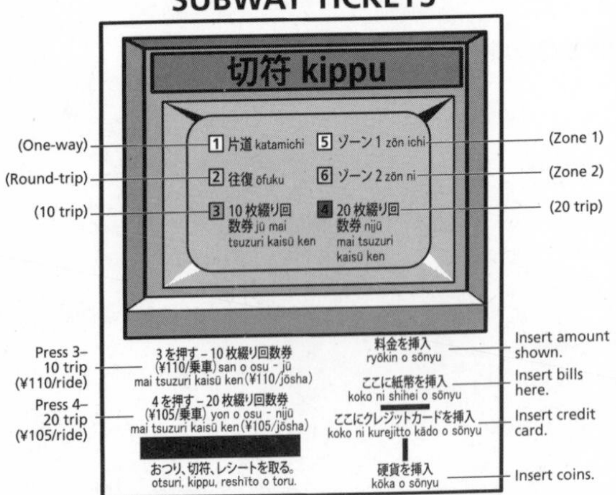

Where do I change to ____?	____へ行くにはどこで乗り換えればよいですか？ *____ e iku niwa doko de norikaereba yoi desu ka.*
What time is the last train to ____?	____行きの最終電車は何時ですか？ *____ yuki no saishū densha wa nanji desu ka.*

CONSIDERATIONS FOR TRAVELERS WITH SPECIAL NEEDS

Do you have wheelchair access?	車椅子で移動できますか？ *kurumaisu de idō dekimasu ka.*
Do you have elevators? Where?	エレベータはありますか？どこですか。 *erebētā wa arimasu ka. doko desu ka.*
Do you have ramps? Where?	スロープはありますか？どこですか。 *surōpu wa arimasu ka. doko desu ka.*
Are the restrooms wheelchair accessible?	トイレには車椅子で入れますか？ *toire niwa kurumaisu de hairemasu ka.*
Do you have audio assistance for the hearing impaired?	聴覚障害者のための補聴アシスタンスがありますか？ *chōkaku shōgaisha no tame no hochō ashisutansu ga arimasu ka.*
I am deaf.	私は耳が聞こえません。 *watashi wa mimi ga kikoe masen.*
May I bring my service dog?	介護犬を連れて行ってもいいですか？ *kaigo ken o tsurete ittemo ii desu ka.*
I am blind.	私は目が見えません。 *watashi wa me ga mie masen.*
I need to charge my power chair.	電動車椅子を充電する必要があります。 *dendō kurumaisu o jūden suru hitsuyō ga arimasu.*

GETTING THERE

Entry Requirements & Customs

For a stay of 90 days or less, tourists from the U.S., Australia, Canada and New Zealand need only a valid passport to enter Japan—no visa is required.

Visitor Information

The **Japan National Tourist Organization** (www.japantravelinfo.com) has a number of publications and maps available for free at its offices in New York (© **212/757-5640**), Los Angeles (© **213/623-1952**) and San Francisco (© **415/292-5686**). There are also three offices in Japan: downtown Tokyo, Tokyo's Narita Airport and Osaka's Kansai International Airport.

Airlines and Airports

Japan is served by a number of major U.S. and foreign airlines, including the two largest Japanese air carriers **Japan Airlines** (JAL) and **All Nippon Airways** (ANA). Direct flights are available from American cities such as Chicago, New York, Los Angeles, Seattle and San Francisco. The major international airports in Japan are **Narita International Airport** (Tokyo), **Kansai International Airport** (Osaka) and **Central Japan International Airport** (Nagoya.) The golden rule for arriving in any of these airports is: Never take a taxi. A taxi ride into the city can easily cost several hundred dollars. The cost-conscious will prefer a clean and comfortable bus or train. Tickets for express buses and trains are available at convenient kiosks inside the public arrival bays of the airport, usually just beyond the restricted access immigration and customs areas.

For domestic air travel, both JAL and ANA, along with some smaller Japanese carriers, serve regional cities such as Hiroshima, Nagasaki, Sendai and Sapporo. Some domestic flights departing or arriving in the Tokyo area use **Haneda Airport** in Tokyo Bay, which is accessible via monorail from Hamamatsu-cho Station on the Yamanote Line loop train.

GETTING AROUND

By Train

Without question, the easiest way to navigate Japan's cities and countryside is by **train**. A vast network of local, limited express and express trains—many of which connect to bus routes—means there's rarely a need to travel by car, rental or otherwise. Japan's former national railroad monopoly has been broken up into several regional companies, but most still go by the old name **Japan Rail** (www.japanrail.com). The trains are uniformly clean, comfortable, and safe—and almost always on time. Keep in mind that while some long-distance trains have sleeper cars, most train service stops near midnight or earlier.

Most Japanese cities also have well-developed **subway** systems whose stations often connect to subterranean shopping centers and above-ground JR sister stations. Like the trains, Japan's subways are clean and safe; in many large cities, the trains announce the next station and transfer options in both English and Japanese. The subway systems also usually shut down at or near midnight.

Japan Rail Pass If you plan on traveling between cities in Japan, be sure to purchase a Japan Rail Pass for unlimited travel on Japan Railways and affiliated trains (including most *shinkansen* bullet trains). It is available only to foreign visitors and, with a few exceptions, *must be purchased before you arrive in Japan*. Buy one from travel agents such as the **Japan Travel Bureau** (**© 800/235-3523**) and Japanese airline offices in the U.S. For details, see www.japanrailpass.net or www.japanrail.com.

By Bus

Buses are just as important to Japanese commuters as trains, but their routes can be more difficult for short-time visitors to decipher. Express buses link major cities and can be a comfortable alternative to trains, especially for mountainous areas where train service is limited. Local buses ferry passengers to all manner of municipal and rural addresses. Moreover, buses are usually by far the cheapest option for travelers on a budget. But be careful not to get stranded, as few buses run after 11pm on weekdays. Many bus fare change machines can break a ¥1,000 bill, but it's a good idea to carry enough change (¥100 or ¥500 coins), just in case.

By Car

Rental cars are rarely a good idea in Japan, especially for big cities such as Osaka and Tokyo, where twisting streets and traffic jams are the norm. A rental car may be more useful in rural areas with limited access to public transportation, but expect to pay rates that are far in excess of what you would expect in the U.S. or many other countries. If you do plan to drive, you will need an international driver's license. Long-term foreign visitors and residents may apply for a Japanese driver's license, but that is an arduous process.

By Taxi

Japanese **taxis** are not the cheapest way to travel since just getting in the cab will set you back about $5. But they can be convenient for short trips across town—especially during rain storms or heat waves. Japanese taxis are as clean as their drivers are courteous. The passenger seats are usually covered with fresh linen, and drivers wear traditional white gloves. Most cabs nowadays boast sophisticated GPS navigational systems that show the shortest and least-crowded routes. In Tokyo, the majority of taxis now accept credit cards, though for shorter trips cash is appreciated. Don't forget to let the driver open the door automatically when you enter and exit a cab. All Japanese taxis come equipped with this function and drivers do not take kindly to riders who grab the rear door handles.

By Ferry

Because Japan is an island nation, an extensive ferry network links the string of islands. Although travel by ferry takes longer, it's also cheaper and can be a pleasant, relaxing experience. For example, you can take a ferry from Osaka to Beppu (on

Kyushu), with fares starting at ¥7,900 for the 11-hour trip. Contact the **Tourist Information Center** (© **03/3201-3311**) for more details concerning ferries, prices, schedules, and telephone numbers of the various ferry companies.

CHAPTER THREE

LODGING

This chapter will help you find the right accommodations, at the right price, and the amenities you might need during your stay.

ROOM PREFERENCES

Please recommend ____	____を選んでいただけますか。 ____*o erande itadake masu ka.*
a clean hostel.	清潔なホステル *seiketsu na hosuteru*
a moderately priced hotel.	手頃な値段のホテル *tegoro na nedan no hoteru*
a moderately priced B&B.	手頃な値段のB & B *tegoro na nedan no B ando B*
a good hotel / motel.	良いホテル / モーテル *yoi hoteru / mōteru*
Does the hotel have ____?	そのホテルに____はありますか? *sono hoteru ni ____ wa arimasu ka.*
a pool	プール *pūru*
a casino	カジノ *kajino*
suites	スイートルーム *suīto rūmu*
a balcony	バルコニー *barukonī*
a fitness center	ジム *jimu*
a spa	スパ *supa*
a private beach	プライベートビーチ *puraibēto bīchi*

a tennis court	テニスコート *tenisu kōto*
I would like a room for ____.	____の部屋をお願いします。 *____ no heya o onegai shimasu.*

For full coverage of number terms, see p6.

I would like ____	____がいいのですが。 *____ ga ii no desuga.*
a king-sized bed.	キングサイズのベッド *kingu saizu no beddo*
a double bed.	ダブル サイズのベッド *daburu saizu no beddo*
twin beds.	ツイン サイズのベッド *tsuin saizu no beddo*
adjoining rooms.	続き部屋 *tsuzuki beya*
a smoking room.	喫煙できる部屋 *kitsuen dekiru heya*
a non-smoking room.	禁煙の部屋 *kin en no heya*

Listen Up: Reservations Lingo

ただいま空室がございません。 *tadaima kūshitsu ga gozaimasen.*	We have no vacancies.
何日ご滞在ですか？ *nan nichi gotaizai desu ka.*	How long will you be staying?
喫煙または禁煙のどちらがよろしいですか？ *kitsuen matawa kin en no dochira ga yoroshii desu ka.*	Smoking or non smoking?

a private bathroom.	プライベート バスルーム *puraibēto basurūmu*
a shower.	シャワー *shawā*
a bathtub.	浴槽 *yokusō*
air conditioning.	エアコン *eakon*
television.	テレビ *terebi*
cable.	ケーブル *kēburu*
satellite TV.	衛星テレビ *eisei terebi*
a telephone.	電話 *denwa*
Internet access.	インターネット接続 *intānetto setsuzoku*
high-speed Internet access.	高速インターネット接続 *kōsoku intānetto setsuzoku*
a refrigerator.	冷蔵庫 *reizōko*
a beach view.	ビーチの見える *bīchi no mieru*
a city view.	街の景色の見える *machi no keshiki no mieru*
a kitchenette.	簡易キッチン *kan i kicchin*
a balcony.	バルコニー *barukonī*
a suite.	スイートルーム *suīto rūmu*
a penthouse.	ペントハウス *pento hausu*

I would like a room ____	____部屋をお願いしたいのですが。 *____ heya o onegai shitai no desuga.*
on the ground floor.	1階にある *ikkai ni aru*
near the elevator.	エレベーターに近い *erevētā ni chikai*
near the stairs.	階段に近い *kaidan ni chikai*
near the pool.	プールに近い *pūru ni chikai*
away from the street.	道路から離れた *dōro kara hanareta*
I would like a corner room.	角部屋をお願いしたいのですが。 *kado beya o onegai shitai no desuga.*
Do you have ____?	____はありますか？ *____ wa arimasu ka.*
a crib	ベビーベッド *bebī beddo*
a foldout bed	折りたたみ式ベッド *oritatami shiki beddo*

FOR GUESTS WITH SPECIAL NEEDS

I need a room with ____	____部屋をお願いします。 *______ heya o onegai shimasu.*
wheelchair access.	車椅子で移動できる *kurumaisu de idō dekiru*
services for the visually impaired.	視覚障害者のための設備のある *shikaku shōgaisha no tame no setsubi no aru.*
services for the hearing impaired.	聴覚障害者のための設備のある *chōkaku shōgaisha no tame no setsubi no aru*

I am traveling with a service dog. | 介護犬を連れているのですが。 *kaigo ken o tsurete iru no desuga.*

MONEY MATTERS

I would like to make a reservation. | 予約をしたいのですが。 *yoyaku o shitai no desuga.*

How much per night? | 一泊の料金はいくらですか? *ippaku no ryōkin wa ikura desu ka.*

Do you have a ____? | ____はありますか? *____ wa arimasu ka.*

weekly / monthly rate | 週 / 月単位の料金 *shū / tsuki tan i no ryōkin*

a weekend rate | 週末料金 *shūmatsu ryōkin*

We will be staying for ____ days / weeks. | ____日間 / 週間滞在する予定です。 *____ nichikan / shūkan taizai suru yotei desu.*

For full coverage of number terms, see p6.

When is checkout time? | チェックアウトの時間はいつですか? *chekku auto no jikan wa itsu desu ka.*

For full coverage of time-related terms, see p13.

Do you accept credit cards / travelers checks? | クレジットカード/トラベラーズ チェックは使えますか? *kurejitto-kādo/toraberāzu-chekku wa tsukae masu ka.*

May I see a room? | お部屋を見せていただけますか? *oheya o misete itadake masu ka.*

How much are taxes? | 税金はいくらですか? *zeikin wa ikura desu ka.*

Is there a service charge? | サービス料はありますか? *sābisu ryō wa arimasu ka.*

I'd like to speak with the manager. | マネージャーとお話ししたいのですが。 *manējā to ohanashi shitai no desuga.*

IN-ROOM AMENITIES

I'd like to place an international call.	国際電話をかけたいのですが。 *kokusai denwa o kaketai no desuga.*
I'd like to place a long-distance call.	市外電話をかけたいのですが。 *shigai denwa o kaketai no desuga.*
I'd like directory assistance in English.	英語の番号案内にかけたいのですが。 *eigo no bangō annai ni kaketai no desuga.*
I'd like room service.	ルーム サービスをお願いします。 *rūmu sābisu o onegai shimasu.*

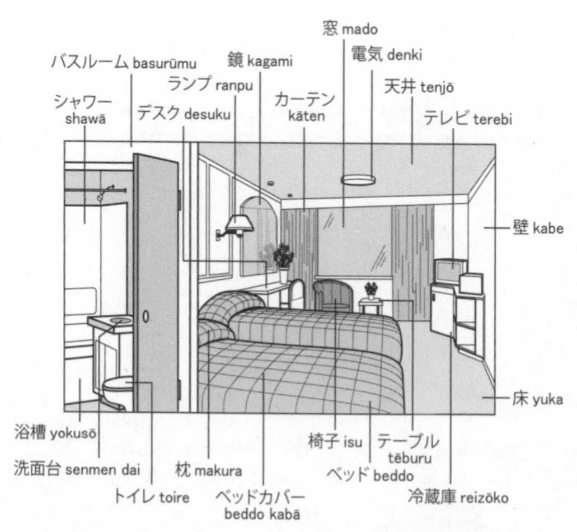

I'd like maid service.	メードのサービスをお願いします。 *mēdo no sābisu o onegai shimasu.*
I'd like the front desk	フロントデスクをお願いします。 *furonto desuku o onegai shimasu.*
Do you have room service?	ルーム サービスはありますか？ *rūmu sābisu wa arimasu ka.*
When is the kitchen open?	食事は何時からできますか？ *shokuji wa nanji kara deki masu ka.*
When is breakfast served?	朝食は何時ですか？ *chōshoku wa nan ji desu ka.*

For full coverage of time-related terms, see p13.

Do you offer massages?	マッサージのサービスはありますか？ *massāji no sābisu wa arimasu ka.*
Do you have a lounge?	ラウンジはありますか？ *raunji wa arimasu ka.*
Do you have a business center?	ビジネス センターはありますか？ *bijinesu sentā wa arimasu ka.*
Do you serve breakfast?	朝食は出ますか？ *chōshoku wa demasu ka.*

Instructions for Dialing the Hotel Phone

他の部屋に電話をかけるには部屋番号をダイヤルします。 *hoka no heya ni denwa o kakeru niwa, heya bangō o daiyaru shimasu.*	To call another room, dial the room number.
市内電話をかけるには、最初に9をダイヤルします。 *shinai denwa o kakeru niwa, saisho ni kyū o daiyaru shimasu.*	To make a local call, first dial 9.
オペレーターを呼びだすには、0をダイヤルします。 *operētā o yobi dasu niwa, zero o daiyaru shimasu.*	To call the operator, dial 0.

Do you have Wi-Fi?	ワイヤーレスインターネット はありますか？ *waiyāresu intānetto wa arimasu ka.*
May I have a newspaper in the morning?	朝、新聞をもらえますか？ *asa, shinbun o morae masu ka.*
Do you offer a tailor service?	仕立屋のサービスはありますか？ *shitateya no sābisu wa arimasu ka.*
Do you offer laundry service?	ランドリー サービスはありますか？ *randorī sābisu wa arimasu ka.*
Do you offer dry cleaning?	ドライ クリーニングのサービスはありますか？ *dorai kurīningu no sābisu wa arimasu ka.*
May we have ____?	____いただけませんか？ _______*itadake masen ka.*
clean sheets today	今日、きれいなシーツ *kyō, kirei na shītsu*
more towels	タオルをもっと *taoru o motto*
more toilet paper	トイレット ペーパーをもっと *toiretto pēpā o motto*
extra pillows	枕をもっと *makura o motto*
Do you have an ice machine?	製氷機はありますか？ *seihyō ki wa arimasu ka.*
Did I receive any ____?	私に____はありますか？ *watashi ni ____ wa arimasu ka.*
messages	伝言 *dengon*
mail	手紙 *tegami*
faxes	ファックス *fakkusu*
A spare key, please.	スペアー キーをください。 *supeā kī o kudasai.*

More hangers please.	ハンガーをもっとください。 *hangā o motto kudasai.*
I am allergic to down pillows.	私は羽毛の枕にアレルギー反応が起きます。 *watashi wa umō no makura ni arerugī hannō ga okimasu.*
I'd like a wake up call.	モーニング コールをお願いします。 *mōningu kōru o onegai shimasu.*

For full coverage of time-related terms, see p13.

Do you have alarm clocks?	目覚まし時計はありますか？ *mezamashi dokei wa arimasu ka.*
Is there a safe in the room?	室内に金庫はありますか？ *shitsu nai ni kinko wa arimasu ka.*
Does the room have a hair dryer?	室内にヘアー ドライヤーはありますか？ *shitsu nai ni heā doraiyā wa arimasu ka.*

HOTEL ROOM TROUBLE

May I speak with the manager?	マネージャーとお話したいのですが。 *manējā to ohanashi shitai no desuga.*
The television does not work.	テレビが見れないんです。 *terebi ga mirenai n desu.*
The telephone does not work.	電話が使えないんです。 *denwa ga tsukaenai n desu.*
The air conditioning does not work.	エアコンがきかないんです。 *eakon ga kikanai n desu.*
The Internet access does not work.	インターネットの接続ができないんです。 *intānetto no setsuzoku ga dekinai n desu.*
The cable TV does not work.	ケーブルテレビが見れないんんです。 *kēburu terebi ga mirenai n desu.*

There is no hot water.	お湯が出ないんです。 *oyu ga denai n desu.*
The toilet is over-flowing!	トイレの水が溢れているんです! *toire no mizu ga afurete irun desu.*
This room is ____	この部屋は *kono heya wa ____*
too noisy.	騒音がひど過ぎます。 *sōon ga hido sugi masu.*
too cold.	寒すぎます。 *samu sugi masu.*
too warm.	暖か過ぎます。 *atataka sugi masu.*
This room has ____	この部屋に____がいます。 *kono heya ni____ ga imasu.*
bugs.	虫 *mushi*
mice.	ねずみ *nezumi*
I'd like a different room.	別の部屋に替えていただけませんか。 *betsu no heya ni kaete itadake masen ka.*
Do you have a bigger room?	これより大きい部屋はありますか? *kore yori ōkii heya wa arimasu ka.*

I locked myself out of my room.
ドアに鍵がかかってしまい部屋に入ることができないんです。
doa ni kagi ga kakatte shimai heya ni hairu koto ga deki nai n desu.

Do you have any fans?
扇風機はありますか？
senpūki wa arimasu ka.

The sheets are not clean.
シーツが汚れています。
shītsu ga yogorete imasu.

The towels are not clean.
タオルが汚れています。
taoru ga yogorete imasu.

The room is not clean.
部屋が汚れています。
heya ga yogorete imasu.

The guests next door / above / below are being very loud.
隣 / 上の階 / 下の階の部屋がとてもうるさいんです。
tonari / ue no kai / shita no kai no heya ga totemo urusai n desu.

CHECKING OUT

I think this charge is a mistake.
この請求額は間違っていると思います。
kono seikyū gaku wa machigatte iru to omoi masu.

Please explain this charge to me.
なぜこの請求額になるのか説明していただけますか。
naze kono seikyūgaku ni naru noka setsumei shite itadake masu ka.

Thank you, we enjoyed our stay.
楽しく滞在しました。ありがとうございました。
tanoshiku taizai shimashita. arigatō gozaimashita.

The service was excellent.
サービスがとてもよかったです。
sābisu ga totemo yokatta desu.

The staff is very professional and courteous.
スタッフはとてもプロフェッショナルで親切です。
sutaffu wa totemo purofesshonaru de shinsetsu desu.

Please call a cab for me.
タクシーを呼んでいただけますか。
takushī o yonde itadake masu ka.

Would someone please get my bags?
どなたか 私の荷物を取ってきていただけませんか？
donata ka watashi no nimotsu o totte kite itadake masen ka.

HAPPY CAMPING

I'd like a site for ____
____場所が欲しいんですが。
_______ basho ga hoshii n desuga.

a tent.
テントを張る
tento o haru

a camper.
キャンパーのための
kyanpā no tame no

Are there ____?
ここに____はありますか？
koko ni ____ wa arimasu ka.

bathrooms
トイレ
toire

showers
シャワー
shawā

Is there running water?
ここに水道水はありますか？
koko ni suidōsui wa arimasu ka.

Is the water drinkable?
この水は飲めますか？
kono mizu wa nome masu ka.

Where is the electrical hookup?
電気の接続部はどこにありますか？
denki no setsuzoku bu wa doko ni arimasu ka.

JAPANESE HOTEL BASICS

Japanese hotels, motels, inns and bed-and-breakfasts embrace the concept of hospitality like those in few other nations. Indeed, it is hard not to be treated like a king or queen, no matter how modest the accommodations. That said, staying overnight in Japan does mean making some adjustments to the local culture. That is especially true in traditional inns (known as *ryokan* or *minshuku*) that predominate in rural areas, but it is also true to some extent in metropolitan hotels operated by global chains. For example, most prices for overnight stays are quoted in yen on a per person basis, not per room. While exceptions are often made for foreign visitors who reserve rooms ahead of time at major hotels, that is rarely the case at smaller hotels, motels and inns. Also, prices often include one or more meals—usually breakfast, but also dinner at *ryokan*.

Most rooms in Japan come complete with disposable toothbrushes (and miniature tubes of toothpaste), razors, slippers and freshly starched *yukata* robes. Interestingly, many hotels here have yet to adopt the larcenous phone-use policies common in the U.S., so calling cards aren't requisite for domestic in-room calls. Yet the size of rooms is almost uniformly small—and downright tiny at no frills "business hotels" or sleeping tube-filled "capsule hotels." Keep in mind that the garish "love hotels" tucked away in urban red light districts or sticking out along rural routes in the countryside charge for "rest" by the hour. Although you can sometimes stay overnight, this may not be ideal. Similarly, nap centers found in big cities charge by the hour—but only for shut-eye.

WESTERN-STYLE HOTELS

Most cities and towns in Japan have many options for travelers who prefer beds to futons (floor mattresses), ranging from five-star resort hotels to more pedestrian "business hotels." Larger rooms with views are, of course, more expensive, but generally speaking, most hotels have uniform and relatively inflexible pricing policies. You are more likely to receive a discount by booking from a package tour operator than by simply calling the front desk. A notable exception is for off-season packages. Note that most Japanese couples prefer to sleep in separate beds, so the majority of rooms at a given hotel come with twin beds. Similarly, while non-smoking rooms are much more widely available today than a few years ago, requesting one may limit options. It is not unusual to find ashtrays in ostensibly non-smoking rooms, particularly in Japan's business hotels.

Internationally known luxury hotel chains have a major presence in Japan—one that seems to be growing every year. The **Hilton** (www.hilton.com) and **Hyatt** (www.hyatt.com) chains have long had a presence in major Japanese cities; newer additions in Tokyo include the **Four Seasons** (www.fourseasons.com), **Mandarin Oriental** (www.mandarinoriental.com/tokyo) and **Peninsula Hotels** (tokyo.peninsula.com). Keep in mind that while the staff at these hotels almost always speak passable English and are used to foreign visitors, most of these chains cater more to domestic tourists and business travelers. A major constituency for these luxury hotels is the weekend wedding party, so it's not unusual for them to sell out entirely on Saturdays.

Japanese chains such as the **ANA** (www.anaihghotels.co.jp/eng), **New Otani** (www.newotani.co.jp/en) and **Prince Hotel** (www.princejapan.com) groups are the dominant players, especially in second-tier cities. Business hotels—often located just outside major train stations—include the budget **APA** (www.apahotel.com), **JAL** (www.jalhotels.com) and **Toyoko** chains (www.toyoko-inn.com/eng).

JAPANESE-STYLE INNS

No trip to Japan is complete without at least one night in a traditional Japanese-style inn. While often very expensive compared to plain vanilla hotels, they offer a cultural immersion you are not soon to forget. The charms range from the *futon* beds on the floor to *shoji* rice paper screens, kimono-clad staff and communal bathing tubs. An overnight stay is usually inclusive of meals—often dinner and breakfast. But don't plan on over-sleeping: even the most expensive resort inns have early riser wake-up policies and mandatory mid-morning check out times.

Broadly speaking, Japanese inns can be divided into two main categories—the more expensive *ryokan* and the cheaper *minshuku*. Whereas staying at a *ryokan* is an all-inclusive package that usually means gourmet Japanese meals (with unfamiliar dishes for adventurous palates) and personalized service, *minshuku* are more akin to bed-and-breakfasts where dinner is optional and guest services are limited. Both types of inns are mostly located in rural areas or second-tier cities, have fewer than 20 to 30 rooms, feature communal bath(s) and always charge by the person (not by the room).

While the concept of a communal bath may seem daunting, it is, in fact, one of the best parts of a visit to Japan. Few experiences are as relaxing as slipping into a steaming pool of water, usually in a giant stone or cypress tub. Some are located outdoors in a fenced off patio. Many ryokan boast several different baths. Communal baths are almost always segregated by sex and completely platonic in nature; no hanky-panky is allowed. A subset of *ryokan* and *minshuku* are located near hot springs and use natural mineral water, which the Japanese believe has beneficial properties for health and overall well-being. It is not uncommon for Japanese to structure an entire holiday around a visit to one of Japan's many famed hot springs.

Inn Ettiquette

It is very important for foreign guests to follow what may seem to be needlessly rigid rules regarding the use of restrooms and communal baths. Inn rest rooms require special slippers (usually green or red) that must be worn in the toilet area—and *only* in the toilet area. Make sure to leave your regular room slippers outside. Failing to do this will bring the wrath of the innkeeper and staff. Similarly important is bathing etiquette, which requires a thorough wash *before* entering a communal bath. All bathing areas have low wash basins with spigots or showers where guests wash with soap and rinse themselves well.

Occasionally, an older Japanese guest will appear to forgo washing, but that is usually because he or she has already soaped up before taking an earlier dip. In any case, few acts in Japan are as taboo for a foreigner as wading into a bath without first subjecting oneself to a proper scrub (and rinse). Note that all Japanese communal baths ban entry to anyone with a tattoo, which is still closely associated with organized crime (sometimes a strategically placed hand towel can prevent problems.) Finally, keep in mind that meals served in *ryokan* and *minshuku* are almost exclusively local cuisine. Even where Western dishes are available, they are rarely authentic. For example, breakfast eggs and toast are often served cold.

CHAPTER FOUR

DINING

This chapter includes a menu reader and the language you need to communicate in a range of dining establishments and food markets.

FINDING A RESTAURANT

Would you recommend a good ____ restaurant?	よい____を教えていただけませんか？ *yoi ____ o oshiete itadake masen ka.*
local	地元のレストラン *jimoto no resutoran*
Chinese	中華料理店 *chūka ryōri ten*
family	ファミリーレストラン *famirī resutoran*
French	フレンス料理のレストラン *furansu ryōri no resutoran*
Indian	インド料理のレストラン *indo ryōri no resutoran*
Italian	イタリア料理のレストラン *itaria ryōri no resutoran*
gastropub / dining bar (izakaya)	居酒屋 *izakaya*
Japanese	和食の店 *washoku no mise*
Korean	韓国料理店 *kankoku ryōri ten*
pizza	ピザ屋 *piza ya*
steakhouse	ステーキハウス *sutēki hausu*

Thai	タイ料理の店 *tai ryōri no mise*
vegetarian	ベジタリアンのレストラン *bejitarian no resutoran*
Western	洋食屋 *yō shoku ya*
buffet	バイキング *baikingu*
inexpensive (budget)	あまり高くないレストラン *amari takaku nai resutoran*
Which is the best restaurant in town?	この街で最高のレストランはどれですか？ *kono machi de saikō no resutoran wa dore desu ka.*
Is there a late-night restaurant nearby?	この近くに深夜営業しているレストランはありますか？ *kono chikaku ni shinya eigyō shite iru resutoran wa arimasu ka.*
Is there a restaurant that serves breakfast nearby?	この近くに朝食を出すレストランはありますか？ *kono chikaku ni chōshoku o dasu resutoran wa arimasu ka.*
Is it very expensive?	値段は高いですか？ *nedan wa takai desu ka.*
Do I need a reservation?	予約が必要ですか？ *yoyaku ga hitsuyō desu ka.*
Do I have to dress up?	正装しなければなりませんか。 *seisō shinakere ba nari masen ka.*
Do they serve lunch?	ランチはやってますか？ *ranchi wa yatte masu ka.*
What time do they open for dinner?	ディナーは何時からですか？ *dinā wa nan ji kara desu ka.*
For lunch?	ランチは何時からですか？ *ranchi wa nan ji kara desu ka.*

What time do they close? 何時に閉店しますか？
nan ji ni heiten shimasu ka.

Do you have a take out menu? 持帰り用のメニューはありますか？
mochi kaeri yō no menyū wa arimasu ka.

Do you have a bar? バーはありますか？
bā wa arimasu ka.

Is there a café nearby? この近くに喫茶店はありますか？
kono chikaku ni kissa ten wa arimasu ka.

GETTING SEATED

Are you still serving? まだ開いていますか？
mada aite imasu ka.

How long is the wait? どのくらい待ちますか？
dono kurai machi masu ka.

Do you have a no-smoking section? 禁煙席はありますか？
kin en seki wa arimasu ka.

A table for ____, please. ____人座れるテーブルをお願いします。
____ nin suwareru tēburu o onegai shimasu.

For a full list of numbers, see p6.

Do you have a quiet table? 静かなテーブル席はありますか？
shizukana tēburu seki wa arimasu ka.

May we sit outside / inside please? 外 / 中に座ってもいいですか？
soto / naka ni suwattemo ii desu ka.

May we sit at the counter? カウンターに座ってもいいですか？
kauntā ni suwatte mo ii desu ka.

A menu please? メニューを見せてください。
menyū o misete kudasai.

Listen Up: Restaurant Lingo

喫煙席と禁煙席、どちらがよろしいですか？ *kitsu en seki to kin en seki, dochira ga yoroshii desu ka.*	Smoking or nonsmoking?
上着とネクタイが要ります。 *uwagi to nekutai ga iri masu.*	You'll need a tie and jacket.
申し訳ございませんが 半ズボンではお入りいただけません。 *mōshiwake gozai masen ga han zubon dewa o hairi itadake masen.*	I'm sorry, no shorts are allowed.
何かお飲み物をお持ちしましょうか？ *nani ka onomimono o omochi shima shō ka.*	May I bring you something to drink?
ワイン リストをご覧になりますか？ *wain risuto o goran ni narimasu ka.*	Would you like to see a wine list?
当店のスペシャルをご説明しましょうか？ *tōten no supesharu o gosetsumei shima shō ka.*	Would you like to hear our specials?
ご注文はお決まりですか？ *gochūmon wa okimari desu ka*	Are you ready to order?
申し訳ございませんが、クレジットカードが拒否されました。 *mōshiwake gozai masen ga, kurejitto kādo ga kyohi sare mashita.*	I'm sorry, sir, your credit card was declined.

ORDERING

Do you have a special tonight?	今夜はスペシャルはありますか？ *konya wa supesharu wa arimasu ka.*
What do you recommend?	何がお勧めですか？ *nani ga osusume desu ka.*
May I see a wine list?	ワインリストを見せていただけますか？ *wain risuto o misete itadake masu ka.*
Do you serve wine by the glass?	グラスワインはありますか？ *gurasu wain wa arimasu ka.*
May I see a drink list?	飲み物のメニューを見せていただけますか？ *nomi mono no menyū o misete itadake masu ka.*
I would like it cooked ____	____でお願いします。 ____ *de onegai shimasu.*
rare.	レア *rea*
medium rare.	ミディアムレア *midiamu rea*
medium.	ミディアム *midiamu*
medium well.	ミディアムウェル *midiamu weru*
well.	ウェルダン *werudan*
charred.	ベリーウェル *berī weru*
Do you have a ____ menu?	____向けメニューはありますか？ ____ *muke menyū wa arimasu ka.*
vegetarian	ベジタリアン *bejitarian*
children's	子供 *kodomo*

What is in this dish?	この料理には何が入っていますか？ *kono ryōri niwa nani ga haitte imasu ka.*
How is it prepared?	どのように調理されていますか？ *donoyō ni chōri sarete imasu ka.*
What kind of oil is that cooked in?	これにはどんなオイルが 使われていますか？ *kore niwa donna oiru ga tsukawarete imasu ka.*
Do you have any low-salt dishes?	減塩の料理はありますか？ *gen en no ryōri wa arimasu ka.*
On the side, please.	横に添えてください。 *yoko ni soete kudasai.*
May I make a substitution?	ほかのものに替えていいですか？ *hoka no mono ni kaete ii desu ka.*
I'd like to try that.	それを食べてみます。 *sore o tabete mimasu.*
Is that fresh?	それは新鮮ですか？ *sore wa shinsen desu ka.*
Excuse me! (to summon a waiter)	すみません！ *sumi masen.*
Extra butter, please.	バターをもう少しください。 *batā o mō sukoshi kudasai.*
No butter, thanks.	バターは要りません。 *batā wa iri masen.*
No cream, thanks.	クリームは要りません。 *kurīmu wa iri masen.*
Dressing on the side, please.	ドレッシングを横に添えてください。 *doressingu o yokoni soete kudasai.*
No salt, please.	塩を入れないでください。 *shio o ire naide kudasai.*
May I have some oil, please?	油をもらえますか？ *abura o morae masu ka.*

More bread, please.	パンをもう少しいただけますか。 *pan o mō sukoshi itadake masu ka.*
I am lactose intolerant.	私は牛乳が飲めません。 *watashi wa gyūnyū ga nome masen.*
Would you recommend something without milk?	牛乳が入っていないものでは何がお勧めですか? *gyūnyū ga haitte inai mono dewa nani ga osusume desu ka.*
I am allergic to ____	____にアレルギーがあります。 *____ ni arerugī ga arimasu.*
seafood.	魚介類 *gyokairui*
shellfish.	貝類 *kai rui*
nuts.	ナッツ類 *nattsu rui*
peanuts.	ピーナッツ *pīnattsu*
Water ____, please.	____水をお願いします。 *____ mizu o onegai shimasu.*
with ice	氷の入っている *kōri no haitte iru*
without ice	氷の入っていない *kōri no haitte inai*
I'm sorry, I don't think this is what I ordered.	すみませんが、これは私が注文したのと違うようです。 *sumi masen ga, kore wa watashi ga chūmon shita no to chigau yō desu.*
My meat is a little over / under cooked.	肉が少し焼けすぎています / よく焼けていません。 *niku ga sukoshi yake sugite imasu / yoku yakete imasen.*

My vegetables are a little over / under cooked.	野菜が少し煮えすぎています / よく煮えていません。 *yasai ga sukoshi nie sugite imasu / yoku niete imasen.*
There's a bug in my food!	食べ物の中に虫が入っています！ *tabemono no naka ni mushi ga haitte imasu.*
May I have a refill?	お代わりをいただけますか？ *okawari o itadake masu ka.*
A dessert menu, please.	デザートのメニューを見せてください。 *dezāto no menyū o misete kudasai.*

DRINKS

alcoholic	アルコール *arukōru*
neat / straight	ストレートで *sutorēto de*
on the rocks	ロックで *rokku de*
with (seltzer or soda) water	(炭酸水または ソーダ)水で *(tansansui / sōda) sui de*
draft beer	生ビール *nama bīru*
bottle beer	ビンビール *bin bīru*
wine	ワイン *wain*
house wine	ハウスワイン *hausu wain*
sweet wine	甘口ワイン *amakuchi wain*
dry white wine	辛口白 ワイン *karakuchi shiro wain*

rosé	ロゼ *roze*
scotch	スコッチ *sukocchi*
red wine	赤ワイン *aka wain*
whiskey	ウイスキー *uisukī*
sparkling sweet wine	甘口スパークリング ワイン *amakuchi supākuringu wain*
chuhai	酎ハイ *chūhai*
liqueur	リキュール *rikyūru*
brandy	ブランデー *burandē*
cognac	コニャック *konyakku*
gin	ジン *jin*
vodka	ウオッカ *uokka*
rum	ラム *ramu*
nonalcoholic	ノン アルコールの *non arukōru no*
hot chocolate	ホット チョコレート *hotto chokorēto*
lemonade	レモネード *remonēdo*
milkshake	ミルクセーキ *miruku sēki*
milk	ミルク *miruku*

tea	紅茶 *kōcha*
coffee	コーヒー *kōhī*
cappuccino	カプチーノ *kapuchīno*
espresso	エスプレッソ *esupuresso*
iced coffee	アイス コーヒー *aisu kōhī*
fruit juice	フルーツ ジュース *furūtsu jūsu*

For a full list of fruits, see p105.

SETTLING UP

I'm stuffed.	お腹が一杯です。 *onaka ga ippai desu.*
The meal was excellent.	とてもおいしかったです。 *totemo oishikatta desu.*
There's a problem with my bill.	お勘定が違うようなんですが。 *okanjō ga chigau yō nan desuga.*
My compliments to the chef!	シェフにとてもおいしかったと伝えてください! *shefu ni totemo oishikatta to tsutaete kudasai.*
Check, please.	お勘定をお願いします。 *okanjō o onegai shimasu.*

MENU READER

Japanese cuisine is far more varied than the offerings of most overseas Japanese restaurants, ranging from astronomically expensive haute cuisine to street food. While this is not a comprehensive guide, it will give you some idea of the diversity of the foods of Japan.

KAISEKI (懐石、会席)

These elaborate multi-course meals are becoming increasingly popular in the US. There are two types of *kaiseki.* One is based on the traditional *cha-kaiseki* (茶懐石), or food served during the traditional tea ceremony. Similar to the French menu *dégustation*, it involves multiple courses of small but elaborate dishes that vary according to season. The courses are predetermined; you do not order individual items. It is usually served at high-end Japanese restaurants known as *ryōtei* (料亭) and *kappō* (割烹), although nowadays, the word has become a catch-all name for any high-end tasting menu, so it is not unusual to find places offering French *kaiseki* menus.

The other form of *kaiseki* (会席) is served at banquets and is tailored toward drinking, featuring many dishes that go well with alcohol, which include *sashimi*, *tempura*, *aemono* and *sunomono.* The first part consists of an appetizer (*zensai*, 前菜), clear soup (*suimono*, 吸い物), and sashimi. The second part includes dishes that are grilled (*yakimono*, 焼物), steamed (*mushimono*, 蒸物), simmered (*nimono*, 煮物) and deep-fried (*agemono*, 揚物). An alternative to these would be a one-pot stew (*nabemono*, 鍋物). A salad, either vinegared (*sunomono*, 酢の物) or marinated (*aemono*, 和え物), also comes with this course. The final part is a course of boiled plain rice (*gohan*, 御飯), miso soup (*miso shiru*, 味噌汁), and pickles (*tsukemono*, 漬け物), served with green tea and some kind of fresh fruit.

BENTO (弁当)

Typically prepared for school and office lunchboxes, the bento is a boxed meal consisting of rice, pickles, and assorted finger foods. These can be found at any convenience store, supermarket or kiosk at a large train station. Bento sold at train stations are called *ekiben* (駅弁), and often contain some local flavor.

TEISHOKU (定食)

Teishoku are inexpensive set meals, usually consisting of meat or fish, some sides, soup and rice, which are all served at once. Restaurants that specialize in them, *teishoku-ya*, are comparable to luncheonettes or diners in the US.

IF YOU KNEW SUSHI

The popular combo of raw fish and vinegar-seasoned rice comes from an ages-old means of preserving fish. Sushi comes in a variety of forms:

Nigirizushi (握りずし): a small handful of rice topped with fish or other seafood and a dab of wasabi paste; also sometimes known as *Edomae* (江戸前) sushi.

Makizushi (巻ずし): rice and fillings rolled inside a wrapping of dried seaweed (*nori*) with the use of a flexible bamboo mat. The best-known example is *tekkamaki* (てっか巻き), or raw tuna.

Chirashizushi (散らしずし): sometimes called *barazushi* (ばらずし), or literally 'scattered sushi.' It consists of various, usually colorful, toppings attractively arranged on top of a bed of seasoned rice. Unlike *nigirizushi* or *makizushi*, which can be eaten by hand, it must be eaten with utensils.

inarizushi (いなりずし): sushi rice stuffed into pockets of sweetened thin, deep-fried tofu called *abura-age* (あぶらあげ). *Inari* is a Shinto deity who is associated with foxes. Foxes were believed to have a fondness for *abura-age*, hence the name.

oshizushi (おしずし): A style of sushi that originated in Osaka, it consists of sushi rice and fish pressed into a rectangular box and then cut into slices. The best-known version is *battera*, which is rice topped with seasoned mackerel and a thin slice of *konbu* (昆布).

FOOD TERMS

CONDIMENTS / SAUCES / SPICES

furikake ふりかけ: topping for hot rice, usually ground dried fish and nori, with salt
goma 胡麻: sesame
karashi からし: Japanese mustard
kinako 黄粉: soybean flour
kōshinryō 香辛料: spice
mirin みりん: sweet liquid flavoring
miso 味噌: fermented soybean paste
ponzu ぽん酢: condiment of citrus juice, vinegar and soy sauce
shōyu 醤油: soy sauce
tare たれ: sauce
tōgarashi 唐辛子: chili pepper
wasabi わさび: Japanese horseradish

GARNISHES / SIDES

fukujinzuke 福神漬け: pickled vegetables
gari がり: thinly sliced vinegared ginger
hijiki ひじき: seaweed
kinpira gobō きんぴらごぼう: burdock

konbu 昆布: kelp
nattō 納豆: fermented soybeans
nori のり: dried laver
shōga 生姜: ginger
takuan 沢庵: pickled daikon radish
tsukemono 漬け物: pickles
umeboshi 梅干し: pickled japanese plum
wakame わかめ: seaweed

GRAINS / RICE / RICE DISHES

chāhan チャーハン: fried rice
donburi 丼: bowl of rice topped with food
genmai 玄米: brown rice
gohan 御飯: cooked rice
gomoku meshi 五目飯: rice dish with chicken and assorted vegetables
kama meshi 釜飯: rice cooked in a large pot over a hearth
katsudon カツ丼: pork donburi
kayu 粥: rice porridge
kome 米: rice
meshi 飯: informal term for food or meal
mochi もち: rice cake
mugi 麦: grain; usually refers to barley
ojiya おじや: rice gruel; also called zōsui **(雑炊)**
oyako donburi 親子丼: chicken and egg donburi

MEATS / POULTRY

butaniku 豚肉: pork
gibie ジビエ: wild game in season
gyūniku 牛肉: beef
hitsuji 羊: lamb
horumon ホルモン: offal, variety meats
kamo 鴨: duck

katsu カツ: breaded and deep-fried meat, fish or chicken
motsu もつ: giblets, viscera
niku 肉: meat
nikujaga 肉じゃが: simmered dish of meat, potatoes and vegetables
shamo しゃも: gamecock, game fowl
tamago 卵 or 玉子: egg
toriniku 鳥肉: chicken meat

NOODLES

kitsune soba / udon きつねそば/うどん: noodles served with abura-age
rāmen ラーメン: Chinese-style noodles served in stock
soba そば: buckwheat noodles
sōmen 素麺: thin wheat noodles
udon うどん: soft, thick wheat noodles
udonsuki うどんすき: udon cooked in clear soup with vegetables and chicken or fish

SEAFOOD

aji あじ: horse mackerel
anago 穴子: saltwater conger eel
ankō あんこう: angler fish
awabi あわび: abalone
ayu 鮎: freshwater sweetfish
dojō どじょう: loach, a freshwater fish
ebi えび: prawn, shrimp, lobster
fugu ふぐ: puffer, blowfish
hamaguri はまぐり: clam
hamo はも: freshwater eel
hokke ほっけ: mackerel
hotategai 帆立て貝: scallop
ika いか: squid

ikura イクラ: salmon eggs
inada いなだ: young yellowtail tuna, also called hamachi **(はまち)**
iwashi いわし: sardine
kai 貝: mollusk
kaki かき: oyster
kamaboko 蒲鉾: processed fish paste
kani かに: crab
karasumi からすみ: dried mullet roe
katsuo かつお: bonito
katsuobushi カツオ節: dried bonito
kazunoko 数の子: herring roe
kegani 毛がに: hairy crab
koi 鯉: carp
maguro まぐろ: northern bluefin tuna
mentaiko 明太子: salted, spicy pollack roe
saba さば: chub mackerel
sakana 魚: fish
sanma さんま: Pacific saury
sake さけ: salmon
shirako 白子: soft roe; fish semen
suppon すっぽん: snapping turtle
surume するめ: dried squid
tai 鯛: sea bream; red snapper
tako たこ: octopus
takoyaki たこやき: grilled chopped octopus in batter
tara たら: cod
toro とろ: fatty tuna meat
unagi うなぎ: sea-born eel that migrates to freshwater
uni うに: sea urchin

SOUPS / STEWS / STOCK

chirinabe ちり鍋: *nabemono* of meat or fish, tofu and vegetables served with dipping sauce
dashi だし: soup stock made with fish and kelp
miso shiru 味噌汁: miso soup
mizutaki 水炊き: chicken *nabemono*
nabemono 鍋物: one-pot dish; stew
suimono 吸い物: clear soup
sumashijiru すまし汁: clear soup
zōni ぞうに: *mochi* in soup

SWEETS / SNACKS / DESSERTS

anko あんこ: sweet red bean paste
annindōfu 杏仁豆腐: almond jelly
kasutera カステラ: Castella cake
manjū まんじゅう: steamed bun with sweet or savory filling
senbei 煎餅: rice cracker
taiyaki たいやき: sweet cake shaped like a sea bream
wagashi 和菓子: Japanese confections, cakes, candy, cookies
yōkan 羊羹: sweet red bean jelly

TEA

bancha 番茶: common green tea
cha 茶: tea
genmaicha 玄米茶: green tea with roasted rice grains added for flavor
hōjicha焙じ茶: roasted green tea
maccha 抹茶: powdered green tea
mugicha 麦茶: barley tea
sencha 煎茶: higher-quality green tea usually reserved for guests

SPECIALTIES

fucha ryōri 普茶料理: Zen Buddhist vegetarian cuisine
izakaya 居酒屋: Japanese gastropub or dining bar
kabayaki かばやき: grilled fish or eel basted in a thick, sweet sauce
kappō 割烹: upscale Japanese restaurant
kushiyaki 串焼き: spit-roasting
kyō ryōri 京料理: Kyoto-style cuisine
oden おでん: Japanese hodgepodge
okonomiyaki お好み焼き: savory pancake
omakase おまかせ: chef's menu
osechi ryōri おせち料理: food for celebrating the New Year
robatayaki ろばたやき: grilled food prepared in front of you
ryōtei 料亭: upscale Japanese restaurant
shabu-shabu しゃぶしゃぶ: *nabemono* of thinly sliced meat and vegetables served with dipping sauce
shōjin ryōri 精進料理: vegetarian cuisine derived from the diet of Buddhist monks
sukiyaki すきやき: *nabemono* of meat and vegetables
sumibiyaki 炭火焼き: charcoal grilling
tempura 天ぷら: battered and deep-fried seafood and vegetables
teppanyaki 鉄板焼き: meat and vegetables grilled on an iron hot plate in front of you, à la Benihana
yakiniku 焼き肉: meat grilled on a griddle, usually over charcoal
yakitori 焼き鳥: chicken meat and parts grilled on a skewer

BUYING GROCERIES

In Japan, groceries can be bought at convenience stores, neighborhood stores, or large supermarkets.

AT THE SUPERMARKET

Where can I find ____?	____はどこにありますか？ ____ *wa doko ni arimasu ka.*
spices	スパイス *supaisu*
toiletries	化粧品 *keshōhin*
paper plates and napkins	紙皿とナプキン *kamizara to napukin*
canned goods	缶詰 *kanzume*
snack food	軽食 *keishoku*
baby food	ベビーフード *bebī fūdo*
water	水 *mizu*
juice	ジュース *jūsu*
bread	パン *pan*
cheese	チーズ *chīzu*
fruit	果物 *kudamono*
cookies	クッキー *kukkī*

AT THE BUTCHER SHOP

Is the meat fresh?	この肉は新鮮ですか？ *kono niku wa shinsen desu ka.*

Do you sell fresh ____ ?	新鮮な____はありますか？ *shinsen na ____ wa arimasu ka.*
beef	牛肉 *gyūniku*
pork	豚肉 *butaniku*
lamb	子羊の肉 *kohitsuji no niku*
Is the ____ fresh?	この____は新鮮ですか？ *kono ____ wa shinsen desu ka.*
fish	魚 *sakana*
seafood	シーフード *shīfūdo*
angler fish	あんこう *ankō*
abalone	あわび *awabi*
bonito	かつお *katsuo*
carp	鯉 *koi*
clam	はまぐり *hamaguri*
crab	かに *kani*
mollusk	貝 *kai*
octopus	たこ *tako*
oyster	かき *kaki*
Pacific saury	さんま *sanma*

prawn; shrimp	えび *ebi*
puffer; blowfish	ふぐ *fugu*
red snapper; sea bream	鯛 *tai*
salmon	さけ *sake*
salmon eggs	イクラ *ikura*
sardine	いわし *iwashi*
sea urchin	うに *uni*
scallop	帆立て貝 *hotategai*
tuna, yellowtail	いなだ or はまち *inada or hamachi*
tuna, northern bluefin	まぐろ *maguro*
tuna belly	とろ *toro*
May I smell it?	そのにおいをかいでもいいですか？ *sono nioi o kaide mo ii desu ka.*
Would you please ____ ?	____いただけませんか？ *____ itadake masen ka.*
filet it	おろして *oroshite*
debone it	骨を取り除いて *hone o tori nozoite*
remove the head and tail	頭と尻尾を取り除いて *atama to shippo o tori nozoite*

AT THE PRODUCE STAND / MARKET

Fruits

persimmon	柿 *kaki*
cherry	さくらんぼ *sakuranbo*
Japanese citron	柚子 *yuzu*
banana	バナナ *banana*
apple	りんご *ringo*
grapes	ぶどう *budō*
orange	オレンジ *orenji*
lime	ライム *raimu*
lemon	レモン *remon*
mango	マンゴー *mangō*
melon	メロン *meron*
cantaloupe	マスクメロン *masuku meron*
watermelon	スイカ *suika*
honeydew	甘露メロン *kanro meron*
cranberry	クランベリー *kuran berī*

peach	もも *momo*
apricot	杏 *anzu*
strawberry	いちご *ichigo*
blueberry	ブルーベリー *burūberī*
kiwi	キーウィー *kīwī*
pineapple	パイナップル *painappuru*
blackberries	ブラックベリー *burakkuberī*
grapefruit	グレープフルーツ *gurēpufurūtsu*
tangerine	みかん *mikan*
plum	プラム *puramu*
pear	梨 *nashi*

Vegetables

Japanese radish	大根 **daikon**
red bean	小豆 **azuki**
soybean	枝豆 **edamame**
winter mushroom	榎 **enoki**
burdock	ごぼう **gobō**

pumpkin	かぼちゃ kabocha
mushroom	きのこ kinoko
chestnut	くり kuri
black bean	黒豆 kuromame
Matsutake mushroom	松茸 matsutake
leek	ねぎ negi
Japanese green pepper	ピーマン pīman
lotus root	れんこん renkon
sweet potato	さつまいも satsumaimo
Shītake mushroom	しいたけ shītake
bamboo shoot	竹の子 takenoko
lettuce	レタス *retasu*
spinach	ほうれん草 *hōrensō*
avocado	アボガド *abogado*
artichoke	アーティチョーク *ātichōku*
beans	豆 *mame*
green beans	青豆 *ao mame*

tomato	トマト *tomato*
potato	じゃがいも *jagaimo*
onion	たまねぎ *tamanegi*
celery	セロリ *serori*
broccoli	ブロッコリー *burokkorī*
cauliflower	カリフラワー *karifurawā*
carrot	にんじん *ninjin*
corn	とうもろこし *tōmorokoshi*
cucumber	きゅうり *kyūri*
bean sprouts	もやし *moyashi*
okra	おくら *okura*
bamboo shoots	たけのこ *takenoko*
eggplant	なす *nasu*
yam	やまいも *yamaimo*
squash	うり *uri*

Fresh Herbs and Spices

black pepper	くろこしょう *kuro koshō*

salt	塩 *shio*
basil	バジル *bajiru*
parsley	パセリ *paseri*
garlic	にんにく *nin niku*
sugar	砂糖 *satō*

WHAT TO EAT

Japan offers an amazing variety of foods from around the world. It's not an overstatement to say that you can enjoy some of the world's finest Chinese, French, Korean and Italian food in big cities such as Osaka and Tokyo. Japan even does American-style fast food pretty well with local hamburger chains such as First Kitchen and Mos Burger. On the other hand, a trip to Japan should include plenty of more typical Japanese cuisine (*washoku*). Consider sampling the following list of traditional favorites:

Chawan-Mushi Egg custard with chunks of chicken or shrimp and gingko nuts.

Fugu Known as blowfish or globefish, this exotic species is a fish whose ovaries and intestines contain deadly poison and must be removed by a specially trained chef before serving, usually raw as sashimi or boiled in a hot pot with vegetables. Not your everyday dish—even for Japanese—*fugu* is considered a delicacy.

Gyoza Pan-fried pork, shrimp or vegetable dumplings.

Kaiseki One of the most expensive and elaborate forms of Japanese cuisine, *kaiseki* is more of a style than any one food. *Kaiseki* meals are always full-course affairs, usually served in a traditional *ryokan* inn or *ryotei* restaurant, starting with a clear broth and ending with rice.

Kama-Meshi A rice casserole with meat, seafood or vegetable toppings that is served in a small cast-iron pot.

Kushiage Japanese-style shish kabobs featuring breaded and deep-fried portions of skewered chicken, beef, seafood or vegetables.

Ocha-Zuki This is a common no-frills breakfast or snack dish that consists of hot green tea poured over a bowl of steaming rice. It is usually accented with small strips of dried seaweed, a pickled plum, or sometimes a piece of charbroiled salmon.

Okonomiyaki Sometimes called "Japanese pizza," this is a specialty of Osaka but can be found in most parts of Japan. It is basically a pancake with pork or seafood and cabbage mixed into the batter that, once cooked, is topped with mayonnaise, dried bonito flakes and Worcestershire sauce.

Ramen White wheat noodles served with slices of cooked pork or vegetables and dried seaweed. There are three main types of broth to choose from: brown soy sauce-flavored (*shoyu*), red or yellowy fermented soy paste (*miso*) or the milky white salty (*shio*.)

Sashimi Sliced raw fish served with a garnish of *wasabi* green horseradish and bright pink pickled ginger (*shoga*).

Shabu-Shabu Thin strips of raw Japanese beef that are dipped momentarily in boiling water to cook and then dipped in either a thin soy-based sauce or a thicker sesame seed-sauce.

Shojin-Ryori A semi-formal style of food created by Zen Buddhist monks that is completely vegetarian and features several types of tofu and vegetable dishes.

Soba Thin brown buckwheat noodles served either chilled in a basket (*zaru-soba*) or hot in a bowl (*kake-soba*), often with tempura or mountain vegetables (*san-sai*).

Sukiyaki Thin strips of Japanese beef which are stewed along with vegetables in a thick sake- and soy-based sauce and served with an (optional) raw egg for dipping.

Sushi Sliced raw fish served atop a bed of vinegar rice. Sushi rolls are called *maki-sushi*.

Tako-Yaki Fried balls of pancake batter mixed with scallions and octopus chunks that are served with a dried bonito flake and Worcestershire sauce topping.

Tempura Lightly deep-fried battered seafood and vegetables, often dipped in a thin soy-based sauce or sea salts.

Tonkatsu Deep-fried breaded pork cutlets, often served with Worcestershire sauce over a bed of rice or inside a white bread sandwich with shredded raw cabbage.

Udon Thick white wheat noodles usually served hot in a bowl with broth.

Unagi Eel broiled with a sweet barbeque sauce served on its own on skewers (*kabayaki*) or over a bed of white rice (*unaju* or *unadon*).

Yakisoba Brown buckwheat noodles stir-fried with cabbage and pork strips.

Yaki-Zakana Any form of grilled fish.

CHEAP EATS

Japanese food isn't always the cheapest option—even in Japan. But that shouldn't stop you from sampling at least some higher-end local fare. Items such as rice balls or bowls of soba are the yen-pinchers' best friend. Other options include a filling snack of *takoyaki* (the Gindaco chain is a safe bet) or a full meal at a teishoku-ya (cheap set menu restaurant) such as **Ootoya**, a chain that has some 80 branches in Tokyo alone.

WHAT TO DRINK

Non-Alcoholic Beverages

Most meals in Japan are served year-round with a cup of hot green tea, which many Japanese do not touch until they are finished eating. Chilled water is often not provided unless asked for—and water glasses are uniformly tiny. In the summertime, **chilled barley tea** or Chinese-style **oolong tea** are popular drinks. Japanese never add sugar or sugar substitutes to chilled or hot tea. It is also still relatively rare for Japanese to consume soft drinks such as cola with meals. Convenience stores are the best bet for a selection of soft drinks—and a hundred types of other chilled beverages such as "Pokari Sweat" and "CC Lemon."

Beer

Japanese are big beer drinkers, especially in the summertime. The four major domestic brands are **Asahi**, **Kirin**, **Sapporo** and **Suntory**, which compete with many microbreweries. Beer lovers say Japanese brew is among the world's best, but Western brands such as Budweiser and Heineken are also available in many urban bars and restaurants. Convenience stores and supermarkets often sell *happo-shu*, which is a beer-like malted beverage that is cheaper than regular beer. Few Japanese drink beer straight from the can or bottle. It is far more common to pour it out into a short glass. Japanese drinking etiquette requires one to keep one's drinking companions' glasses full (never pour your own). Also, be sure to use both hands when pouring—or receiving—a refill. Another option is draft beer, which is usually served in a chilled mug called a *jokki*. Note that unlike American beer drinkers, Japanese like large foam heads on their beers.

Liquor & Wine

Whiskey cut with water and served in a highball glass with ice is the national drink of Japan's salarymen, who fondly refer to it as *mizu-wari*. But other than whiskey, Western style hard liquor is uncommon in Japan outside of some big city bars and clubs.

Sake

Japanese rice wine, or sake, is a fermented drink served hot or cold. Most Japanese use the term *nihon-shu* to refer to sake, since the word sake can mean any alcoholic beverage. Sake can be divided into three main categories: *seishu*, which is cheap, lower quality sake with added non-rice alcohol that is often served warm; *ginjo* (or *dai-gingo*), a higher quality sake with added alcohol that can be served either warm or chilled; and *junmai*, a high quality sake with no added alcohol that is almost always served chilled. There are thousands of brands and dozens of distinctions such as *taru-zake* (cask-brewed sake). One good way to gauge sake is to look for the "+" or "-" sign on a menu or bottle. A higher plus sign indicates a drier sake, whereas a minus sign indicates a sweeter taste.

Shochu

Even more popular than sake in Japan these days, believe it or not, is a traditional distilled drink made from sweet potatoes or wheat called *shochu*. This vodka-like drink is often served with soda water and called a *chu-hai*. It can also be served straight at room temperature or warmed. This type of alcohol is also popular in China and South Korea.

A WORD ON TIPPING

Don't. No matter how hard you may find it to break the habit—or how good the service may have been—gratuitous gratuities are almost always unwelcome in Japan. Occasionally, a service charge of 10% or 15% may be tacked onto bills of large parties or at high-end restaurants in big cities. Some restaurants with views have a flat table charge.

CHAPTER FIVE
SOCIALIZING

Whether you're meeting people in a bar or a park, you'll find the language you need, in this chapter, to make new friends.

GREETINGS

Hello.	こんにちは。 *kon nichi wa.*
How are you?	お元気ですか？ *ogenki desu ka.*
Fine, thanks.	元気です。どうもありがとう。 *genki desu. dōmo arigatō.*
And you?	あなたもお元気ですか？ *anata mo ogenki desu ka.*
I'm exhausted from the trip.	旅行で疲れました。 *ryokō de tsukare mashita.*
I have a headache.	頭痛がしています。 *zutsū ga shite imasu.*
I'm terrible.	体の調子が悪いです。 *karada no chōshi ga warui desu.*
I have a cold.	カゼを引きました。 *kaze o hiki mashita.*
Good morning.	おはようございます。 *ohayō gozai masu.*
Good evening.	こんばんは。 *kon ban wa.*
Good afternoon.	こんにちは。 *kon nichi wa.*
Good night.	おやすみなさい。 *oyasumi nasai.*

Listen Up: Common Greetings

お会いできて嬉しいです。 *oai dekite ureshii desu.*	It's a pleasure.
とても嬉しいです。 *totemo ureshii desu.*	Delighted.
ご用を承ります。/ ご希望通りに。 *goyō o uke tamawari masu. / gokibō dōrini.*	At your service. / As you wish.
嬉しいです。 *ureshii desu.*	Charmed.
ごきげんよう。 *gokigen yō.*	Good day. (shortened)
こんにちは。 *kon nichi wa.*	Hello.
お元気ですか? *ogenki desu ka.*	How's it going?
最近どう? *saikin dō?*	What's up?
何をしているのですか? *nani o shite iru no desu ka*	What's going on?
さよなら! *sayonara*	Bye!
さようなら。 *sayōnara*	Goodbye.
それじゃ、また後で。 *soreja, mata ato de.*	See you later.

OVERCOMING THE LANGUAGE BARRIER

I don't understand.	わかりません。 *wakari masen.*
Please speak more slowly.	もっとゆっくり話してください。 *motto yukkuri hanashi te kudasai.*
Please speak louder.	もっと大きな声で話してください。 *motto ōkina koe de hanashi te kudasai.*
Do you speak English?	英語を話しますか？ *eigo o hanashi masu ka.*
I speak ____ better than Japanese.	日本語より____の方がうまく話せます。 *nihongo yori ________ no hō ga umaku hanase masu.*
Please spell that.	つづりを言ってもらえますか。 *tsuzuri o itte morae masu ka.*
Please repeat that?	もう一度お願いします。 *mō ichido onegai shimasu.*
How do you say ____?	____は何と言いますか？ ________ *wa nan to iimasu ka.*
Would you show me that in this dictionary?	それをこの辞書で示してもらえますか。 *sore o kono jisho de shimeshite morae masu ka.*

GETTING PERSONAL

People in Japan are generally friendly, but more formal than Americans or Europeans.

INTRODUCTIONS

What is your name?	あなたの名前は何ですか？ *anata no namae wa nan desu ka.*
My name is ____.	私は____です。 *watashi wa ________ desu.*
I'm very pleased to meet you.	お会いできて嬉しいです。 *oai dekite ureshii desu.*
May I introduce my ____	私の____を紹介します。 *watashi no ____ o shōkai shimasu.*
How is your ____?	____はお元気ですか？ *______ wa ogenki desu ka.*
wife	奥さん *oku san*
husband	ご主人 *go shujin*
child	お子さん *oko san*
friends	お友達 *o tomodachi*
boyfriend / girlfriend	ボーイフレンド / ガールフレンド *bōi furendo / gāru furendo*
family	ご家族 *go kazoku*
mother	お母さん *okā san*
father	お父さん *otō san*

brother / sister	ご兄弟 / ご姉妹 *go kyōdai / go shimai*
friend	お友達 *o tomodachi*
neighbor	ご近所の方 *go kinjo no kata*
boss	上司 *jōshi*
cousin	いとこ *itoko*
aunt / uncle	おばさん / おじさん *oba san / oji san*
fiancée / fiancé	婚約者 *kon yaku sha*
partner	パートナー *pātonā*
niece / nephew	姪御さん / 甥御さん *meigo san / oigo san*
parents	ご両親 *go ryōshin*
grandparents	お祖父さん、お祖母さん *ojīsan, obāsan*
Are you married / single?	ご結婚していますか / 独身ですか？ *go kekkon shite imasu ka / dokushin desu ka.*
I'm married.	結婚しています。 *kekkon shite imasu.*
I'm single.	独身です。 *dokushin desu.*
I'm divorced.	離婚しました。 *rikon shima shita.*

I'm a widow / widower.	未亡人 / やもめです。 *mibōjin / yamome desu.*
We're separated.	別居しています。 *bekkyo shite imasu.*
I live with my boyfriend / girlfriend.	ボーイフレンド / ガールフレンドと一緒に暮らしています。 *bōi furendo / gāru furendo to issho ni kurashite imasu.*
How old are you?	何歳ですか？ *nan sai desu ka.*
How old are your children?	お子さんは何歳ですか？ *oko san wa nan sai desu ka.*
Wow! That's very young.	まあ! とてもお若いですね。 *ma! totemo owakai desu ne.*
No you're not! You're much younger.	違いますよ! あなたの方がずっと若いです。 *chigai masuyo. anata no hō ga zutto wakai desu.*
Your wife / daughter is beautiful.	あなたの奥さん / お嬢さんは美人ですね。 *anata no oku san / ojō san wa bijin desu ne.*
Your husband / son is handsome.	あなたのご主人 / 息子さんはハンサムですね。 *anata no goshujin / musuko san wa hansamu desu ne.*
What a beautiful baby!	可愛い赤ちゃんですね! *kawaii aka chan desu ne.*
Are you here on business?	ここへは商用で来られましたか？ *koko ewa shōyō de korare mashita ka.*
I am vacationing.	私は休暇で来ました。 *watashi wa kyūka de kimashita.*

I'm attending a conference. 会議に参加します。
kaigi ni sanka shimasu.

How long are you staying? どのくらい滞在しますか？
dono kurai taizai shimasu ka.

What are you studying? 何を勉強していますか？
nani o benkyō shite imasu ka.

I'm a student. 私は学生です。
watashi wa gakusei desu.

Where are you from? どこから来ましたか？
doko kara kimashita ka.

PERSONAL DESCRIPTIONS

blond(e) 金髪
kinpatsu

brunette ブルネット
burunetto

redhead 赤毛
aka ge

straight hair 直毛
choku mō

curly hair 巻き毛
maki ge

kinky hair ちじれ毛
chijire ge

long hair 長い髪
nagai kami

short hair 短い髪
mijikai kami

tanned 日焼けした
hiyake shita

pale 青白い
ao jiroi

mocha-skinned 茶色い皮膚
chairoi hifu

black 黒人
koku jin

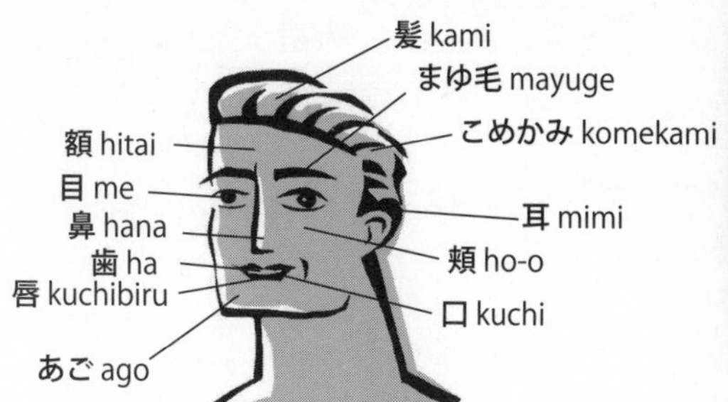

white	白人 *haku jin*
Asian	アジア人 *ajia jin*
African-American	アフリカ系アメリカ人 *afurika kei amerika jin*
caucasian	白人 *hakujin*
biracial	人種の混じった *jinshu no majitta*
tall	背が高い *se ga takai*
short	背が低い *se ga hikui*
thin	痩せている *yasete iru*
fat	太っている *futotte iru*
blue eyes	青い目 *aoi me*
brown eyes	茶色い目 *chairoi me*

green eyes	緑の目 *midori no me*
hazel eyes	薄茶色の目 *usucha iro no me*
eyebrows	まゆ毛 *mayu ge*
eyelashes	まつ毛 *matsu ge*
freckles	そばかす *sobakasu*
moles	ほくろ *hokuro*
face	顔 *kao*

DISPOSITIONS & MOODS

sad	悲しい *kanashii*
happy	嬉しい *ureshii*
angry	怒っている *okotte iru*
tired	疲れている *tsukarete iru*
anxious	心配している *shinpai shite iru*
confused	混乱している *konran shite iru*
enthusiastic	熱心である *nesshin de aru*

Listen Up: Nationalities

私は台湾人です。 *watashi wa taiwan jin desu.*	I'm Taiwanese.
私はチベット人です。 *watashi wa chibetto jin desu.*	I'm Tibetan.
私は韓国人です。 *watashi wa kankoku jin desu.*	I'm Korean.
私はフィリピン人です。 *watashi wa firipin jin desu.*	I'm Filipino.
私は中国人です。 *watashi wa chūgoku jin desu.*	I'm Chinese.
私はマカオ人です。 *watashi wa makao jin desu.*	I'm Macanese.
私はタイ人です。 *watashi wa tai jin desu.*	I'm Thai.
私はマレーシア人です。 *watashi wa marēshiya jin desu.*	I'm Malaysian.
私はベトナム人です。 *watashi wa betonamu jin desu.*	I'm Vietnamese.
私はネパール人です。 *watashi wa nepāru jin desu.*	I'm Nepalese.
私はラオス人です。 *watashi wa raosu jin desu.*	I'm Laotian.
私はヒンズー人です。 *watashi wa hinzū jin desu.*	I'm Indian.
私はビルマ人です。 *watashi wa biruma jin desu.*	I'm Burmese.
私はイタリア人です。 *iwatashi wa itaria jin desu.*	I'm Russian.
私は日本人です。 *watashi wa nihon jin desu.*	I'm Japanese.

For a full list of nationalities, see English / Japanese dictionary.

PROFESSIONS

What do you do for a living?	仕事は何をされていますか? *shigoto wa nani o sarete imasu ka.*
Here is my business card.	私の名刺をお渡しします。 *watashi no meishi o owatashi shimasu.*
I am ____	私は____です。 *watashi wa ____ desu.*
a doctor.	医者 *isha*
an engineer.	エンジニア *enjinia*
a lawyer.	弁護士 *bengoshi*
a salesperson.	販売員 *hanbai in*
a writer.	作家 *sakka*
an editor.	編集者 *henshū sha*
a designer.	デザイナー *dezainā*
an educator.	教育者 *kyōiku sha*
an artist.	芸術家 *geijutsu ka*
a craftsperson.	職人 *shoku nin*
a homemaker.	主婦 *shufu*
an accountant.	会計士 *kaikei shi*
a nurse.	看護師 *kango shi*

a musician.	音楽家 *ongaku ka*
a military professional.	職業軍人 *shokugyō gunjin*
a government employee.	公務員 *kōmu in*

DOING BUSINESS

I'd like an appointment.	面会の約束をしたいのですが。 *menkai no yakusoku o shitai no desuga.*
I'm here to see ____.	______に会いに来ました。 *______ ni ai ni ki mashita.*
May I photocopy this?	これをコピーしてもいいですか？ *kore o kopī shitemo ii desu ka.*
May I use a computer here?	ここでコンピュータを使用できますか？ *koko de konpyūtā o shiyō deki masu ka.*
What's the password?	パスワードは何ですか？ *pasuwādo wa nan desu ka.*
May I access the Internet?	インターネットにアクセスできますか？ *intānetto ni akusesu deki masu ka.*
May I send a fax?	ファックスを送信できますか？ *fakkusu o sōshin deki masu ka.*
May I use the phone?	電話を使用できますか？ *denwa o shiyō deki masu ka.*

PARTING WAYS

Keep in touch.	連絡を取り合いましょう。 *renraku o toriai mashō.*
Please write or email.	手紙かＥメールをください。 *tegami ka E mēru o kudasai.*

Here's my phone number.	私の電話番号をお渡しします。 *watashi no denwa bangō o owatashi shimasu.*
Call me.	私に電話をください。 *watashi ni denwa o kudasai.*
May I have your phone number / e-mail please?	あなたの電話番号 / E メールアドレスをいただけますか？ *anata no denwa bangō / E mēru adoresu o itadake masu ka.*
May I have your card?	あなたの名刺をいただけますか？ *anata no meishi o itadake masu ka.*
Give me your address and I'll write you.	あなたの住所を教えてください。手紙を書きます。 *anatao no jūsho o oshiete kudasai. tegami o kaki masu.*

TOPICS OF CONVERSATION

As in the United States or Europe, the weather and current affairs are common conversation topics.

THE WEATHER

It's so ____	とても____。 *totemo* ________。
Is it always so ____ ?	いつもそんなに____か？ *itsumo sonna ni* ________ *ka.*
sunny	晴れています *harete imasu*
rainy	雨が降ります *amega furi masu*
cloudy	曇っています *kumotte imasu*
humid	湿気が多いです *shikke ga ōidesu*

warm	暖かいです *atatakai desu*
cool	涼しいです *suzushii desu*
windy	風が強いです *kaze ga tsuyoi desu*
Do you know the weather forecast for tomorrow?	明日の天候予報を知っていますか? *ashita no tenki yohō o shitte imasu ka.*

THE ISSUES

What do you think about ____?	______について どう思いますか? ______ *ni tsuite dō omoi masu ka.*
democracy	民主主義 *minshu shugi*
socialism	社会主義 *shakai shugi*
American Democrats	アメリカの民主党 *amerika no minshutō*
American Republicans	アメリカの共和党 *amerika no kyōwatō*
monarchy	君主政治 *kunshuseiji*
the environment	環境 *kankyō*
climate change	気候変動 *kikōhendō*
the economy	経済 *keizai*
What political party do you belong to?	あなたはどの政党に属していますか? *anata wa dono seitō ni zokushi imasu ka.*

What did you think of the election in ____?	____の選挙についてどう思いましたか？ *________ no senkyo ni tsuite dō omoi mashita ka?*
What do you think of the war in ____?	____の戦争についてどう思いますか？ *________ no sensō ni tsuite dō omoi masu ka.*

RELIGION

Do you go to church / temple / mosque?	教会 / 寺院 / モスクへ行きますか？ *kyōkai / jiin / mosuku e ikimasu ka.*
Are you religious?	宗教を信仰していますか？ *shūkyō o shinkō shiteimasu ka.*
I'm ____ / I was raised ____	私は____です / 私は____として育ちました。 *watashi wa ________ desu / watashi wa ________ toshite sodachi mashita.*
Protestant.	プロテスタント *purotesutanto*
Catholic.	カトリック *katorikku*
Jewish.	ユダヤ教徒 *yudaya kyōto*
Muslim.	イスラム教徒 *isuramu kyōto*
Buddhist.	仏教徒 *bukkyōto*
Greek Orthodox.	ギリシャ正教徒 *girisha seikyōto*
Hindu.	ヒンズー教徒 *hinzū kyōto*
agnostic.	不可知論者 *fuka chiron sha*
atheist.	無神論者 *mu shinron sha*

I'm spiritual but I don't attend services.	私は信心深いですが、教会の礼拝には参加しません。 *watashi wa shinjin bukai desuga, kyōkai no reihai niwa sanka shimasen.*
I don't believe in that.	それは信じません。 *sore wa shinji masen.*
That's against my beliefs.	それは私の信仰に反します。 *sore wa watashi no shinkō ni hanshi masu.*
I'd rather not talk about it.	そのことについては話したくありません。 *sono koto ni tsuite wa hanashi taku arima sen.*

GETTING TO KNOW SOMEONE

Following are some conversation starters.

MUSICAL TASTES

What kind of music do you like?	どのような音楽が好きですか？ *dono yō na ongaku ga suki desu ka.*
I like _____	_____が好きです。 _________ *ga suki desu.*
rock 'n' roll.	ロックンロール *rokkun rōru*
hip hop.	ヒップ ホップ *hippu hoppu*
techno.	テクノ *tekuno*
soul.	ソウル *sōru*
classical.	クラシック *kurashikku*
jazz.	ジャズ *jazu*

country and western.	カウントリー アンド ウェスタン *kantorī ando uesutan*
reggae.	レゲー *regē*
calypso.	カリプソ *karipuso*
opera.	オペラ *opera*
show-tunes / musicals.	映画音楽 / ミュージカル *eiga ongaku / myūjikaru*
New Age.	ニューエイジ *nyū eiji*
pop.	ポップ *Poppu*

HOBBIES

What do you like to do in your spare time?	開いている時間には何をするのが好きですか? *aite iru jigan niwa nani o suru noga suki desu ka.*
I like ____	____のが好きです。 ________ *no ga suki desu.*
playing guitar.	ギターを弾く *gitā o hiku*
piano.	ピアノを弾く *piano o hiku*

For other instruments, see the English / Japanese dictionary.

painting.	絵を描く *e o kaku*
drawing.	スケッチする *sukecchi suru*
dancing.	ダンスをする *dansu o suru*
reading.	本を読む *hon o yomu*

watching TV.	テレビを見る *terebi o miru*
shopping.	買い物をする *kaimono o suru*
going to the movies.	映画を観に行く *eiga o mini iku*
hiking.	ハイキングをする *haikingu o suru*
camping.	キャンプをする *kyanpu o suru*
hanging out.	ぶらぶらする *bura bura suru*
traveling.	旅行する *ryokō suru*
eating out.	外食する *gaishoku suru*
cooking.	料理をする *ryōri o suru*
sewing.	裁縫をする *saihō o suru*
sports.	スポーツをする *supōtsu o suru*
Do you like to dance?	踊るのは好きですか？ *odoru nowa suki desu ka.*
Would you like to go out?	外に出かけたいですか？ *soto ni dekake tai desu ka.*
May I buy you dinner sometime?	いつか夕食をご馳走させてください。 *itsuka yūshoku o gochisō sasete kudasai.*
What kind of food do you like?	どんな料理が 好きですか？ *donna ryōri ga suki desu ka.*

For a full list of food types, see Dining in Chapter 4.

Would you like to go ____?	____行きたいですか? *________ ikitai desu ka.*
to a movie	映画を観に *eiga o mini*
to a concert	コンサートに *konsāto ni*
to the zoo	動物園に *dōbutsu en ni*
to the beach	ビーチに *bīchi ni*
to a museum	美術館に *bijutsu kan ni*
for a walk in the park	公園に散歩しに *kōen ni sapo shini*
dancing	ダンスをしに *dansu o shini*
Would you like to get ____?	____に行きたいですか? *________ ni ikitai desu ka.*
lunch	お昼ごはんを食べ *ohiru gohan o tabe*
coffee	コーヒーを飲み *kōhī o nomi*
dinner	夕食を食べ *yūshoku o tebe*
What kind of books do you like to read?	どんな本を読むのが好きですか? *donna hon o yomu noga suki desu ka.*
I like ____	_____が好きです。 *__________ ga suki desu.*
mysteries.	ミステリー *misuterī*
Westerns.	西部劇物 *seibu geki mono*
dramas.	劇の脚本 *geki no kyakuhon*

novels.	小説 *shōsetsu*
biographies.	伝記物 *denki mono*
auto-biographies.	自叙伝 *jijoden*
romance.	恋愛小説 *renai shōsetsu*
history.	歴史物 *rekishimono*

SOCIALIZING

While most Japanese are unfailingly polite and courteous toward visitors, getting beyond mere formalities can be difficult. Japanese society does not embrace spontaneous gatherings and instantaneous friendships. And even close friends in Japan seldom visit one another's homes. Of course, the Japanese can be very warm toward outsiders—particularly when a little effort is made to pick up some of the local lingo.

Among the best opportunities a visitor has for interacting with Japanese in an informal setting are the many annual festivals and cultural events. Most local shrines and temples have an annual festival featuring traditional dancing, food and game vendors. There are plenty of regional cultural events as well, some of which draw people from all over Japan. Check exact dates with the Japan National Tourist Organization or look up listings in local English language newspapers such as **The Japan Times** (www.japantimes.co.jp).

JAPANESE FESTIVALS

January

New Year's Day This is the most important national holiday in Japan – so important, in fact, that the celebrations last the better part of a week. Unlike in the U.S., most Japanese choose to spend the time quietly at home with their families; however, most shrines and temples remain open, and many Japanese visit them to pray dressed in colorful kimonos. *January 1.*

Coming-of-Age Day This holiday on the second Monday in January honors young people who have turned 20, the traditional first day of adulthood. Ceremonies are held throughout the country, and many 20-year-olds visit shrines or temples in kimonos. *Second Monday in January.*

February

Setsubun (Bean Throwing Festival) Held on the last day of winter on the lunar calendar, this festival involves trips to temples, where visitors toss dried beans while yelling "Evil out, Luck in!" *February 3 or 4.*

Lantern Festival An event at Kasuga Shrine in Nara featuring the lighting of more than 3,000 bronze and stone lanterns. *February 3 or 4.*

Snow Festival A world-renowned week-long festival staged along Odori Boulevard in Sapporo starring life-size snow and ice sculptures of famous buildings and characters. *Early February.*

Plum Blossom Viewing Festivals Events are held in parks, shrines and temples calling attention to plum blossoms, which are similar to cherry blossoms. *Late February.*

March

Hinamatsuri (Doll Festival) A rite of passage for families with girls in which figurines of the emperor, empress and other dignitaries are put on display in their homes. *March 3.*

April

O-Hanami Matsuri (Cherry Blossom Viewing Festivals) This traditional event starts as early as late March in southern Japan, but peaks in early-to-mid April in central Japan. *Early to Mid-April.*

Kanamara Matsuri This famed fertility festival at Kanayama Shrine in Kawasaki (near Tokyo) features a parade of giant phalluses, some carried by transvestites. *First Sunday in April.*

Takayama Spring Festival Dating back to the 15th century, this festival features dozens of elaborate floats wheeled through the streets of Takayama. *April 14 and 15.*

Gunmonji-do (Firewalking ceremonies) Held at Daishoin Temple, this event in Miyajima features firewalking on live coals for purification. *April 15 and November 15.*

May

Golden Week A nearly week-long stretch of national holidays. Many companies and shops close down entirely as the Japanese rush to the airports and train stations for vacations in the countryside or overseas. *April 29 to May 5.*

Children's Day This national holiday honors children. To commemorate the day off, boys often string up kites that look like carp from their roofs. *May 5.*

Toshogu Shrine Grand Festival More than 1,000 armor-clad participants escort three palanquins through the streets of Nikko to commemorate the day in 1617 when the great shogun Tokugawa Ieyasu's remains were interred there. *May 17 and 18.*

Sanja Matsuri Tokyo's most celebrated festival features some 100 portable shrines carried on the shoulders of men and women dressed in traditional garb near Asakusa Shrine. Friday, Saturday, and Sunday closest to *May 18.*

June

Hyakumangoku Festival A series of events held in Kanazawa celebrating Lod Maeda Toshiie's triumphant arrival in1583. The highlight is a parade with lion dances, ladder-top acrobatics and a torch-lit outdoor Noh performance. *June 8 to 14.*

Cormorant Fishing From June through September cormorants can be seen diving from small wooden boats to catch Japanese river trout called ayu in Kyoto, Nagoya and Gifu. *June to September.*

July

Gion Festival This is Kyoto's grandest spectacle, when more than 30 elaborate wheeled floats make their way through city streets accompanied by traditional music and dance. *July 16 and 17.*

Tenjin Festival One of Osaka's biggest festivals, this event at Temmangu Shrine features a procession of more than 100 sacred river boats, a 3,000-person parade with traditional costumes and a fireworks show. *July 24 and 25.*

Tokyo Fireworks Festival This fascinating display of advanced pyrotechnics on the banks of the Sumida River near Asakusa draws tens of thousands dressed in summer yukata robes—and millions more via television. *Last Saturday of July.*

August

Obon Festival This national event commemorates the dead who, according to Buddhist beliefs, revisit the world during this period. Many companies and stores close for the week-long period, during which Japanese often return to their hometowns to pay their respects. *Mid-July or Mid-August, depending on the area in Japan.*

Peace Ceremony A ceremony held in Hiroshima at Peace Memorial Park to remember those who perished in the atomic bomb blast on August 6, 1945. Thousands of lit lanterns are set adrift on the Ota River in their honor. (A similar ceremony is held in Nagasaki on August 9.) *August 6.*

Daimonji Bonfire A huge bonfire in the shape of the Chinese character for dai, which means "large, " is set ablaze near the peak of Mount Nyoigadake near Kyoto. *Mid-August.*

September

Yabusame Archery is performed on horseback at Kamakura's Tsurugaoka Shrine. *September 16.*

October

Takayama Autumn Festival See description under month of April. *October 9 and 10.*

Nagoya Festival The city's biggest festival is held the second week of October and features a parade with traditional floats and marching bands to commemorate three historical shoguns who hailed from Nagoya—including the great Tokugawa Ieyasu. *Second weekend in October.*

November

Shichi-Go-San Matsuri (Children's Shrine Visiting Day) Children aged three, five or seven years-old are dressed up in kimonos and escorted to shrines to pray for good fortune. *November 15.*

December

Gishi-sai A memorial at Tokyo's Sengakuji Temple honoring 47 ronin (masterless samurai) of yore who avenged their departed master's chief rival. *December 14.*

Hagoita-Ichi (Battledore Fair) A feudal-era festival held at Tokyo's Sensoji Shrine, showcasing elaborately decorated paddles with designs of famous kabuki actors. These make great souvenirs. *December 17 to 19.*

CHAPTER SIX

MONEY & COMMUNICATIONS

This chapter covers money, the mail, phone, Internet service, and other tools you need to connect with the outside world.

MONEY

Do you accept ____ ?	____は使えますか? *____ wa tsukae masu ka.*
Visa / MasterCard / Discover / American Express / Diners' Club credit cards	ビザカード / マスターカード / ディスカバー / アメリカン エキスプレス / ダイナーズ クラブ クレジットカード *biza kādo/ masutā kādo / disukabā / amerikan ekisupuresu / daināzu kurabu kurejitto kādo*
bills	紙幣 *shihei*
coins	硬貨 *kōka*
travelers checks	トラベラーズ チェック *toraberāzu chekku*
money transfer	振り込み *furikomi*
May I wire transfer funds here?	ここから電信振り込みできますか? *koko kara denshin furikomi deki masu ka.*
Would you please tell me where to find ____ ?	____はどこにありますか。 *____ wa doko ni arimasu ka.*
a bank	銀行 *ginkō*

a credit bureau	クレジット部 *kurejitto bu*
an ATM	ATM *ATM*
a currency exchange	通貨両替所 *tsūka ryōgae jo*
A receipt, please.	レシートをください。 *reshīto o kudasai.*
Would you tell me ____ ?	____は何ですか。 ____*wa nan desu ka.*
the exchange rate for dollars to ____	ドルから____への交換レート *doru kara ____ eno kōkan rēto*
the exchange rate for pounds to ____	ポンドから____への変換レート *pondo kara ____ eno kōkan rēto*
Is there a service charge?	サービス料は取られますか? *sābisu ryō wa torare masu ka.*
May I have a cash advance on my credit card?	このクレジットカードでキャッシングできますか? *kono kurejitto kādo de kyasshingu deki masu ka.*
Will you accept a credit card?	クレジットカードを使えますか? *kurejitto kādo o tsukae masu ka.*
May I have smaller bills, please.	両替してもらえますか。 *ryōgae shite morae masu ka.*
Can you make change?	おつりをもらえますか? *otsuri o morae masu ka.*
I only have bills.	お札しかありません。 *osatsu shika ari masen.*
Some coins, please.	小銭もまぜてください。 *kozeni mo mazete kudasai.*

Listen Up: Bank Lingo

ここに署名してください。 *koko ni shomei shite kudasai.*	Please sign here.
レシートのお返しです。 *reshīto no okaeshi desu.*	Here is your receipt.
身分証明書を見せてください。 *mibun shōmeisho o misete kudasai.*	May I see your ID, please?
トラベラーズ チェックが使えます。 *toraberāzu chekku ga tsukae masu.*	We accept travelers checks.
現金のみです。 *genkin nomi desu.*	Cash only.

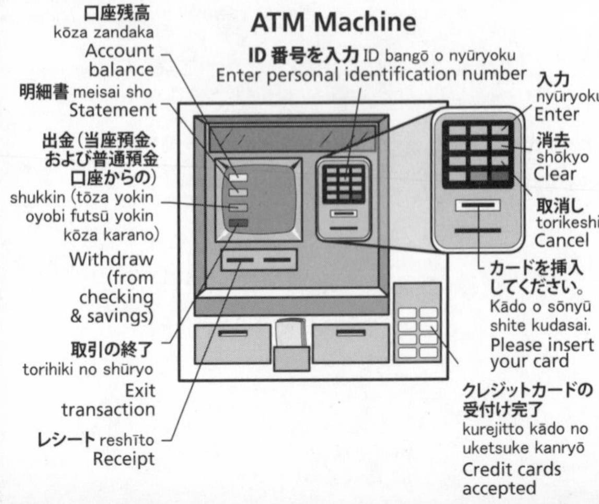

PHONE SERVICE

Where can I buy or rent a cell phone?	携帯電話はどこで借りるか買うことができますか？ *keitai denwa wa dokode kariru ka kau koto ga deki masu ka.*
What rate plans do you have?	どんな料金プランがありますか？ *donna ryōkin puran ga arimasu ka.*
Is this good throughout the country?	これは国中どこでも通用しますか？ *kore wa kunijū dokodemo tsūyō shimasu ka.*
May I have a prepaid phone?	プリペイドの電話をください。 *puri peido no denwa o kudasai.*
Where can I buy a phone card?	テレフォン カードはどこで買えますか？ *terefon kādo wa doko de kae masu ka.*
May I add more minutes to my phone card?	テレフォン カードにもっと時間を追加できますか？ *terefon kādo ni motto jikan o tsuika deki masu ka.*

MAKING A CALL

May I dial direct?	直通電話はできますか？ *chokutsū denwa wa deki masu ka.*
Operator please.	オペレーターをお願いします。 *operētā o onegai shimasu.*
I'd like to make an international call.	国際電話をかけたいのですが。 *kokusai denwa o kake tai no desuga.*
I'd like to make a collect call.	コレクト コールをお願いします。 *korekuto kōru o onegai shimasu.*
I'd like to use a calling card.	コーリングカードを使います。 *kōringu kādo o tsukai masu.*

Listen Up: Telephone Lingo

もしもし。 *moshi moshi.*	Hello?
お電話番号をお願いします。 *odenwa bangō o onegai shimasu.*	What number?
申し訳ございませんが、相手先の電話は話し中です。 *mōshiwake gozai masen ga, aite saki no denwa wa hanashi chū desu.*	I'm sorry, the line is busy.
一度切ってからおかけ直しください。 *ichido kitte kara mata okake naoshi kudasai.*	Please, hang up and redial.
申し訳ございませんが、どなたも電話にでられません。 *mōshiwake gozai masen ga, donata mo denwa ni derare masen.*	I'm sorry, nobody is answering.
カードの残り時間は10分です。 *kādo no nokori jikan wa juppun desu.*	Your card has ten minutes left.

Bill my credit card.	私のクレジットカードに請求してください。 *watashi no kurejitto kādo ni seikyū shite kudasai.*
May I bill the charges to my room?	私の部屋に請求してもらえますか？ *watashi no heya ni seikyū shite morae masu ka.*
May I bill the charges to my home phone?	これはわたしの家の電話に請求していただけますか？ *kore wa watashi no ie no denwa ni seikyū shite itadake masu ka.*
Information, please.	インフォメーションをお願いします。 *infomēshon o onegai shimasu.*
I'd like the number for ____.	____の番号をお願いします。 *____no bangō o onegai shimasu.*
I just got disconnected.	電話が切れてしまいました。 *denwa ga kirete shimai mashita.*
The line is busy.	只今話し中です。 *tadaima hanashi chū desu.*
I lost the connection.	電話が切れてしまいました。 *denwa ga kireteshimai mashita.*

INTERNET ACCESS

Where is an Internet café?	インターネット カフェはどこにありますか？ *intānetto kafe wa doko ni arimasu ka.*
Is there a wireless hub nearby?	この近くにワイヤーレス ハブはありますか？ *kono chikaku ni waiyā resu habu wa arimasu ka.*
How much do you charge per minute / hour?	1分 / 1時間いくらですか？ *ippun / ichi jikan ikura desu ka.*
Can I print here?	ここで印刷できますか？ *koko de insatsu deki masu ka.*
Can I burn a CD?	CDに書き込めますか？ *CD ni kaki kome masu ka.*
Would you please help me change the language preference to English?	言語を英語に変えるのを手伝っていただけませんか？ *gengo o eigo ni kaeru no o tetsudatte itadake masen ka.*
May I scan something?	何かスキャンしてもいいですか？ *nanika sukyan shitemo ii desu ka.*
Can I upload photos?	写真をアップロードできますか？ *shashin o appu rōdo deki masu ka.*

Do you have a USB port so I can download music?	**音楽をダウンロードできるUSBポートはありますか?** *ongaku o daun rōdo dekiru USB pōto wa arimasu ka.*
Do you have a machine compatible with iTunes?	**iTuneと互換性のある機械はありますか?** *iTune to gokansei no aru kikai wa arimasu ka.*
Do you have a Mac?	**Macはありますか?** *Makku wa arimasu ka.*
Do you have a PC?	**PCはありますか?** *PC wa arimasu ka.*
Do you have a newer version of this software?	**このソフトウェアの新しいバージョンはありますか?** *kono sofuto uea no atarashii bājon wa arimasu ka.*
Do you have broadband?	**ブロードバンドはありますか?** *burōdo bando wa arimasu ka.*
How fast is your connection speed here?	**この回線速度は何ですか?** *kono kaisen sokudo wa nan desu ka.*

GETTING MAIL

Where is the post office?	**郵便局はどこにありますか?** *yūbin kyoku wa doko ni arimasu ka.*
May I send an international package?	**外国に小包を送れますか?** *gaikoku ni kozutsumi o okure masu ka.*
Do I need a customs form?	**関税申告用紙に記入しなければなりませんか?** *kanzei shinkoku yōshi ni kinyū shi nakere ba nari masen ka.*
Do you sell insurance for packages?	**小包に保険をかけられますか?** *kozutsumi ni hoken o kakerare masu ka.*

Please, mark it fragile.	「割れ物注意」の印を付けてください。 *「waremono chūi」 no shirushi o tsukete kudasai.*
Please, handle with care.	丁寧に扱ってください。 *teinei ni atsukatte kudasai.*
Do you have twine?	ひもはありますか？ *himo wa arimasu ka.*
Where is a DHL office?	DHL はどこにありますか？ *DHL wa doko ni arimasu ka.*

Listen Up: Postal Lingo

次の方どうぞ！ *tsugi no kata dōzo.*	Next!
ここに置いてください。 *koko ni oite kudasai.*	Please, set it here.
どのクラスですか？ *dono kurasu desu ka.*	Which class?
どのサービスになさいますか？ *dono sābisu ni nasai masu ka.*	What kind of service would you like?

Do you sell stamps?	切手を売っていますか？ *kitte o utte imasu ka.*
Do you sell postcards?	はがきを売っていますか？ *hagaki o utte imasu ka.*
May I send that first class?	それをファースト クラスで送れますか？ *sore o fāsuto kurasu de okure masu ka.*
How much to send that express / air mail?	それを 速達 / 航空便で送るといくらかかりますか？ *sore o sokutatsu / kōkū bin de okuru to ikura kakari masu ka.*
Do you offer overnight delivery?	翌日配達のサービスはありますか？ *yokujitsu haitatsu no sābisu wa arimasu ka.*
How long will it take to reach the United States?	何日くらいでアメリカに届きますか？ *nan nichi kurai de amerika ni todoki masu ka.*
I'd like to buy an envelope.	封筒を１枚ください。 *fūtō o ichi mai kudasai.*
May I send it airmail?	それを航空便で送ってください。 *sore o kōkū bin de okutte kudasai.*
I'd like to send it certified / registered mail.	それを配達証明郵便 / 書留郵便で送ってください。 *sore o haitatsu shōmei yūbin / kakitome yūbin de okutte kudasai.*

MONEY

The currency in Japan is called the yen, which comes in coin denominations of ¥1, ¥5, ¥10, ¥50, ¥100 and ¥500, and bills of ¥1,000, ¥2,000, ¥5,000 and ¥10,000. A change purse definitely comes in handy because the very smallest denomination bill, the ¥1,000 note, is worth about $10 at current exchange rates.

Getting Cash

While Japan possibly has more **ATM** machines than any other country on the planet, most of them do not accept cash cards issued by foreign banks. Your best bet for withdrawing cash is to find a post office where the ATMs accept cards with the Cirrus or PLUS system marks. Be aware that, unlike in the U.S., many Japanese ATMs are not available 24 hours a day. Some shut off their ATMs as early as 5pm and many shut them down entirely on Japanese national holidays.

Credit Cards

Even though **credit cards** have made rapid inroads in Japan in recent years, cash is still king. Many smaller shops and restaurants take cash only, and others accept only Japanese credit cards (such as JCB). What's more, American travelers sometimes find that their U.S.-issued Mastercard and Visa cards are rejected in Japan as part of fraud prevention policies. If you're using a credit card in Japan, remember:

- Call your card issuer before you leave to let them know your overseas travel plans.
- Ask your card issuer about exchange rate fees on foreign currency transactions, which can often add up quickly.
- Don't forget to sign the back of your card, as many Japanese retailers will not accept an unsigned card.

In Japan, it is common to be asked at the register if the method of card payment is *ikkai-barai* ("one-time payment") or *sukkai-barai* ("revolving credit"). Japanese banks require you to make a decision at the point of purchase. A one-time payment means the balance will be paid off at the end of the month, whereas revolving credit allows payment with interest over a longer time period. This usually does not affect cards issued by foreign banks, so if you're asked, it's best to choose the one-time payment option.

Checks

Personal checks are not used in Japan and will not be accepted anywhere in the country, even with a valid passport. **Traveler's checks** are widely accepted at banks, major department stores and hotels in Japan. However, in remoter areas of the country, banks and stores may refuse to cash them.

STAYING CONNECTED

As home to some of the leading global mobile phone handset manufacturers, Japan has one of the highest per capita mobile phone rates in the industrialized world. The bad news is that few mobile phones from abroad can be used on the Japanese mobile network. The good news is that renting a phone is a relatively cheap and easy thing to do. While not an absolute necessity, even in 21st- century Japan, having access to a mobile phone during your stay is definitely an asset.

Because most Japanese rely on their mobile phones' e-mail functions, there are fewer Internet cafes than in other Asian countries. While most luxury hotels offer high-speed Internet access in rooms, mid-tier and regional hotels usually do not. As far as rural inns are concerned, most are "off the grid." In fact, many inns in mountainous areas are also well outside mobile phone networks and may not have any international phone service.

TELEPHONES & INTERNET

Fixed Phones

Calling to Japan Calls to Japan use the country code **81** before the regional area codes and local numbers. When dialing from the U.S., press 011 for an international call. All regional codes for big cities in Japan start with a zero (Tokyo is 03 and Osaka is 06), but that is only used when dialing domestically—it should be dropped while dialing from overseas. In other words, when calling to Japan from the U.S., dial 011-81-3 for Tokyo numbers and 011-81-6 for Osaka).

Calling within Japan Within Japan, you can make local, domestic and international calls from most hotel rooms. Green-colored public phones can make local or domestic calls in denominations of ¥10 or ¥100, or by using a ¥1,000 phone card sold at convenience stores, newspaper kiosks or vending machines.

Calling from Japan For international calls, use 001 (KDDI) or 0041 (Japan Telecom), 0033 (NTT-Com) or 0061 (Japan Telecom IDC) to access an international line. You must then dial the country code (1 for the U.S.) followed by the area code and local number. For assistance or a collect call, dial 0051 to speak with a KDDI international telephone operator. Outside your hotel room, look for the gray-colored ISDN public phones, which can be used for local, domestic and international calls. They also have data ports for Internet access. However, these phones generally only accept phone cards (not coins), and regular phone cards cannot be used for international calls. For calls outside of Japan, you must purchase a special prepaid international dialing card, which can be purchased at most convenience stores.

Mobile Phones Japan's mobile phone networks use a system that is incompatible with most European and North American mobile phones. You can, however, use your own mobile phone number in Japan via **SoftBank Mobile** (www.softbank-rental.jp) or **NTT DoCoMo's** 3G service area if you bring a SIM card and insert it into a rental phone or your own 3G handset (http://roaming.nttdocomo.co.jp). Otherwise, you can rent a mobile phone before leaving for Japan through an operator such as **InTouch USA** (✆ **800/872-7626**; www.intouchglobal.com).

The most convenient option, however, is to rent a mobile phone once you arrive—either right at the airport terminal or, if you're staying at a luxury hotel, the front desk. At Narita airport, for example, you can sign up for a short-term plan from Nokia, NTT DoCoMo or SoftBank Mobile. Any rental phone can receive calls from overseas, but if you plan to make calls to numbers outside Japan, make sure to choose the international dialing package option.

Internet

Both cybercafes and wireless Internet hot spots have yet to catch on in a big way in Japan, so your best bet may be to use a local access number from your Internet service provider at home. While luxury hotels in major cities generally offer high-speed access for your laptop, you may be forced to use dial-up service via a regular phone line at mid-tier hotels and rural inns. That can pose challenges because some require users to dial a 0 or 9 to connect to external numbers. Laptops can be hooked up to mobile phones via a special Ethernet card and cable, but this set up is not practical for short-term stays. Many hotel business centers, while not cheap, offer default Internet access via PC. Remember to pack an adapter for the three-prong plug-ins used by most laptops in the U.S. because Japanese electrical outlets only fit two-pronged plugs. It's also not a bad idea to carry an extra Ethernet and/or telephone wire as not all hotels or inns provide them to guests.

CHAPTER SEVEN
CULTURE

CINEMA

Is there a movie theater nearby?	この近くに映画館はありますか？ *kono chikakuni eiga kan wa arimasu ka.*
What's playing tonight?	今夜上映されるのは何ですか？ *kon ya jōei sareru nowa nan desu ka.*
Is that in English or Japanese?	それは英語ですか、それとも日本語ですか？ *sore wa eigo desuka, sore tomo nihongo desu ka.*
Are there English subtitles?	英語の字幕は出ますか？ *eigo no jimaku wa demasu ka.*
Is the theater air conditioned?	館内は冷房が効いていますか？ *kan nai wa reibō ga kiite imasu ka.*
How much is a ticket?	チケットはいくらですか？ *chiketto wa ikura desu ka.*
Do you have a ____ discount?	____割引きはありますか？ *____ waribiki wa arimasu ka.*
senior	高齢者 *kōreisha*
student	学生 *gakusei*
children's	児童 *jidō*
What time is the movie showing?	映画は何時に始まりますか？ *eiga wa nanji ni hajimeri masu ka.*
How long is the movie?	上映時間はどのくらいですか？ *jōei jikan wa dono kurai desu ka.*

May I buy tickets in advance?
前もってチケットを買えますか？
mae motte chiketto o kae masu ka.

Is it sold out?
売り切れですか？
urikire desu ka.

When does it begin?
いつ始まりますか？
itsu hajimari masu ka.

PERFORMANCES

Do you have ballroom dancing?
社交ダンスは開かれますか？
shakō dansu wa hirakare masu ka.

Are there any plays showing right now?
現在上演されている劇はありますか？
genzai jōen sarete iru geki wa arimasu ka.

Where can I buy tickets?
チケットはどこで買えますか？
chiketto wa doko de kae masu ka.

Are there student discounts?
学生割引きはありますか？
gakusei waribiki wa arimasu ka.

I need ____ seats.
____席ください。
____ seki kudasai.

For a full list of numbers, see p6.

An aisle seat.
通路側の座席。
tsūro gawa no zaseki.

Orchestra seat, please.
オーケストラ席をお願いします。
ōkesutora seki o onegai shimasu.

What time does the play start?
劇は何時に始まりますか？
geki wa nanji ni hajimari masu ka.

Is there an intermission?
途中で休憩はありますか？
tochū de kyūkei wa arimasu ka.

Do you have an opera house?
オペラハウスはありますか？
opera hausu wa arimasu ka.

Is there a local symphony?
地方交響楽団はありますか？
chihō kōkyō gakudan wa arimasu ka.

Listen Up: Box Office Lingo

何をご覧になりますか？ *nani o goran ni nari masu ka.*	What would you like to see?
何枚ですか？ *nan mai desu ka.*	How many?
大人２枚ですか？ *otona nimai desu ka.*	For two adults?
バターは？ 塩は？ *batā wa? shio wa?*	With butter? Salt?
ほかにも何かございますか？ *hoka nimo nani ka gozai masu ka.*	Would you like anything else?

May I purchase tickets over the phone?	電話でチケットを買えますか？ *denwa de chiketto o kae masu ka.*
What time is the box office open?	チケット売り場は何時に開きますか？ *chiketto uriba wa nanji ni hiraki masu ka.*
I need space for a wheelchair, please.	車椅子が入れるくらいの空間が必要です。 *kuruma isu ga haireru kurai no kūkan ga hitsuyō desu.*
Do you have private boxes available?	ボックス席はありますか？ *bokkusu seki wa arimasu ka.*
Is there a church that gives concerts?	コンサートを催す教会はありますか？ *konsāto o moyōsu kyōkai wa arimasu ka.*

A program, please.	プログラムをください。 *puroguramu o kudasai.*
Please show us to our seats.	座席まで案内していただけますか。 *zaseki made annai shite itadake masu ka.*

MUSEUMS, GALLERIES & SIGHTS

Do you have a museum guide?	美術館ガイドはいますか？ *bijutsukan gaido wa imasu ka.*
Do you have guided tours?	ガイドが付いて説明しますか？ *gaido ga tsuite setsumei shimasu ka.*
What are the museum hours?	美術館の開館時間は何時から何時までですか。 *bijutsukan no kaikan jikan wa nanji kara nanji made desu ka.*
Do I need an appointment?	予約が必要ですか？ *yoyaku ga hitsuyō desu ka.*
What is the admission fee?	入場料はいくらですか？ *nyūjō ryō wa ikura desu ka.*
Do you have ____?	____はありますか？ ____ *wa arimasu ka.*
student discounts	学生割引き *gakusei waribiki*
senior discounts	高齢者割引き *kōreisha waribiki*

Do you have services for the hearing impaired?
聴覚障害者のためのサービスはありますか？
chōkaku shōgaisha no tame no sābisu wa arimasu ka.

Do you have audio tours in English?
英語の音声ガイドはありますか？
eigo no onsei gaido wa arimasu ka.

JAPANESE PERFORMING ARTS

Kabuki Kabuki is traditional and highly stylized Japanese theater dating back to the Edo period (1603-1867). All roles, male and female, are played by men. Enjoy the gorgeous costumes, the elaborate use of makeup, and the unique sounds of traditional Japanese instruments. The best place to watch kabuki is in the Kabukiza Theater in the Ginza District of Tokyo, where you can rent headphones and hear a running commentary in English on the story, music, and actors.

Noh Noh is more traditional and aristocratic than Kabuki, which was developed as a form of entertainment for the masses. Noh is calculated, slow and restrained, and it is one of the oldest forms of theater in the world; the form hasn't changed much in the past six centuries, and even the Japanese themselves can't understand much of the archaic language. The audience can participate in the drama by projecting feelings into the carved faces; the range of emotions is extraordinary.

Bunraku Bunraku is traditional Japanese puppet theater, which has been popular in Japan since the 17th century. You will see the puppeteers dressed in black to make them less intrusive, right on stage with their puppets. Three skillful puppeteers control each puppet, which is about three-fourths human size. The narrator tells the story and speaks the various parts, accompanied by a traditional three-stringed Japanese instrument called a *shamisen*.

Takarazuka Kagekidan While Kabuki performers are all men, Takarazuka performers are all women. The troupe stages elaborate musical revues with dancing, singing and gorgeous costumes. Performances range from Japanese versions of Broadway hits to original Japanese works based on local legends.

JAPAN'S MOST UNIQUE MUSEUMS

Benesse Art Site Naoshima, Takamatsu This is one of the most unusual museums in Japan since its cutting edge artworks are not confined to one building but rather spread out over an entire island devoted to the displays. The two main facilities are designed by famed architect Tadao Ando and include works by Jasper Johns, Robert Rauschenberg, Frank Stella, Pollock and Warhol—each of whom contributed specifically for this site. www.naoshima-is.co.jp.

Disaster Reduction and Human Renovation Institution, Kobe Despite the clunky name, this is a fascinating museum chronicling the devastating magnitude 7.3 earthquake that hit Kobe in 1995 (killing some 6,000 people) and the recovery efforts in its aftermath. Films, dioramas and exhibits play out the natural disaster and the lessons learned from it. www.dri.ne.jp.

Edo-Tokyo Museum, Tokyo This museum vividly traces the history of Tokyo from its beginning in 1590 to 1964, when Tokyo hosted the Olympics. The modern, high-tech building features plenty of models, replicas, artifacts and dioramas. www.edo-tokyo-museum.or.jp.

Hakone Open-Air Museum, Hakone Spectacularly landscaped grounds and beautiful scenery showcase nearly 700 sculptures from 20th-century artists, from Henry Moore to Rodin. You can also visit the Picasso Pavilion, which houses some 200 works by the artist. www.hakone-oam.or.jp.

Hida Minzoku Mura Folk Village, Takayama This restored feudal era village features 30 thatched farmhouses ringing a picturesque pond in the middle of the Japan Alps. Inside the high-peaked structures, objects provide insight into daily life 100-500 years ago. Artisans demonstrate the production of traditional crafts, such as laquerware and woodcarvings **© 05/7734-4711**.

Ishikawa Prefectural Museum for Traditional Products and Crafts, Kanazawa Famed Kutani pottery, Kaga Yuzen tie-dying, and Kanazawa gold leaf and lacquerware are among the handcrafted items on display in one of the finest museums of its type in Japan. English language explanations, pamphlets and audio guides make it easy to appreciate the works of artisanship. **© 07/6262-2020**.

Japan Ukiyo-e Museum, Matsumoto Come for one of the finest collections of woodblock prints in the world displayed on a rotating basis changing every three months. A 10-minute English language slide show presentation introduces the exhibit and shows how the prints are painstakingly made. www.ukiyo-e.co.jp.

Museum Meiji Mura, Nagoya Another open-air architectural museum featuring more than 60 original buildings and structures dating from the Meiji era (1868-1912) set on 250 acres of marvelously landscaped gardens. Sip a cup of tea in the lobby of the original Imperial Hotel, which was designed by Frank Lloyd Wright. www.meijimura.com.

Tokyo National Museum, Tokyo The largest and oldest museum in Japan, Tokyo National Museum opened in 1872 and still holds what many consider the most comprehensive collection of everything from Japanese samurai armor and swords to ancient pottery and scrolls. About 4,000 items are displayed at any one time. www.tnm.jp.

Yasukuni Shrine Yushukan, Tokyo Located on the grounds of the controversial Yasukuni Shrine, which commemorates some 2.5 million Japanese war dead (including WWII war criminals), this museum takes a fascinating look at the country's modern wars dating from 1868. Though the English language explanations are poor and the displays tend to gloss over Japanese war atrocities, the museum hosts a sweeping collection of historical memorabilia—from samurai armor and flags to WWI–era guns, tanks and a kamikaze suicide attack plane. www.yasukuni.or.jp.

CHAPTER EIGHT

SHOPPING

This chapter covers the phrases you'll need to shop in a variety of settings, from the mall to street vendors. We also threw in the terminology you'll need to visit the barber or hairdresser.

For coverage of food and grocery shopping, see p102.

GENERAL SHOPPING TERMS

Please tell me ____	____を教えてください。 ____ *o oshiete kudasai.*
how to get to a mall?	ショッピングセンターへの行き方 *shoppingu sentā eno iki kata*
the best place for shopping?	ショッピングに一番よいところ *shoppingu ni ichiban yoi tokoro*
how to get downtown?	繁華街への行き方 *hanka gai eno iki kata*
Where can I find a ____?	____はどこにありますか? ____ *wa doko ni arimasu ka.*
shoe store	靴屋 *kutsu ya*
men's / women's / children's clothing store	紳士 / 婦人 / 子供服の店 *shinshi / fujin / kodomo fuku no mise*
designer fashion shop	デザイナー ブランドの店 *dezainā burando no mise*
vintage clothing store	ビンテージ物を売っている洋服屋 *bintēji mono o utteiru yōfuku ya*
jewelry store	宝石店 *hōseki ten*
bookstore	本屋 *hon ya*
toy store	おもちゃ屋 *omocha ya*

stationery store	文房具店 *bunbōgu ten*
antique shop	骨董品店 *kottōhin ten*
cigar shop	タバコ屋 *tabako ya*
souvenir shop	お土産屋 *omiyage ya*
Where can I find a flea market?	フリーマーケットはどこでやっていますか？ *furī māketto wa doko de yatte imasu ka.*

CLOTHES SHOPPING

I'd like to buy ____	____を買いたいのですが。 ____ *o kaitai no desuga.*
men's shirts.	紳士用のシャツ *shinshi yō no shatsu*
women's shoes.	婦人用の靴 *fujin yō no kutsu*
children's clothes.	子供服 *kodomo fuku*
toys.	オモチャ *omocha*

For a full list of numbers, see p6.

I'm looking for a size ____	____サイズを探しています。 ____ *saizu o sagashite imasu.*
small.	S *esu*
medium.	M *emu*
large.	L *eru*
extra-large.	LL *eru eru*

イヤリング
iyaringu

シャツ
shatsu

ネクタイ
nekutai

腕時計
ude dokei

ジャケット
jaketto

ワンピース
wan pīsu

ベルト
beruto

ズボン
zubon

靴
kutsu

I'm looking for ____	____ を探しています。 ____ *o sagashite imasu.*
a silk blouse.	シルクのブラウス *shiruku no burausu*
cotton pants.	コットンのズボン *kotton no zubon*
a hat.	帽子 *bōshi*
sunglasses.	サングラス *san gurasu*
underwear.	下着 *shitagi*
cashmere.	カシミヤの *kashimiya no*
socks.	靴下 *kutsu shita*
sweaters.	セーター *sētā*

a coat.	コート *kōto*
a swimsuit.	水着 *mizugi*
May I try it on?	これを試着していいですか？ *kore o shichaku shite ii desu ka.*
Do you have fitting rooms?	試着室はありますか？ *shichaku shitsu wa arimasu ka.*
This is ____	これは____ *kore wa ____*
too tight.	きつすぎます。 *kitsu sugi masu.*
too loose.	ゆるすぎます。 *yuru sugi masu.*
too long.	長すぎます。 *naga sugi masu.*
too short.	短かすぎます。 *mijika sugi masu.*

This fits great!	これはぴったりです! *kore wa pittari desu.*
Thanks, I'll take it.	ありがとうございます。これにします。 *arigatōgozaimasu. kore ni shimasu.*
Do you have that in ____?	これと同じで____はありますか? *kore to onaji de ___ wa arimasu ka.*
a smaller / larger size	小さい / 大きいサイズ *chiisai / ōkii saizu*
a different color	違う色 *chigau iro*
How much is it?	それはいくらですか? *sore wa ikura desu ka.*

ARTISAN MARKET SHOPPING

Is there a craft / artisan market?	工芸 / 職人市場はありますか? *kōgei / shokunin ichiba wa arimasu ka.*
That's beautiful. May I look at it?	それはきれいですね。それを見せていただけますか? *sore wa kirei desu ne. sore o misete itadake masu ka.*
When is the farmers' market open?	朝市は何時からですか? *asaichi wa nanji kara desu ka.*
Is that open every day of the week?	それは毎日開いていますか? *sore wa mai nichi aite imasu ka.*
How much does that cost?	それはいくらしますか? *sore wa ikura shimasu ka.*
That's too expensive.	それは高すぎます。 *sore wa taka sugi masu.*
How much for two?	2つだといくらですか? *futatsu dato ikura desu ka.*
Do I get a discount if I buy two or more?	2つ以上買うと割引がありますか? *futatsu ijō kau to waribiki ga arimasu ka.*

Listen Up: Market Lingo

品物を扱う前に(店の人に)たずねてください。 *shinamono o atsukau mae ni (miseno hito ni) tazunete kudasai.*	Please ask (the store employee) for help before handling goods.
____円のお返しです。 *____ en no okaeshi desu.*	Here is your change.
2つで40円です。 *futatsu de yon jū en desu.*	Two for forty, sir.

Do I get a discount if I pay in cash? 現金で支払うと割引がありますか?
genki de shiharau to waribiki ga arimasu ka.

No thanks, maybe I'll come back. いいえ、いりません。でもまた後で戻ってくるかもしれません。
iie, iri masen. demo mata ato de modotte kuru kamo shirema sen.

Would you take ¥____? ____円で買えますか?
____ en de kae masu ka.

For a full list of numbers, see p6.

That's a deal! では買います!
dewa kai masu.

Do you have a less expensive one? もう少し安いのはありますか?
mō sukoshi yasui nowa arimasu ka.

Is there tax? 税金はかかりますか?
zeikin wa kakari masu ka.

May I have the VAT forms? VAT付加価値税用紙をください。
VAT fuka kachi zei yōshi o kudasai.

BOOKSTORE / NEWSSTAND SHOPPING

Is there a ____ nearby?	この近くに____はありますか? *kono chikaku ni ____ wa arimasu ka.*
a bookstore	本屋 *hon ya*
a newsstand	新聞売り場 *shinbun uriba*
Do you have ____ in English?	英語の____はありますか? *eigo no ____ wa arimasu ka.*
books	本 *hon*
newspapers	新聞 *shinbun*
magazines	雑誌 *zasshi*
books about local history	地方の歴史に関する本 *chihō no rekishi ni kansuru hon*
picture books	絵本 *ehon*

SHOPPING FOR ELECTRONICS

Can I play this in the United States / United Kingdom?	これはアメリカ／イギリスでつかえますか? *kore wa amerika / igirisu de tsukae masu ka.*
Will this game work on my game console in the United States / United Kingdom??	このゲームは、アメリカ／イギリスにある私のゲーム 機で使用できますか? *kono gēmu wa, amerika/igirisu ni aru watashi no gēmu ki de shiyō dekimasu ka.*

Do you have this in a U.S. / U.K. market format?	これと同じものでアメリカ／イギリス対応のものがありますか？ *koreto onaji mono de amerika/ igirisu taiō no mono ga arimasu ka.*
Can you convert this to a U.S. / U.K. market format?	これはアメリカ／イギリスの形式に変換できますか？ *kore wa amerika/igirisu no keishiki ni henkan deki masu ka.*
Will this work with a 110 VAC adapter?	これは 110VのAC アダプターで動きますか？ *kore wa hyaku jū boruto no AC adaputā de ugoki masu ka.*
Do you have an adapter plug for 110 to 220?	110 から 220 に変換するのアダプタープラグはありますか？ *hyaku jū kara ni hyaku ni jū ni henkan suru adaputā puragu wa arimasu ka.*
Do you sell electronics adapters here?	電子アダプターは売っていますか？ *denshi adaputā wa utte imasu ka.*
Is it safe to use my laptop with this adapter?	このアダプターで私のラップトップを使っても大丈夫ですか？ *kono adaputā de watashi no rappu toppu o tsukattemo daijōbu desu ka.*
If it doesn't work, may I return it?	もし使えなかった場合返品できますか？ *moshi tsukaenakatta baai henpin deki masu ka.*
May I try it here in the store?	これをここで試してみることはできますか？ *kore o koko de tameshite miru koto wa deki masu ka.*

AT THE BARBER / HAIRDRESSER

Do you have a style guide?	スタイル ブックはありますか？ *sutairu bukku wa arimasu ka.*
A trim, please.	髪をそろえてください。 *kami o soroete kudasai.*
I'd like it bleached.	ブリーチしてください。 *burīchi shite kudasai.*
Would you change the color ____?	____色に変えてください。 *____ iro ni kaete kudasai.*
darker	もっと濃い *motto koi*
lighter	もっと明るい *motto akarui*
Would you just touch it up a little?	少し修正してください。 *sukoshi shūsei shite kudasai.*
I'd like it curled.	カールしてください。 *kāru shite kudasai.*
Do I need an appointment?	予約する必要がありますか？ *yoyaku suru hitsuyō ga arimasu ka.*
Shampoo, cut, and perm.	シャンプー、カット、パーマ。 *shanpū, katto, pāma.*
Do you do permanents?	パーマはできますか？ *pāma wa deki masu ka.*
May I make an appointment?	予約できますか？ *yoyaku deki masu ka.*
Please use low heat.	低温でお願いします。 *teion de onegai shimasu.*
Please don't blow dry it.	ブローしないでください。 *burō shinaide kudasai.*
Please dry it curly / straight.	カール / ストレートにドライしてください。 *kāru / sutorēto ni dorai shite kudasai.*

Would you fix my braids?	編んだ髪を直してください。 *anda kami o naoshite kudasai.*
Would you fix my highlights?	ハイライトを直してください。 *hai raito o naoshite kudasai.*
Do you wax?	ワックスはできますか？ *wakkusu wa deki masu ka.*
Please wax my ____	私の____をワックスしてください。 *watashi no ____ o wakkusu shite kudasai.*
legs.	足 *ashi*
bikini line.	ビキニの線 *bikini no sen*
eyebrows.	まゆ毛 *mayu ge*
under my nose.	鼻の下 *hana no shita*
Please trim my beard.	ひげを揃えてください。 *hige o soroete kudasai.*
A shave, please.	剃ってください。 *sotte kudasai.*
Use a fresh blade please.	良く切れる刃を使ってください。 *yoku kireru ha o tsukatte kudasai.*
Sure, cut it all off.	はい、全部切ってください。 *hai, zenbu kitte kudasai.*

WHERE TO BUY

Department Stores

Department stores in Japan carry everything from soup to nuts. Most have huge food emporiums in their basements followed by floor after floor of fashionable clothes, shoes and accessories. In addition, there are almost always one or two floors of home wares such as duvets, crystal goblets and children's toys. The highest floors often have a large selection of restaurants and coffee shops where you can stop for a meal or snack. Many department stores have service desks on the ground floor with English speaking staff or floor guides written in English. Also, for purchases over ¥10,000 don't forget to head to the department store's duty free counter for an immediate refund of Japan's 3% sales tax. The downside is that true bargains are rare, so expect to pay at or close to the manufacturers suggested retail price.

Some major department stores in Tokyo are: **Matsuya** (**© 03/3567-1211**), **Mitsukoshi** (**© 03/3241-3311**), **Seibu** (**© 03/3981-0111**) and **Wako** (**© 03/3562-2111**). Some major department stores in Osaka are: **Daimaru** (www.daimaru.co.jp/English) and **Takashimaya** (**© 06/6631-1101**).

Flea Markets

Flea markets are good places to shop for antiques and delightful junk. You can pick up a secondhand kimono at a very reasonable price, as well as kitchenware, vases, cast-iron teapots, small chests, woodblock prints, dolls, and odds and ends. The markets usually begin as early as dawn or 6am and last until 3 or 4pm, but go early if you want to pick up bargains. Bargaining is expected. Note that since most markets are outdoors, they tend to be canceled if it rains.

Togo Shrine, on Meiji Dori in Harajuku, has an antiques market on the first, fourth, and fifth Sunday of every month from 4am to 2pm. It's great for used kimono and curios.

Nogi Shrine, a 1-minute walk from Nogizaka Station, has an antiques flea market from dawn to about 2pm the second Sunday of each month except November.

Hanazono Shrine, near the Yasukuni Dori/Meiji Dori intersection east of Shinjuku Station, has a flea market every Sunday from dawn to about 2pm (except in May and Nov).

Ameya Yokocho is the closest thing Tokyo has to a permanent flea market. It is a narrow street near Ueno Park that runs underneath the elevated tracks of the JR Yamanote Line between Ueno and Okachimachi stations. There are about 400 stalls here selling discounted items ranging from fish to seaweed, handbags, cosmetics, and watches. Hours are usually daily from 10am to 7pm; early evening is the most crowded time.

Shopping Malls

Japan traditionally has not been a haven for Western-style shopping malls. However, this has begun to change with the revitalization of formerly shabby urban districts in the 2000s. Where tired concrete office buildings once stood, there are now row upon row of aesthetically pleasing towers of steel and glass. These are not the type of places to buy traditional handicrafts, but you will probably find some things to your liking. Here are some shopping malls:

Omotesando Hills Omotesando Hills, near Shibuya, was designed by famed architect Tadao Ando and dubbed "Tokyo's Champs-Elysees" when it opened in 2005. www.omotesandohills.com.

Roppongi Hills The Roppongi Hills complex opened in spring 2003 with shops spread throughout several buildings in the Roppongi district. Roppongi Hills is also anchored by the **Mori Art Museum** (www.mori.art.museum), a movie theater and the **Grand Hyatt Tokyo** (www.tokyo.grandhyatt.com). www.roppongihills.com.

Shin-Marunouchi Building The futuristic new **Shin-Marunouchi Building** near JR's Tokyo station opened in the fall of 2002 with 740 retail tenants, mostly upscale shops and restaurants. www.shinmaru.jp.

Tokyo Midtown In addition to shops and restaurants, Tokyo Midtown, which opened in early 2007, includes the relocated **Suntory Museum of Art**, the new **Ritz-Carlton Tokyo**, and even a medical center. www.tokyo-midtown.com.

BEST BUYS

Japanese Crafts

There are a number of craft shops along the paths to major temples such as Kiyomizu-dera in Kyoto and Sensoji in Tokyo's

Asakusa district. The latter is concentrated on an Asakusa side street called Nakamise-Dori. There you'll find traditional crafts and goods including wooden geta shoes (traditional wooden sandals) and hairpins worn by geisha. Major department stores also have sections devoted to ceramics, pottery, bamboo ware, flower-arranging accessories and fabrics. For the largest selection of kitsch and touristy souvenirs, try **Oriental Bazaar** (**© 03/3400-3933**) in Tokyo's Omotesando district near Shibuya.

Bookstores

While most books are published in Japanese, the larger bookstores stock an impressive selection of English titles. Fans of Japanese anime, literature, culture and history are in for a treat because the selection of English-language books on these topics is astounding. In Tokyo, the Jimbocho district, anchored by a large outlet of **Sanseido** (**© 03/3293-8119**), has dozens of small bookstores. **Maruzen** is another major chain with a great selection, particularly at its outlet across from **Tokyo Station** (**© 03/5288-8881**). The top floor of the **Tower Records** branch in Shibuya (**© 03/3496-3661**) has an eclectic collection of books on pop culture. Perhaps Tokyo's best know bookstore chain is **Kinokuniya**, which has an entire floor devoted to English language publications (including magazines) at its two Tokyo locations, in East Shinjuku and (the flagship store) in South Shinjuku (**© 03/5361-3301**).

Electronics & Software

For decades, the epicenter of Japan's electronics and electrical-appliance shops has been in the Tokyo district of Akihabara called **Denkigai ("Electric Avenue")**. Though it still boasts hundreds of stores, the spread of discount audio-visual stores nationwide has eroded the Akihabara mystique. Even so, it may be worth a visit because the larger stores have duty-free floors where products are made for export. Two of the largest are **Yamagiwa** (**© 03/3253-2111**) and **Laox** (**© 03/3255-5301**). Or check out **AKKY International** (**© 03/5207-5027**), which has knowledgeable salespeople.

Before you purchase anything, make sure the item will be compatible with your hardware and electric current back home. If you do buy, always ask a salesperson for an English language manual—sometimes these are available upon request.

Kitchenware

When the selection at department stores just won't do, then the place for serious chefs is Tokyo's **Kappabashi** district near Asakusa. This is Japan's largest wholesale area for cookware, where some 150 specialty stores sell everything from sukiyaki pots to woks, lunch boxes, pots and pans, aprons, knives, china and lacquerware. The mom-and-pop stores of Kappabashi are closed on Sunday, but are otherwise open from about 10am to 5pm.

Pearls

There are many pearl retailers in Japan—home to the world's first cultured pearls—and most department stores will have a decent selection, too. It is said by some Japanese that the best pearls can only be bought in Wakayama, a rural peninsula near Kyoto where Japan's pearl industry is based. But unless you are planning a major detour, consider instead heading straight to the mother of all pearl shops, the flagship store of **Mikimoto** (**© 03/3535-4611**), Japan's most famous pearl producer, in Tokyo's Ginza district. The main store is open every day except Wednesday, but there are other outlets in Tokyo and most major cities in Japan.

Swords

It is possible to purchase a real samurai sword at a specialty shop. The prices can be truly astronomical however, so it isn't a practical purchase for all but the most dedicated and wealthy of collectors. Two of the most well-regarded sword shops in Tokyo are **Ginza Choshuya** in Ginza (**© 03/3541-8371**) and **Japan Sword** in Toranomon (**© 03/3434-4321**). Note that it is possible to purchase fairly authentic (and decidedly non-lethal) replica swords at many souvenir shops for a fraction of the cost of the real deal.

Toys

Kiddy Land in Omotesando near Shibuya (**© 03/3409-3431**; www.kiddyland.co.jp) is a toy store that sells a variety of modern anime and other character goods such as Hello Kitty-themed mobile phone straps and Pokemon cards. There's also a **Kitty Land** in Osaka in the **Hankyu** department store (**© 06/6372-7701**). For diehard fans of anime figurines and other paraphernalia, a visit to the **Sakuraya Hobby Kan** in Shinjuku (**© 03/3226-6868**) is a must.

CHAPTER NINE
SPORTS & FITNESS

GETTING FIT

Is there a gym nearby?	この近くにジムはありますか? *kono chikaku ni jimu wa arimasu ka.*
Do you have free weights?	フリーウェイトはありますか? *furī ueito wa arimasu ka.*
I'd like to go for a swim.	泳ぎに行きたいのですが。 *oyogi ni ikitai no desuga.*
Do I have to be a member?	会員でなければなりませんか? *kai in de nakere ba narima sen ka.*
May I come here for one day?	一日ここに来ることはできますか? *ichi nichi koko ni kuru koto wa deki masu ka.*
How much does a membership cost?	会員になるにはいくらかかりますか? *kaiin ni naru niwa ikura kakari masu ka.*
I need to get a locker please.	ロッカーを使いたいのですが。 *rokkā o tsukai tai no desuga.*
Do you have a lock?	鍵はありますか? *kagi wa arimasu ka.*

Do you have a treadmill?	トレッドミルはありますか? *toreddo miru wa arimasu ka.*
Do you have a stationary bike?	エアロ バイクはありますか? *earo baiku wa arimasu ka.*
Do you have handball / squash courts?	ハンドボール / スカッシュ コートはありますか? *hando bōru / sukasshu kōto wa arimasu ka.*
Are they indoors?	それは屋内にありますか? *sore wa okunai ni arimasu ka.*
I'd like to play tennis.	テニスをしたいのですが。 *tenisu o shitai no desuga.*
Would you like to play?	プレイしませんか? *purei shima sen ka.*
I'd like to rent a racquet.	ラケットを借りたいのですが。 *raketto o kari tai no desuga.*
I need to buy some ____	____を買わなければなりません。 *____ o kawa nakere ba nari masen.*
new balls.	新しいボール *atarashii bōru*
safety glasses.	セーフティーグラス *sēfutī gurasu*
May I rent a court for tomorrow?	明日、コートを借りたいのですが。 *ashita, kōto o karitai no desuga.*
May I have clean towels?	きれいなタオルをいただけますか。 *kirei na taoru o itadake masu ka.*
Where are the showers / locker-rooms?	シャワー / ロッカールームはどこにありますか? *shawā/rokkā rūmu wa doko ni arimasu ka.*

Do you have a workout room for women only?	女性専用のワークアウト ルームはありますか? *josei senyō no wāku auto rūmu wa arimasu ka.*
Do you have aerobics classes?	エアロビクスのクラスはありますか? *earobikusu no kurasu wa arimasu ka.*
Do you have a women's pool?	女性用のプールはありますか? *josei yō no pūru wa arimasu ka.*
Let's go for a jog.	ジョギングに行きましょう。 *jogingu ni iki ma shō.*
That was a great workout.	とてもよい運動でした。 *totemo yoi undō deshita.*

CATCHING A GAME

Where is the stadium?	スタジアムはどこですか? *sutajiamu wa doko desu ka.*
Where can I see a cockfight?	闘鶏はどこで見ることがますか? *tōkei wa doko de miru koto ga deki masu ka.*
Do you have a bullfight?	闘牛は行われますか? *tōgyū wa okonaware masu ka.*

Who is your favorite toreador / matador?	好きな闘牛士は誰ですか? *suki na tōgyūshi wa dare desu ka.*
Who is the best goalie?	最高のゴールキーパーは誰ですか? *saikō no gōru kīpā wa dare desu ka.*
Are there any women's teams?	女性チームはありますか? *josei chīmu wa arimasu ka.*
Do you have any amateur / professional teams?	アマチュア / プロのチームはありますか? *amachua / puro no chīmu wa arimasu ka.*
Is there a game I could play in?	私も参加できるゲームはありますか? *watashi mo sanka dekiru gēmu wa arimasu ka.*
Which is the best team?	最高のチームはどれですか? *saikō no chīmu wa dore desu ka.*
Will the game be on television?	この試合はテレビでも放送されますか? *kono shiai wa terebi demo hōsō sare masu ka.*
Where can I buy tickets?	チケットはどこで買えますか? *chiketto wa doko de kae masu ka.*
The best seats, please.	一番よい席をお願いします。 *ichiban yoi seki o onegai shimasu.*
The cheapest seats, please.	一番安い席をお願いします。 *ichiban yasui seki o onegai shimasu.*
How close are these seats?	これらの席はどれくらい近いですか? *korera no seki wa dore kurai chikai desu ka.*
May I have box seats?	ボックス シートをいただけますか? *bokksu shīto o itadake masu ka.*

Wow! What a game! うわぁ! すごい試合だ!
uwa! sugoi shiai da.

Go Go Go! 行け、行け、行け!
ike, ike, ike!

Oh No! あ、だめだ!
a, dame da!

Give it to them! 彼らにあげろ!
karera ni agero!

Go for it! がんばれ!
ganbare!

Score! 入れろ!
irero!

What's the score? 何点ですか?
nan ten desu ka.

Who's winning? どっちが勝ってますか?
docchi ga katte masu ka.

HIKING

Where can I find a guide to hiking trails? ハイキング トレイルのガイドはどこで見つけられますか?
haikingu toreiru no gaido wa doko de mitsuke rare masu ka.

Do we need to hire a guide? ガイドを雇う必要がありますか?
gaido o yatou hitsuyō ga arimasu ka.

Where can I rent equipment? 装具はどこで借りられますか?
sōgu wa doko de kari rare masu ka.

Do they have rock climbing there? そこにはロック クライミングがありますか?
soko niwa rokku kuraimingu ga arimasu ka.

We need more ropes and carabiners. ロープとカラビナがもっと必要です。
rōpu to karabina ga motto hitsuyō desu.

Where can we go mountain climbing? どこで登山ができますか?
doko de tozan ga deki masu ka.

Are the routes ____ ?	ルートは____ されていますか？ *rūto wa ____ sarete imasu ka.*
well marked	標識が完備 *hyōshiki ga kanbi*
in good condition	整備 *seibi*
What is the altitude there?	標高はいくらですか？ *hyōkō wa ikura desu ka.*
How long will it take?	どのくらい時間がかかりますか？ *dono kurai jikan ga kakari masu ka.*
Is it very difficult?	とても難しいですか？ *totemo muzukashii desu ka.*
I'd like a challenging climb - but I don't want to take oxygen.	登りがいのある山は好きですが、酸素補給器は携帯したくありません。 *nobori gai no aru yama wa suki desuga, sanso hokyūki wa keitai shitaku arima sen.*
I want to hire someone to carry my excess gear.	残りの装具を運んでくれる人を雇いたいのですが。 *nokori no sōgu o hakonde kureru hito o yatoi tai no desuga.*

We don't have time for a long route.	長いルートを行く時間はありません。 *nagai rūto o iku jikan wa arima sen.*
I don't think it's safe to proceed.	先に進むのは安全ではないと思います。 *saki ni susumu nowa anzen dewa nai to omoi masu.*
Do we have a backup plan?	第２プランはありますか？ *dai ni puran wa arimasu ka.*
If we're not back by tomorrow, send a search party.	私たちが明日までに戻らなければ、捜索隊を送ってください。 *watashi tachi ga ashita made ni modora nakere ba, sōsaku tai o okutte kudasai.*
Are the campsites marked?	キャンプサイトには標識が整備されていますか？ *kyanpu saito niwa hyōshiki ga seibi sarete imasu ka.*
Can we camp off the trail?	トレイル外でキャンプはできますか？ *toreiru gai de kyanpu wa deki masu ka.*
Is it okay to build fires here?	ここで火をおこしてもいいですか？ *koko de hi o okoshite mo ii desuka.*
Do we need permits?	許可が要りますか？ *kyoka ga iri masu ka.*

For more camping terms, see p79.

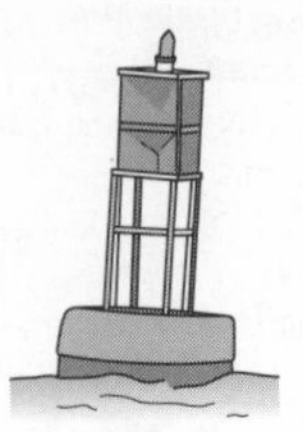

BOATING OR FISHING

When do we sail?	いつ出航しますか？ *itsu shukkō shimasu ka.*
Where are the life preservers?	救命用具はどこにありますか？ *kyūmei yōgu wa doko ni arimasu ka.*
Can I purchase bait?	えさを買えますか？ *esa o kae masu ka.*
Can I rent a pole?	釣竿を借りられますか？ *tsurizao o kari rare masu ka.*
How long is the voyage?	航海はどれくらいですか？ *kōkai wa dorekurai desu ka.*
Are we going up river or down?	川を上りますかそれとも下りますか？ *kawa o nobori masu ka, soretomo kudari masu ka.*
How far are we going?	どのくらい遠くまで行きますか？ *dono kurai tōku made iki masu ka.*
How fast are we going?	どのくらいの速度で行きますか？ *dono kurai no sokudo de iki masu ka.*
How deep is the water here?	ここの水深はどのくらいありますか？ *koko no suishin wa dono kurai arimasu ka.*
I got one!	かかった！ *kakatta!*

I can't swim. 泳げません。 *oyoge masen.*

Can we go ashore? 岸に上がれますか？ *kishi ni agare masu ka.*

For more boating terms, see p60.

DIVING

I'd like to go snorkeling. スノーケルをしたいのですが。 *sunōkeru o shitai no desuga.*

I'd like to go scuba diving. スキューバ ダイビングをしたいのですが。 *sukyūba daibingu o shitai no desuga.*

I have a NAUI / PADI certification. 私は NAUI / PADI の資格証明書を持っています。 *watashi wa NAUI / PADI no shikaku shōmei sho o motte imasu.*

I need to rent gear. 道具を借りる必要があります。 *dōgu o kariru hitsuyō ga arimasu.*

We'd like to see some shipwrecks if we can. できれば難破船を見たいです。 *deki reba nanpa sen o mitai desu.*

Are there any good reef dives? さんご礁のあるダイビング場所はありますか？ *sango shō no aru daibingu basho wa arimasu ka.*

I'd like to see a lot of sea-life. 海の生き物をたくさん見たいです。 *umi no ikimono o takusan mitai desu.*

Are the currents strong? 潮の流れは強いですか？ *shio no nagare wa tsuyoi desu ka.*

How clear is the water? 海の中の透明度はどうですか？ *umi no naka no tōmeido wa dō desu ka.*

I want / don't want to go with a group.	グループで行きたい / 行きたくないです。 *gurūpu de ikitai / ikitaku nai desu.*
Can we charter our own boat?	私たちだけで行くボートをチャーターできますか？ *watashi tachi dake de iku bōto o chātā deki masu ka.*

SURFING

I'd like to go surfing.	サーフィンをしたいのですが。 *sāfin o shitai no desuga.*
Are there any good beaches?	よいビーチはありますか？ *yoi bīchi wa arimasu ka.*
Can I rent a board?	ボードを借りることはできますか？ *bōdo o karirukoto wa deki masu ka.*
How are the currents?	潮の流れはどうですか？ *shio no nagare wa dō desu ka.*
How high are the waves?	波の高さはどれくらいですか？ *nami no takasa wa dore kurai desu ka.*
Is it usually crowded?	たいていいつも混んでいますか？ *taitei itsumo konde imasu ka.*
Are there facilities on that beach?	そのビーチにシャワーやトイレはありますか？ *sono bīchi ni shawā ya toire wa arimasu ka.*
Is there wind surfing there also?	そこにはウィンド サーフィンもありますか？ *soko niwa uindo sāfin mo arimasu ka.*

GOLFING

'd like to reserve a ee-time, please.
ティータイムの予約をお願いします。
tī taimu no yoyaku o onegai shimasu.

Do we need to be nembers to play?
会員でないとプレイできませんか?
kaiin de nai to purē deki masen ka.

How many holes is your course?
このコースは何ホールありますか?
kono kōsu wa nan hōru arimasu ka.

What is par for the course?
このコースのパーはいくつですか?
kono kōsu no pā wa ikutsu desu ka.

need to rent clubs.
クラブを借りなければなりません。
kurabu o kari nakereba narimasen.

need to purchase a leeve of balls.
ボール一箱買わなければなりません。
bōru hito hako kawa nakereba narimasen.

need a glove.
手袋が必要です。
tebukuro ga hitsuyō desu.

need a new hat.
新しい帽子が必要です。
atarashii bōshi ga hitsuyō desu.

Do you require soft spikes?
ソフトスパイクを履かなければなりませんか?
sofuto supaiku o haka nakere ba narima sen ka.

Do you have carts?
カートはありますか?
kāto wa arimasu ka.

I'd like to hire a caddy.
キャディを雇いたいのですが。
kyadī o yatoi tai no desuga.

Do you have a driving range?
ゴルフ練習場はありますか？
gorufu renshū jō wa arimasu ka.

How much are the greens fees?
グリーン料金はいくらですか？
gurīn ryōkin wa ikura desu ka.

Can I book a lesson with the pro?
プロ レッスンの予約はできますか？
puro ressun no yoyaku wa deki masu ka.

I need to have a club repaired.
クラブの修理が必要です。
kurabu no shūri ga hitsuyō desu.

Is the course dry?
コースは乾いていますか？
kōsu wa kawaite imasu ka.

Are there any wildlife hazards?
野生動物に遭遇する危険はありますか？
yasei dōbutsu ni sōgu suru kiken w arimasu ka.

How many meters is the course?
このコースは一周何メートルありますか？
kono kōsu wa isshū nan mētoru arimasu ka.

Is it very hilly?
急な斜面が多いですか？
kyū na shamen ga ōi desu ka.

THE BEST ACTIVE SPORTS

Bicycling

What Tokyo lacks in amenities for pedestrians and joggers, it more than makes up for in terms of ease of use for bicyclists. It is pretty easy to get anywhere in Tokyo by bike. Renting a bike can be a great way to explore Tokyo—all the more so because many train stations have bike parking nearby. Bike rental shops in the Tokyo area include **Mujirushi Ryouhin** near Yurakucho Station (✆ **03/5208-8241**); **Green-Chari Tokyo** near Jinbocho Station (✆ **03/3512-2817**); and **RE/Bike Station** near Shibuya (✆ **03/3407-3344**).

Golfing

If baseball is Japan's national pastime, then golf is a close second. The sport is something of a required skill set for salarymen on Japan Inc.'s fast track, and it's not unusual for enthusiasts to spend nearly every Saturday either on the links or in batting cages. During the heyday of Japan's "bubble" economy of the 1980s and early 1990s, memberships at key courses traded like commodities for tens of thousands of dollars. But today, it is much easier to play a round of golf without paying outrageous green or membership fees. Formerly private courses outside Tokyo that have opened their doors to non-members include the Jack Nicklaus-designed **Kazusa Monarch Country Club** in Chiba prefecture, which boasts a bathhouse (www.giganet.net/kmcc/english); and **Sakawa Royal Golf Club** in Kanagawa prefecture, which features views of Mt. Fuji (✆ **04/6577-2226**).

Hiking

Japan is in many ways a hiker's paradise with thousands of miles of well-marked trails up and down its spine. The Japan Alps offers some of the finest trails and most spectacular scenery in North Asia. But even a 40-minute train trip outside Tokyo yields some impressive hikes for both the amateur and seasoned hiker alike. One of the most popular half-day trips near Tokyo is a hike up **Mount Takao**, which is conveniently located at one end of the Chuo Line that runs from Tokyo Station. Mt. Takao is a relatively easy hike that is fun any time of year, but especially so during the autumn when the mountainside's Japanese maples burst out in a riot of color—reds, oranges and yellows. For information on more adventurous hikes, you might want to read up in advance by checking out books like *Hiking in Japan: An Adventurer's Guide to the Mountain Trails* (Origami/Kodansha) and *Day Walks Near Tokyo* (Origami/Kodansha).

Ice Skating

Winter or summer, ice skating is a popular diversion for Japanese children and adults alike. In Tokyo, major rinks include the **Kokuritsu Kyogijyo** near Harajuku Station (**© 03/3468-1171**) and the **Meiji Jingu Skate Rink** near Shinanomachi Station (**© 03/3403-3456**).

Jogging

Japan offers a challenge to joggers because sidewalks and streets tend to be crowded and narrow. However, outside the most congested urban areas there is plenty of well-paved territory to explore. In cities like Tokyo, your best bet will be to look for major parks or paths along the many rivers. Running around the **Imperial Palace** grounds in central Tokyo is a popular route. Tokyo's **Yoyogi Park** near Harajuku/Shibuya and **Shinjuku Gyoen Park** also have nice paths for joggers. The Kanda River and Zenpukuji River west of Shinjuku are favorites because they emanate from pretty Inogashira Park in the suburb of Kichijoji.

Martial Arts

Japan is the birthplace of some of the world's most popular martial arts, including *aikido*, *jujitsu*, *karate-do* and *kendo*. While most Japanese experience at least one of these traditional sports during their early school years, relatively few continue to practice much beyond college. However, there are devoted martial artists in most cities and towns —often practicing in single room *dojo* off side alleys and up or down several flights of stairs. Generally speaking, training sessions at dojo in Japan are more intense than in the U.S. and require regular attendance if you're going to stay in the good graces of fellow students and teachers. A working knowledge of Japanese language is also very helpful. Nevertheless, it can be a unique experience to participate once in the training involved in one of these Japanese sports.

Skiing

Many visitors to Japan are surprised by how mountainous the country is outside of major urban areas. In fact, much of the archipelago is dominated by major mountain ranges such as the Japan Alps, which run along the spine of Japan. Therefore, it should come as no surprise that the country is dotted with ski resorts, particularly in central Japan and on the northeastern island of Hokkaido, where the snowfall is heaviest. From Tokyo, it is relatively easy to journey by express or bullet train to resorts such as **Echigo-Yuzawa** or **Shiga-Kogen**. In Hokkaido, **Niseko** and **Rusutsu** are two of the many options for avid skiers. Best of all, most ski areas in Japan rent high quality equipment and gear—from poles to down jackets and boots.

THE BEST BEACHES

A trip to a popular beach in Japan can easily conjure up the Japanese expression for overcrowding, *imo-arai* ("potato wash"), as swimmers bob up and down in the waves. Needless to say, the best white sand beaches are those that are furthest from major cities such as Osaka and Tokyo, and that take the better part of a day to reach. Shark attacks are extremely rare, but rip tides have been known to drown more than a few swimmers each year, so exercise caution and plan to swim with a buddy. Some of the better known spots near Tokyo include Chiba prefecture's **Chosi**, **Kujukurihama** and **Onjuku** beaches, and Kanagawa prefecture's **Enoshima**, **Yuigahama** and **Zushi** beaches.

SPECTATOR SPORTS

Baseball

Japanese baseball has a surprisingly long history and, despite the defections of several top stars to the U.S. major league, Japan's 12 professional teams remain quite popular. The best way to catch a game in Tokyo is at **Tokyo Dome** (✆ **03/5800-9999**), home to the Yomiuri Giants franchise.

Horse Racing

While Tokyo has no casinos, it does have two horse racing tracks where spectators are free to bet on their favorite steeds—**Oi Keibajo** (✆ **03/3763-2151**) and **Tokyo Keibajo** (✆ **04/2363-3141**). Both have tried to market themselves as a date spot for the younger crowd they tend to attract, but that campaign has met with mixed success.

Soccer

Football, or soccer to Americans, is newer to Japan as a professional sport, but the 12 teams of the J-League have developed a wide following throughout the country (especially after Japan's co-hosting of the 2002 World Cup with South Korea). Games are played regularly at the **Kokuritsu Kyogijo** in central Tokyo (✆ **03/3403-1151**).

Sumo

Traditional wrestling bouts, featuring two jumbo-size contestants squaring off in loin cloths, are held six times a year around the country and are televised live on NHK, the quasi-governmental national broadcaster. The Tokyo tournaments are held in January, May and September at the **Kokugikan Stadium** in Ryogoku (✆ **03/3263-5111**).

CHAPTER TEN

NIGHTLIFE

For coverage of movies and cultural events, *see p152, Chapter Seven, "Culture."*

CLUB HOPPING

Where can I find ____ ?	____はどこにありますか？ *____ wa doko ni arimasu ka.*
a good nightclub	よいナイトクラブ *yoi naito kurabu*
a club with a live band	ライブ演奏のあるクラブ *raibu ensō no aru kurabu*
a reggae club	レゲー クラブ *regē kurabu*
a hip hop club	ヒップホップ クラブ *hippu hoppu kurabu*
a techno club	テクノ クラブ *tekuno kurabu*
a jazz club	ジャズ クラブ *jazu kurabu*
a country-western club	カントリー ウエスタン クラブ *kantorī uesutan kurabu*
a gay / lesbian club	ゲイ / レスビアン クラブ *gei / resubian kurabu*
a club where I can dance	踊れるクラブ *odoreru kurabu*
a club with Spanish / Mexican music	スペイン / メキシコ音楽が聴けるクラブ *supein / mekishiko ongaku ga kikeru kurabu*
the most popular club in town	街で一番人気があるクラブ *machi de ichiban ninki ga aru kurabu*

a singles bar	独身が集まるバー *dokushin ga atsumaru bā*
a piano bar	ピアノ バー *piano bā*
the most upscale club	最高級バー *sai kōkyū bā*
What's the hottest bar these days?	最近最も人気があるのはどんなバーですか？ *saikin mottomo ninki ga aru nowa donna bā desu ka.*
What's the cover charge?	カバー チャージはいくらですか？ *kabā chāji wa ikura desu ka.*
Do they have a dress code?	服装に規則はありますか？ *fukusō ni kisoku wa arimasu ka.*
Is it expensive?	値段は高いですか？ *nedan wa takai desu ka.*
What's the best time to go?	いつ行くのが一番いいですか？ *itsu iku noga ichiban ii desu ka.*
What kind of music do they play there?	どんな音楽を演奏していますか？ *donna ongaku o ensō shite imasu ka.*
Is it smoking?	タバコを吸えますか？ *tabako o sue masu ka.*
Is it nonsmoking?	禁煙ですか？ *kin en desu ka.*
I'm looking for ____	____を探しています。 *____ o sagashite imasu.*
a good cigar shop.	よいタバコ屋 *yoi tabako ya*
a pack of cigarettes.	タバコ１箱 *tabako hito hako*

I'd like ____	____ください。 ____ *kudasai.*
a drink please.	飲み物を *nomi mono o*
a bottle of beer please.	ビールを１本 *bīru o ippon*
a beer on tap please.	生ビールを *nama bīru o*
a shot of ____ please.	____を1杯 ____ *o ippai*

For a full list of drinks, see p91.

Make it a double please!	ダブルにしてください！ *daburu ni shite kudasai.*
With ice, please.	氷を入れてください。 *kōri o irete kudasai.*
And one for the lady / the gentleman!	1つはこのご婦人 / 男性に！ *hitotsu wa kono gofujin / dansei ni.*
How much for a bottle / glass of beer?	ビール１本 / １杯はいくらですか？ *bīru ippon / ippai wa ikura desu ka.*

Do You Mind If I Smoke?

タバコはありますか？ *tabako wa arimasuka.*	Do you have a cigarette?
火はありますか？ *hi wa arimasuka.*	Do you have a light?
火をおかししましょうか？ *hi o okashi shimashō ka.*	May I offer you a light?
禁煙です。 *kin en desu.*	Smoking not permitted.

NIGHTLIFE

I'd like to buy a drink for that woman / man over there.
あそこの女性 / 男性に私のおごりで一杯あげてください。
asoko no josei / dansei ni watashi no ogori de ippai agete kudasai.

A pack of cigarettes, please.
タバコを１箱ください。
tabako o hito hako kudasai.

Do you have a lighter or matches?
ライターかマッチを持ってますか？
raitā ka macchi o motte masu ka.

Do you smoke?
タバコを吸いますか？
tabako o suimasu ka.

Would you like a cigarette?
タバコ1本いかがですか？
tabako ippon ikaga desu ka.

May I run a tab?
つけにしていいですか？
tsuke ni shite ii desu ka.

What's the cover?
カバーチャージはいくらですか？
kabā chāji wa ikura desu ka.

ACROSS A CROWDED ROOM

Excuse me; may I buy you a drink?
あの一、私のおごりで１杯いかがですか？
anō, watashi no ogori de ippai ikaga desu ka.

You look amazing.	すてきですね。 *suteki desu ne.*
You look like the most interesting person in the room.	あなたはここで一番魅力的です。 *anata wa koko de ichiban miryoku teki desu.*
Would you like to dance?	ダンスしませんか？ *dansu shima sen ka.*
Do you like to dance fast or slow?	ダンスは速いのとスローなのとどちらが好きですか？ *dansu wa hayai noto surōna noto dochira ga suki desu ka.*
Give me your hand.	手をかしてください。 *te o kashite kudasai.*
What would you like to drink?	飲み物は何がいいですか？ *nomi mono wa nani ga ii desu ka.*
You're a great dancer.	踊りが上手ですね。 *odori ga jōzu desu ne.*
I don't know that dance!	あれは私の知らないダンスです！ *are wa watashi no shira nai dansu desu*
Do you like this song?	この歌は好きですか？ *kono uta wa suki desu ka.*
You have nice eyes!	あなたの目はとても素敵ですね！ *anata no me wa totemo suteki desu ne.*

For a full list of features, see p120.

May I have your phone number?	あなたの電話番号を教えてくれますか？ *anata no denwa bangō o oshiete kureru masu ka.*

IN THE CASINO

How much is this table?	このテーブルでは最低いくらのかけですか? *kono tēburu dewa saitei ikura no kake desu ka.*
Deal me in.	私も入れてください。 *watashi mo irete kudasai.*
Put it on red!	赤に置いてください! *aka ni oite kudasai.*
Put it on black!	黒に置いてください! *kuro ni oite kudasai.*
Let it ride!	つづけるよ! *tsuzukeru yo!*
21!	21! *nijū ichi!*
Snake-eyes!	スネークアイだ! *sunēku ai da!*
Seven.	7。 *shichi/nana.*

For a full list of numbers, see p6.

Damn, eleven.	残念、11だ。 *zannen, jū ichi da.*
I'll pass.	パスします。 *pasu shimasu.*
Hit me!	もう1枚! *mō ichi mai.*
Split.	2手に分けるよ。 *futa te ni wakeru yo.*
Are the drinks complimentary?	飲み物はタダですか? *nomi mono wa tada desu ka.*
May I bill it to my room?	わたしの部屋につけてくれますか? *watashi no heya ni tsukete kure masu ka.*

I'd like to cash out.	清算してください。 *seisan shite kudasai.*
I'll hold.	パスします。 *pasu shimasu.*
I'll see your bet.	それにあわせます。 *sore ni awasemasu.*
I call.	コール。 *kōru.*
Full house!	フルハウス! *furu hausu.*
Royal flush.	ロイヤル フラッシュ。 *roiyaru furasshu.*
Straight.	ストレート。 *sutorēto.*

NIGHTLIFE ESSENTIALS

Japan offers the traveler many diversions once the sun goes down and the neon signs begin to flicker. Japanese night spots can be fairly easily categorized into three groups:

Izakaya The most widespread of Japan's nightspots is the informal *izakaya*. These watering holes, many of which are mom-and-pop affairs, typically serve hearty helpings of Japanese grub such as grilled fish and deep-fried croquettes, along with draft beer, sake and other beverages. *Izakaya* tend to be cheap by Japanese standards and offer an excellent window into the local character. Places like Tokyo's **Shinjuku district** or **Dotombori** in Osaka are positively overflowing with *izakaya*. Often, there's no sign in English, but they can usually be identified by the half-curtains (called *noren*) hanging outside the entrance and the smell of grilled chicken or fish from within. Most *izakaya* open at 6pm and close by 11pm.

The Hostess Club Decidedly more upscale, these nightspots are usually tiny spaces with low-slung chairs and tables, chatty female staffers, $200 bottles of whiskey and an imperious *mama-san* owner-operator. Many are outfitted with ice machines for the ubiquitous *mizuwari* (whiskey and water on the rocks) and karaoke machines for the quickly inebriated clientele. But the appeal may be limited to all but the initiated because the food and drink selection is usually poor—and expensive.

The Western Bar Popular with both Japanese and foreign visitors alike, these are no different than most bars or clubs anywhere outside Japan, although some liquors may be harder to find (such as tequila). Western-style bars and clubs are usually concentrated in big urban areas, although any decent-sized suburb is likely to have one or two. There is rarely a cover charge at bars, and most drinks are paid for at the time of purchase. Dance and jazz clubs do charge hefty covers.

TOKYO AFTER DARK

Roppongi

Roppongi earned its reputation as a hangout for foreign expatriates and visitors after World War II, when many G.I.s frequented its garish precincts. Today, it is still a popular nightspot for foreigners, along with Japanese who like the Western-style bars and clubs that predominate. It is one of the few districts in Tokyo that is truly open 24 hours a day.

Imoarai-zaka ("Potato Wash Hill") is a central strip that is filled with watering holes such as **Café Mogumbo** (© **03/3403-4833**), where a ring of the bell means drinks are on the house. Not far away is the ear-splitting **Hard Rock Café Tokyo** (© **03/3408-7018**) and financial community favorites **Wall Street** (© **03/3478-7659**) and **Trading Places** (© **03/3589-2442**). Other bar hopping spots include **Motown House** (© **03/5474-4605**), the Irish themed **Paddy O'Folleys** (© **03/3423-2239**) and **Tokyo Sports Café** (© **03/3404-3675**). **Bar Isn't It?** (www.isnt-it.info) and **Gas Panic** (www.gaspanic.co.jp) are chains that can be found among dozens of other singles-friendly dive bars down the twisting backstreets of Roppongi.

NIGHTLIFE

Popular dance clubs include hip-hop and trance specialist **Vanilla** (© **03/3401-6200**), **Lexington Queen** (© **03/3401-1661**), and the Latin dance mecca **Salsa Susada** (© **03/5474-8806**).

Shinjuku

The center of nightlife in central Tokyo's westernmost hub is **Kabuki-cho**, an area located northeast of Shinjuku Station. On the one hand, there are an estimated 200 sex-related businesses in operation—from strip joints to massage parlors to peep shows. On the other, it hosts some of the most advanced video game parlors in Japan and a smorgasbord of fast food restaurants. While it's safe to walk through, it probably isn't wise to dally.

Nowadays, outside of a smattering of small clubs, the only major disco in the district is Club Code (© **03/3209-0702**), which boasts three dance floors. To the east of Kabuki-cho, just west of Hanazono Shrine, is a run-down warren of alleys called **Goruden Gai** ("Golden Street"), dating from the immediate post-WWII period, where 6-seat bars predominate. If you go farther east, you'll find the gay-bar district called "**Shinjuku 2-chome**" (pronounced "knee-chomay"), where clubs such as **Advocates Café** (**© 03/3358-3988**) attract a male crowd.

Ginza

Ginza is quieter and more sophisticated than Roppongi and Shinjuku. Here you'll find what the Japanese call *ichi-ryu* ("first-grade") bars and hostess clubs. But they don't come cheap and aren't necessarily the most foreigner-friendly establishments due to the intricate protocol involved. A better choice is one of the many bars and restaurants off the main drag, *Harumi-dori*, where young Japanese head for dinner and drinks after a long day at work in the nearby business districts. Here you can find large branches of the Ginza Lion beer hall and Kirin City pub chains, along with smaller mom-and-pop bars.

Shibuya

As a major transportation hub, Shibuya is one of the most popular spots for bars and clubs in Tokyo for all age groups. Teens and young adults flock here for the highest density of discos, lounges, and love hotels in Tokyo. The bars are too numerous to list, but a stroll up Dogenzaka or Tokyu Hoten-dori, both of which branch out from the JR train station, will give you plenty of options. After midnight, the pace picks up at some of the trendiest clubs in the city, such as **Club Asia** (**© 03/5458-2551**) for trance; underground music spot **Module** (**© 03/3464-8432**); and **Womb** (**© 03/5459-0039**) for techno. Shibuya also has its share of live jazz clubs, such as **JZ Brat** (**© 03/5728-0168**) and, in nearby Omotesando, the **Blue Note Tokyo** (**© 03/5485-0088**).

OSAKA AFTER DARK

Japan's Second City abounds in nightlife: from the most faddish clubs to age-old *ryotei* restaurants. The liveliest and most budget-friendly area to sample Osaka's various offerings after dark is **Dotombori**, which flanks the southern bank of the Dotombori Canal. A two-minute walk from exit 14 of Namba station, it's a fun place to people-watch, even if you're not up for a night of drinking. There are dozens of *izakaya* with Japanese cuisine and drinks. Irish pub **Murphy's (© 06/6213-6911)** is a western-style bar that never fails to attract a crowd. There are also several local bar chains with outlets in the area such as pool hall favorite **Sam & Dave Four (© 06/6251-5333)**, **Pig & Whistle (© 06/6213-6911)** and raging hormone hotspot **Bar Isn't It? (© 06/6363-4001)**. For a more sophisticated evening out, try the microbrew and tofu at **Bar Tachibana (© 06/6212-6074)** in Dotombori. Or head to the Nishi-Umeda station area for a glass or two of fine wine at **Enoteca (© 06/6343-7175)**, followed by a jazz set at the **Blue Note Osaka (© 06/6342-7788)**.

KYOTO AFTER DARK

The **Gion** district has traditionally been the heart of Kyoto's nightlife, but while it still has its share of geisha houses and high-end bars, these are not open to what the Japanese refer to as *ichigen-sans* ("first timers"). Still, it can be worth a stroll down the narrow alleys if only to hear the occasional sound of a Japanese lute or perhaps a burst of tittering laughter. For more hearty fare, head to the **Pontocho** district running parallel to the Kamo River, or nearby Kiyamachi. Popular Western bars include **Pig & Whistle (© 075/761-6022)** and **Rub-A-Dub (© 075/256-3122)**. For live jazz, check out **Hello Dolly (© 075/241-1728)** in Pontocho, or for live Irish music, head to **The Hill of Tara (© 075/213-3330)**, beside the Kyoto Hotel.

CHAPTER ELEVEN

HEALTH & SAFETY

This chapter covers the terms you'll need to maintain your health and safety—including the most useful phrases for the pharmacy, the doctor's office, and the police station.

AT THE PHARMACY

Please fill this prescription.	この薬を処方してください。 *kono kusuri o shohō shite kudasai.*
Do you have something for ____ ?	____に効く薬はありますか？ *____ ni kiku kusuri wa arimasu ka.*
a cold	カゼ *kaze*
a cough	咳 *seki*
I need something ____	____が欲しいのですが。 *____ ga hoshii no desuga.*
to help me sleep.	眠れるようになるもの *nemureru yōni naru mono*
to help me relax.	気を静められるもの *ki o shizume rareru mono*
I want to buy ____	____をください。 *____ o kudasai.*
condoms.	コンドーム *kondōmu*
an antihistamine.	抗ヒスタミン剤 *kō hisutamin zai*
antibiotic cream.	抗生物質クリーム *kōsei busshitsu kurīmu*
aspirin.	アスピリン *asupirin*

non-aspirin pain reliever.	アスピリン以外の鎮痛剤 *asupirin igai no chintsūzai*
medicine with codeine.	コデインを含む薬 *kodein o fukumu kusuri*
insect repellant.	虫除けローション *mushi yoke rōshon*
I need something for ____	____に効くものが欲しいのですが。 *____ ni kiku mono ga hoshii no desuga.*
corns.	うおのめ *uonome*
congestion.	充血 *jūketsu*
warts.	いぼ *ibo*
constipation.	便秘 *benpi*
diarrhea.	下痢 *geri*
indigestion.	消化不良 *shōka furyō*
nausea.	吐き気 *hakike*
motion sickness.	乗り物酔い *norimono yoi*
seasickness.	船酔い *funayoi*
acne.	ニキビ *nikibi*

AT THE DOCTOR'S OFFICE

I would like to see ____	____に診ていただきたいのですが。 *____ ni mite itadaki tai no desuga.*
a doctor.	医者 *isha*

a chiropractor.	カイロプラクター *kairo purakutā*
a gynecologist.	婦人科医 *fujinka i*
an eye / ears & nose / throat specialist.	眼科 / 耳鼻科 / 咽喉科医 *ganka / jibika / inkōka i*
a dentist.	歯医者 *haisha*
an optometrist.	検眼師 *kenganshi*
Do I need an appointment?	予約が必要ですか？ *yoyaku ga hitsuyō desu ka.*
I have an emergency.	緊急なんです。 *kinkyū nan desu.*
My prescription has run out and I need a refill.	薬がなくなってしまったので薬をいただきたいのですが。 *kusuri ga nakunatte shimatta node kusuri o itadakitai no desuga.*
Please call a doctor.	医者を呼んでください。 *isha o yonde kudasai.*
I need an ambulance.	救急車を呼んでください。 *kyūkyū sha o yonde kudasai.*

SYMPTOMS

For a full list of body parts, see p205.

My ____ hurts.	____が痛いんです。 *____ ga itain desu.*
My ____ is stiff.	____が凝っています。 *____ ga kotte imasu.*
I think I'm having a heart attack.	心臓発作を起こしたみたいです。 *shinzō hossa o okoshita mitai desu.*
I can't move.	動けません。 *ugoke masen.*
I fell.	転びました。 *korobi mashita.*

I fainted.	気を失いました。 *ki o ushinai mashita.*
I have a cut on my ____.	____を切りました。 *____ o kiri mashita.*
I have a headache.	頭痛がします。 *zutsū ga shimasu.*
My vision is blurry.	物がぼやけて見えます。 *mono ga boyakete mie masu.*
I feel dizzy.	めまいがします。 *memai ga shimasu.*
I think I'm pregnant.	妊娠したみたいなんです。 *ninshin shita mitai nan desu.*
I don't think I'm pregnant.	妊娠ではないと思います。 *ninshin dewa nai to omoi masu.*
I'm having trouble walking.	歩行が困難なんです。 *hokō ga konnan nan desu.*
I can't get up.	立ち上がれません。 *tachi agare masen.*

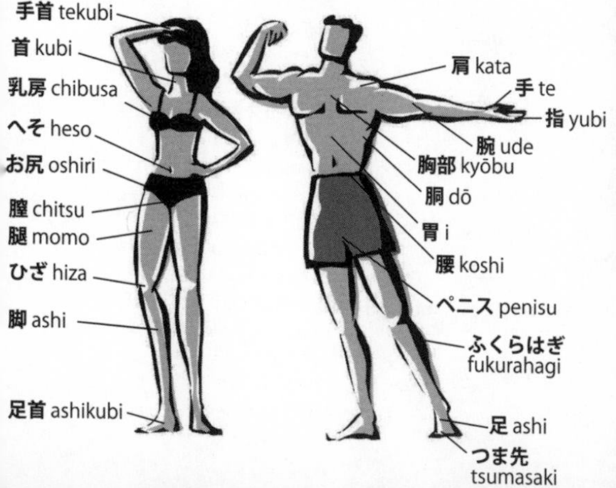

I was mugged.	襲われました。 *osoware mashita.*
I was raped.	強姦されました。 *gōkan sare mashita.*
A dog attacked me.	犬に襲われました。 *inu ni osoware mashita.*
A snake bit me.	蛇にかまれました。 *hebi ni kamare mashita.*
I can't move my ____ without pain.	____を動かすと痛みます。 *____ o ugokasu to itami masu.*

MEDICATIONS

I need morning-after pills.	モーニングアフター ピルが欲しいのですが。 *mōningu afutā piru ga hoshii no desuga.*
I need birth control pills.	避妊薬が欲しいのですが。 *hinin yaku ga hoshii no desuga.*
I lost my eyeglasses and need new ones.	眼鏡をなくしたので、新しいのが必要なんですが。 *megane o nakushita node, atarashii noga hitsuyō nan desuga.*
I need new contact lenses.	新しいコンタクトレンズが必要なんですが。 *atarashii kontakuto renzu ga hitsuyō nan desuga.*
I need erectile dysfunction pills.	勃起不全改善薬が欲しいのですが。 *bokki fuzen kaizen yaku ga hoshii no desuga.*
Please fill this prescription.	処方箋がほしいのですが。 *shohōsen ga hoshi no desuga.*

I need a prescription for ____.	______の薬を処方してほしいのですが。 *______ no kusuri o shoho shite hoshii no desuga.*
I am allergic to ____	私は____にアレルギーがあります。 *watashi wa____ ni arerugī ga arimasu.*
penicillin.	ペニシリン *penishirin*
antibiotics.	抗生物質 *kōsei busshitsu*
sulfa drugs.	サルファー剤 *sarufā zai*
steroids.	ステロイド *suteroido*
I have asthma.	私は喘息を持っています。 *watashi wa zensoku o motte imasu.*

DENTAL PROBLEMS

I have a toothache.	歯が痛みます。 *ha ga itami masu.*
I chipped a tooth.	歯が欠けました。 *ha ga kake mashita.*
My bridge came loose.	ブリッジがゆるんできました。 *burijji ga yurunde kimashita.*
I lost a crown.	歯にかぶせていたものがとれてしまいましたしました。 *ha ni kabusete ita mono ga torete shimai mashita.*
I lost a denture plate.	義歯がとれてしまいました。 *gishi ga torete shimai mashita.*

AT THE POLICE STATION

I'm sorry, did I do something wrong?	すみません、私がなにか悪いことをしましたか？ *sumima sen, watashi ga nani ka warui koto o shimashita ka.*
I am ____	私は____です。 *watashi wa ____ desu.*
an American.	アメリカ人 *amerika jin*
British.	イギリス人 *igirisu jin*
a Canadian.	カナダ人 *kanada jin*
Irish.	アイルランド人 *airurando jin*
an Australian.	オーストラリア人 *ōsutoraria jin*
a New Zealander.	ニュージーランド人 *nyūjīrando jin*
The car is a rental.	車はレンタ カーです。 *kuruma wa rentakā desu.*
Do I pay the fine to you?	罰金を払うのですか？ *bakkin o harau no desu ka.*
Do I have to go to court?	裁判所に行かなければなりませんか？ *saiban sho ni ikana kereba narima sen ka.*
When?	いつですか？ *itsu desu ka.*
I'm sorry, my Japanese isn't very good.	すみません、日本語はあまり上手に話せません。 *sumima sen, nihon go wa amari jōzuni hanase masen.*

Listen Up: Police Lingo

免許証、登録証、保険証を見せてください。 *menkyo shō, tōroku shō, hoken shō o misete kudasai.*	Your license, registration and insurance, please.
罰金は 1000 円です。私に直接払ってもかまいません。 *bekkin wa sen en desu. watashi ni chokusetsu harattemo kamai masen.*	The fine is ¥1000. You can pay me directly.
パスポートを見せてください。 *pasupōto o misete kudasai.*	Your passport please?
どこに行くんですか? *doko ni ikun desu ka.*	Where are you going?
なぜそんなに急いでいますか? *naze sonnani isoide imasu ka.*	Why are you in such a hurry?

I need an interpreter.	通訳が必要です。 *tsūyaku ga hitsuyō desu.*
I'm sorry, I don't understand the ticket.	すみません、このチケットの意味がわかりません。 *sumima sen, kono chiketto no imi ga wakari masen.*
May I call my embassy?	私の国の大使館に電話をかけてもいいですか? *watashi no kuni no taishi kan ni denwa o kaketemo ii desu ka.*
I was robbed.	強盗に遭いました。 *gōtō ni ai mashita.*
I was mugged.	襲われました。 *osoware mashita.*

I was raped.
強姦されました。
gōkan sare mashita.

Do I need to make a report?
警察に届け出る必要がありますか？
keisatsu ni todokeru hitsuyō ga arimasu ka.

Somebody broke into my room.
誰かが私の部屋に侵入しました。
dareka ga watashi no heya ni shin nyū shima shita.

Someone stole my purse / wallet.
誰かが私のハンドバッグ/財布を盗みました。
dareka ga watashi no hando baggu/saifu o nusumi mashita.

SAFETY FAST FACTS

Crime

The general crime rate in Japan is well below the average in the U.S. and most other industrialized countries. Petty theft such as pick-pocketing is the biggest risk most travelers will face and even that is a statistical anomaly. However, it is wise to keep your money and passport tucked safely away after use, particularly right after landing in Japan. In the recent past, the U.S. Embassy has reported a handful of incidents involving lost or stolen American passports at Narita airport.

Most parts of Tokyo are safe any time of day, but it's wise to exercise some caution when walking alone late at night in deserted parks or in some red-light districts, such as Shinjuku's Kabukicho or Shibuya's Dogenzaka.

Drugs

Japanese law treats drug law offenders harshly, so do not even consider possessing or trafficking in any illegal narcotics, including marijuana. Detainees are often held in solitary confinement and sentences usually result in large fines or long jail sentences. About half of all Americans currently incarcerated in Japan are serving time for drug-related offenses, including some who were paid couriers for traffickers operating out of Europe or Southeast Asia, according to the U.S. State Department.

Embassies & Consulates

The **U.S. Embassy** in Tokyo is located at 1-10-5 Akasaka, Minato-ku, Tokyo 107-8420, near the Tameike-Sanno and Toranomon subways stations (© **03/3224-5000**; http://tokyo.usembassy.gov). The **U.S. Consulate** in Osaka-Kobe is located at 2-11-5 Nishitenma, Kita-ku, Osaka 530-8543 (© **06/6315-5900**).

The **Canadian Embassy** in Tokyo is located at 7-3-38 Akasaka, Minato-ku, Tokyo, near the Aoyama-Itchome subway station (© **03/5412-6200**). The **British Embassy** is located in Tokyo at 1 Ichibancho, Chiyoda-ku, near Hanzomon subway station

(© **03/3265-5511**). The **Embassy of Ireland** is located in Tokyo on the 5th floor at 2-10-7 Kojimachi, Chiyoda-ku, near Hanzomon Station (© **03/3263-0695**). The **Australian Embassy** is located at 2-1-14 Mita, Minato-ku (© **03/5232-4111**), and the **New Zealand Embassy** is located at 20-40 Kamiyama-cho, Shibuya-ku (© **03/3467-2271**)—both are in Tokyo.

Emergency Contacts

Police can be summoned throughout Japan by dialing © **110**. Ambulance and fire services can be reached by dialing © **119**. Be aware that these numbers do not always work from mobile phones and that English-speaking dispatchers may not be available.

Food & Water

All Japanese food venders are subject to regular inspection by Japanese health authorities, so food sold almost anywhere in the country should be safe to eat in most circumstances. Raw fish requires special handling and storage, but the Japanese have this down to a fine art. **Tap water** is safe to drink anywhere in Japan, although some people claim it is too highly chlorinated. Bottled water is also widely available.

Lost and Found

Almost every long-term foreign resident—and a few tourists—have a tale of a dropped or misplaced valuable that somehow found its way back to its owner. Even in a big city like Tokyo, little miracles like that seem to happen with surprising frequency. If you forget something in a taxi, ask someone who speaks Japanese to contact the **Tokyo Taxi Center** (© **03/3648-0300**). It helps if you have the printed receipt, which Japanese taxi drivers rarely fail to proffer. For items lost on JR trains, call or go to the Lost & Found Rooms at **JR Tokyo Station** (© **03/3231-1880**) or **JR Ueno Station** (© **03/3841-8069**). The lost and found section of the **Tokyo Metropolitan Government** (© **03/3812-2011**) may be able to track down something lost on a bus or subway after a three-day waiting period.

Natural Disasters

Japan is one of the most earthquake-prone nations in the world, and the threat of deadly typhoons—mostly from landslides—reaches a fever pitch in the autumn. Don't be too alarmed by minor tremors, as they occur frequently, but if there is a major strike, take cover under a doorway or large table indoors and stay away from power lines, trees and the walls of buildings. Never use elevators during an earthquake. Hotels should supply in-room flashlights for emergencies, but packing a small spare won't hurt.

MEDICAL CARE

The quality of care at Japanese clinics and hospitals is good, but keep in mind that relatively few nurses and physicians are fluent in English, especially in rural areas. Moreover, medical facilities and drugs that fully cater to the preferences of Americans and other foreigners are expensive and not very widespread. More importantly, Japan's nationalized health insurance system is available only to non-Japanese with long-term visas. So any treatment must be paid for immediately, in cash, at the time of treatment unless the patient can provide some form of concrete proof of ability to pay at a later date—preferably written in Japanese. Note that U.S. prescriptions are not honored in Japan, so visitors should arrive with their own supply of medications.

The American Embassy in Tokyo has a full list of medical facilities in Japan with English-speaking staff available on its website at: http://tokyo.usembassy.gov/e/acs/tacs-tokyodoctors. Some medical facilities in Tokyo where English is spoken include:

- **International Medical Center of Japan** at 1-21-1 Toyama, Shinjuku-ku, Tokyo 162-8655. © **03/3202-7181**.
- **Sanno Hospital** at 8-10-16 Akasaka, Minato-ku, Tokyo 107-0052. © **03/3402-2187**; www.sannoclc.or.jp.

- **Tokyo British Clinic** at Daikanyama Y Bldg. 2F, 2-13-7 Ebisu-Nishi, Shibuya-ku, Tokyo 150-0021. © **03/5458-6099**; www.tokyobritishclinic.com.
- **Tokyo Medical & Surgical Clinic** at No. 32 Mori Bldg. 2F, 3-4-30 Shiba Koen, Minato-ku, Tokyo 105-0011. © **03/3436-3028**; www.tmsc.jp.

INSURANCE

Check your existing insurance polices and credit card coverage before you buy travel insurance. You may already be covered for lost luggage, canceled tickets or medical expenses. The cost of travel insurance varies widely, depending on the cost and length or your trip, your age, your health and the type of trip you're taking. You can get estimates from a number of providers through www.InsureMyTrip.com.

Trip Cancellation Insurance Contact **Access America** (© **866/807-3982**; www.AcessAmerica.com), **Travel Guard International** (© **800/826-4919**; www.TravelGuard.com), **Travel Insured International** (© **800/243-3174**; www.TravelInsured.com), or **Travelex Insurance Services** (© **888/457-4602**; www.travelex-insurance.com).

Medical Insurance Most health plans (including Medicare and Medicaid) do not provide coverage for travel overseas, and the ones that do usually require filling out extensive paperwork for reimbursement. As an extra precaution, you may consider buying travel medical insurance from providers such as **MEDEX Assistance** (© **410/453-6300**; www.MedexAssist.com) or **Travel Assistance International** (© **800/821-2828**; www.TravelAssistance.com).

CHAPTER TWELVE

CULTURE GUIDE

GREAT MOMENTS

Making a Pilgrimage to a Temple or Shrine

From mountaintop shrines to neighborhood temples, Japan's religious structures rank among the nation's most popular attractions. Usually devoted to a particular deity, they're visited for specific reasons: Shopkeepers call on Fushimi-Inari Shrine outside Kyoto, dedicated to the goddess of rice and therefore prosperity, while couples wishing for a happy marriage head to Kyoto's Jishu Shrine, a shrine to the deity of love. Shrines and temples are also the sites for most of Japan's major festivals.

Taking a Communal Hot-Spring Bath

No other people on earth bathe as enthusiastically, as frequently, and for such duration as Japanese. Their many hot-spring resorts—thought to cure all sorts of ailments as well as simply make you feel good—range from hangarlike affairs to outdoor baths with views of the countryside. No matter what the setup, you'll soon warm to the ritual of soaping up, rinsing off, and then soaking in near-scalding waters. Hot-spring spas are located almost everywhere in Japan, from Kyushu to Hokkaido.

Participating in a Festival

With Shintoism and Buddhism as its major religions, and temples and shrines virtually everywhere, Japan has multiple festivals every week. These celebrations, which range from huge processions of wheeled floats to those featuring horseback archery and ladder-top acrobatics, can be lots of fun; you may want to plan your trip around one.

Dining on Japanese Food

There's more to Japanese cuisine than sushi, and part of what makes travel here so fascinating is the variety of national and regional dishes. Every prefecture, it seems, has its own style of noodles, its special vegetables, and its delicacies. If money is no object, order kaiseki, a complete meal of visual and culinary finesse.

Viewing the Cherry Blossoms

Nothing symbolizes the coming of spring so vividly to Japanese as the appearance of the cherry blossoms—and nothing so amazes visitors as the way Japanese gather under the blossoms to celebrate the season with food, drink, dance, and karaoke.

Riding the Shinkansen Bullet Train

Asia's fastest train whips you across the countryside at more than 290km (180 miles) an hour as you relax, see the country's rural countryside, and dine on boxed meals filled with local specialties of the area through which you're speeding.

Staying in a Ryokan

Japan's legendary service reigns supreme in a top-class ryokan, a traditional Japanese inn. Staying in one is the height of both luxury and simplicity: You'll bathe in a Japanese tub, feast your eyes on lovely views (usually a Japanese garden) past shoji screens, dine like a king in your own room, and sleep on a futon.

Attending a Traditional Tea Ceremony

Developed in the 16th century as a means to achieve inner harmony with nature, the highly ritualized ceremony is carried out in teahouses throughout the country, including those set in Japan's many parks and gardens. Several Tokyo hotels offer English-language instruction in the tea ceremony.

Shopping in a Department Store

Japan's department stores are among the best in the world, offering everything from food to designer clothing to electronics to kimono and traditional crafts. Service also is among the best in the world: If you arrive when the store opens, staff will be lined up at the front door to bow as you enter.

Attending a Kabuki Play

Based on universal themes and designed to appeal to the masses, Kabuki plays are extravaganzas of theatrical displays, costumes, and scenes—but mostly they're just plain fun.

Strolling Through Tokyo's Nightlife District

Every major city in Japan has its own nightlife district, but probably none is more famous, more wicked, or more varied than Tokyo's Kabuki-cho in Shinjuku, which offers everything from hole-in-the-wall bars to strip joints, discos, and gay clubs.

Seeing Mount Fuji

It may not seem like much of an accomplishment to see Japan's most famous and tallest mountain, visible from 161km (100 miles) away. But the truth is, it's hardly ever visible except during the winter months and rare occasions when the air is clear. Catching your first glimpse of the giant peak is truly breathtaking and something you'll never forget, whether you see it from aboard the Shinkansen, from a Tokyo skyscraper, or from a nearby national park. If you want to climb it, be prepared for a group experience—600,000 people climb Mount Fuji every year.

Spending a Few Days in Kyoto

If you see only one city in Japan, Kyoto should be it. Japan's capital from 794 to 1868, Kyoto is one of Japan's finest ancient cities, boasting some of the country's best temples, Japanese-style inns, traditional restaurants, shops, and gardens.

Attending a Sumo Match

There's nothing quite like watching two monstrous sumo wrestlers square off, bluff, and grapple as they attempt to throw each other on the ground or out of the ring. Matches are great cultural events, but even if you can't attend one, you can watch them on TV during one of six annual 15-day tournaments.

Wandering through a Japanese Garden

Most of Japan's famous gardens are relics of the Edo Period, when the shogun, daimyo feudal lords, imperial family, and even samurai and Buddhist priests developed private gardens for their own viewing pleasure. Each step in a strolling garden brings a new view to die for.

Shooting the Kumagawa Rapids in Kumamoto

You can glide down one of Japan's most rapid rivers in a long, traditional wooden boat, powered by men with poles.

Getting a Shiatsu Massage

Shiatsu, or pressure-point massage, is available in virtually all first-class accommodations in Japan and at most moderately priced ones as well. After a hard day of work or sightseeing, nothing beats a relaxing massage in the privacy of your room.

Cheering at a Baseball Game

After sumo, baseball is Japan's most popular spectator sport. Watching a game with a stadium full of avid fans can be quite fun and can shed new light on America's favorite pastime.

Visiting Tsukiji Fish Market in Tokyo

One of the largest wholesale fish markets in the world, this indoor market bustles with activity from about 3am on as frozen tuna is unloaded from boats, auctions are held, and vendors sell octopus, fish, squid, and everything else from the sea that's edible to the city's restaurants.

Seeing Tokyo from the TMG

On the 45th floor of the Tokyo Metropolitan Government Office (TMG), designed by well-known architect Kenzo Tange, an observatory offers a bird's-eye view of Shinjuku's cluster of skyscrapers, the never-ending metropolis and, on fine winter days, Mount Fuji. Best of all, it's free.

ETIQUETTE

Like all peoples, the Japanese have idiosyncrasies, mannerisms and superstitions that can escape even the most astute visitor. Below is a list of "do's" and "don'ts" to help you avoid any embarrassments during your visit:

- **Don't** leave chopsticks sticking out of a bowl of rice (this is considered a funeral rite for the dead).
- **Do** take off your shoes (but not socks) before entering a Japanese home and many Japanese restaurants (there will usually be an internal foyer with a place to store shoes).
- **Do** wash and rinse your body thoroughly before entering a communal bath (baths are for soaking, not washing).
- **Don't** eat while walking (while not a grave taboo, it will cause quite a few raised eyebrows).
- **Don't** blow your nose in public (Japanese usually seek relief in private, where others aren't watching).
- **Do** bring a small gift when visiting a client, friend or family member at their home or office (a gift-wrapped box of cookies or Japanese sweets is always a safe choice).
- **Don't** force an answer to a yes or no question when the response is a wan smile, a sigh through clenched teeth, or a "maybe" (all of which mean "no").

- **Don't** be offended if someone closes his or her eyes while listening to a conversation or speech (it often signals concentration).
- **Do** allow enough distance between yourself and a Japanese to bow and **don't** overdo physical contact (most Japanese like their personal space respected).

ORIGINS OF JAPANESE

Japanese is an Altaic language, one of a Eurasian family of tongues including Korean and Mongolian, but not Chinese. Written Japanese, however, is a hodgepodge of Altaic-style phonetic and Chinese characters. The origins of the language provide insight into the early history of Japan, which was first populated about 30,000 years ago with people who crossed over from the Asian mainland. For thousands of years after that, Japan continued to draw upon the continent for cultural, economic, political, religious and technological innovations that blended with indigenous beliefs and practices.

JAPANESE HISTORY IN A NUTSHELL

Although the Japanese imperial family's lineage dates back at least to the 4th century, emperors often ruled in name only. By the early 7th century written history shows the emperor had become little more than a figurehead. It was under military dictatorships, called *shogunates*, that the country became unified and transformed itself into one of the world's first true nation-states. The *shogun* leaders and their samurai retainers grabbed power from Kyoto-based monks and nobles in the 12th century and ruled until 1867. During this feudal era, Japan increasingly focused inward, eventually cutting off most of its ties with Asia and the world at large. Modern Japanese history began in 1868 with the country's reopening to the outside world and the rapid industrialization that followed. After a tumultuous 20th century, including its defeat in World War II, Japan today is a mature parliamentary democracy with a modern post-industrial economy.

HISTORICAL TIMELINE

Ancient History (30,000 B.C.-A.D. 710)

Japanese prehistory begins around 30,000 years ago when the first peoples are thought to have crossed over to Japan via a land bridge. In what is known as the **Jomon period**, an early civilization of hunter-gatherers developed a distinctive style of cord-patterned pottery. The Jomon era gave way around 400 B.C. to the **Yayoi period**, which lasted until A.D. 300 and saw the spread of metalworking technology and rice farming.

Written Japanese history began around A.D. 600, but modern historians say the country was first unified politically in the 4th century by the **Yamato dynasty**, the originators of Japan's imperial line. According to Japanese legend, the first emperor, **Jimmu**, established the imperial line in 600 B.C. and was a descendent of two mythological deities, the male creator god Izanagi and his mate Izanami. (Those two are said to have created the Japanese archipelago by slashing the Sea of Japan with a holy, bejeweled sword.) Blending the political with the mythological, the emperor was seen not only as a political leader but as the head of the animistic Shinto religion native to Japan. By the 7th century, Japan's emperors had ceded control to a series of regents, and **Buddhism** had begun to take hold as the major religion. Among those to embrace Buddhism was **Prince Regent Shotoku**, who emerged as a great historical figure calling for political reforms and also drafting one of the world's first constitutions.

The Nara and Heian Periods (710-1185)

Nara, near Kyoto, became the site of the first permanent capital of Japan in 710, giving rise to a period of history during which government-sponsored Buddhist art, culture and religion flourished. By 794, the capital had moved to **Kyoto**, where it remained—officially, at least—until 1868. The **Heian Period** is best known as a golden age for Japanese architecture, art and literature—much of it inspired by the influence of Chinese culture. It ended when the aristocrats who ruled in Kyoto grew increasingly out of touch and failed to grasp the threat posed by warlord clans in the countryside. Eventually, two main warrior families—the **Taira** (also called the Heike) and the **Minamoto** (or Genji) set off a civil war that effectively ended the reign of the nobility in Kyoto.

The Rise and Fall of the Shoguns (1192-1333)

During the **Kamakura Period**, the Minamoto clan subdued their arch rivals in an epic battle that concluded in 1192 and established a de facto capital in Kamakura, hundreds of miles northeast of the imperial capital in Kyoto. **Minamoto Yoritomo**, the first shogun, or military dictator, set about transforming Japanese society from top to bottom by implementing the **code of Bushido**, the Confucian and Zen Buddhist-influenced way of the warrior. While this Spartan model of government stifled artistic and cultural innovation, it served Japan well in helping it stave off two waves of Mongol invasions, in 1274 and 1281, staged by forces loyal to Kublai Khan.

The Muromachi Period (1333-1573)

By 1333, the Kamakura shogunate was on its last legs and the capital reverted back to Kyoto for a brief period while various warlords battled one another for territory. This feudal period of fighting, called the *Sengoku-jidai* ("Age of the Warring States"), lasted for about 200 years. Despite the political turmoil, Japanese culture and arts once again blossomed under the patronage of various warlords and armies led by Buddhist monks. It was this period that saw the construction in Kyoto of the Golden and Silver pavilions and the famous **rock gardens of Ryoanji Temple**. Arts such as flower arrangement, Noh theater and tea ceremony also rose to prominence, developing a large following among upper class merchants, nobles and samurai.

The Azuchi-Momoyama Period (1573-1603)

As the 16th century dawned, Japan was split up into a number of feudal regimes, each with its own warlord and castle. Out of this chaos a military leader named **Oda Nobunaga** (1534-1582) almost succeeded in unifying Japan, thanks to brilliant battlefield tactics. But Nobunaga's quest ended when he was assassinated by one of his own samurai in 1582. His successor, another general named **Toyotomi Hideyoshi**, succeeded in crushing opposition armies and established himself as supreme leader. It was he who built the grandest fortress of them all—the magnificent **Osaka Castle**, outside of Kyoto.

The Edo Period (1603-1867)

Hideyoshi had little time to savor his achievement as he died in 1598, setting off a new round of squabbling for power. At the **Battle of Sekigahara**, two years later, General **Tokugawa Ieyasu** smote his main rivals and set up a new capital in Edo (present day Tokyo). Yet it wasn't until the defeat of Hideyoshi's son at the **Battle of Osaka Castle** in 1615 that the Tokugawa legacy was ensured. For the next 250 years, Ieyasu's heirs ruled the country with an iron hand, setting up a caste system with samurai at the apex and forcing farmers, craftsmen and merchants to serve them.

The Tokugawas also sealed the country's borders in 1639 to stem the incursion of Christianity and the flow of foreign-made guns into Japan. But even as the Japanese were forced to retreat inward and trade links were severed, the local culture and economy began to flourish anew with peace finally achieved throughout the archipelago. The Edo period saw the development of Japan's main transportation arteries, the spread of literacy and schooling, and the growing popularity of Kabuki theater and woodblock prints. Although the merchants technically were at the bottom of the totem pole, they grew increasingly prosperous and influential with time—largely at the expense of the cash-poor samurai class.

The Meiji Era (1868-1912)

Japan's era of isolation ended with the blast of a ship's cannon in 1853, when American Commodore Matthew Perry sailed into Yokohama seeking to establish a trading relationship. Rebuffed at first, Perry returned the next year and forced the shogun to open up the country to foreign trade. That set off a chain of events culminating with the overthrow of the shogunate in 1867 by an alliance of old warlord families who had the tacit approval of the emperor. This became known as the **Meiji Restoration**, after the name of the young emperor in Kyoto.

The next year, the imperial family moved from Kyoto to Tokyo (which literally means "Eastern Capital") and set about reasserting its authority by stripping the samurai of their right to bear swords and wear the warrior's top-knot. Japan quickly began a crash course in **Westernization**, with the promulgation of a constitution, the convening of a parliament and the naming of a prime minister and cabinet—composed primarily of members of the old warlord alliance. At the same time, Japan began modernizing its economy by adopting Western technology and creating a modern army by arming peasants with firearms. In 1895, Japan marked its arrival on the world stage by fighting and winning a war against Imperial China. It then stunned the world with a quick naval victory over Imperial Russia in 1905.

The Taisho Era (1912-1926)

All the while, Japan's factories began churning out more and more manufactured products, and its economy boomed. Parliamentary democracy took hold under the **Taisho Emperor**, who took over in 1912 with the death of Emperor Meiji, and the right to vote was extended to all men (but not women). By World War I, Japan had developed a modern military second to none in Asia and ranked among the top powers globally. Like many of its new peers, it took on colonies by annexing Taiwan (1895) and Korea (1910)—and then setting up a sphere of influence in Northern China. In the 1920s, a series of financial panics and political corruption scandals began to erode public support in Japan for both capitalism and democracy.

The Showa Era (1927-1989)

Five years after the adolescent **Emperor Hirohito** (posthumously known as the **Showa Emperor**) took the chrysanthemum (Imperial) throne, Japan set up a puppet state in Manchuria in 1931. That was a step too far for the international community and Japan was effectively forced out of the League of Nations (the predecessor of the United Nations). At home, the Japanese military began asserting more and more control over the economy and politics. Another war with China in 1937 set off a chain of events culminating in Japan's embrace of militaristic government and the surprise attack on Pearl Harbor on December 7, 1941.

World War II took a devastating toll on Japan—from the atomic destruction of two major cities (Hiroshima and Nagasaki) to the complete collapse of its economy and the occupation of its territory by Allied Forces. Under the leadership of U.S. General Douglas MacArthur, Japan's armed forces were abolished in 1945 and Japanese business and political circles were subsequently "purged" of military sympathizers. The emperor, however, was allowed to remain the "symbol of the state," even though he was stripped of power and had to renounce his status as a living deity. In 1947, new elections for Japan's parliament were held and a pacifist constitution was enacted which, among other things, gave women the right to vote. The occupation officially ended five years later, by which time the Japanese economy had started to recover from demand spurred by the outbreak of the Korean War.

Under the ruling **Liberal Democratic Party** (LDP), Japan began to play "catch-up" with the U.S. and other industrialized economies. The government funneled precious capital and resources to export industries while protecting them from foreign competition. In 1964, the Japanese "economic miracle" was on full display to the world as Tokyo successfully hosted the **Summer Olympic Games**. Incomes soared throughout the 1960s and 1970s, and, by the 1980s, **Japan Inc.** had become a feared and respected rival of Corporate America. Economic friction with the U.S., Japan's biggest trading partner, led to a series of "voluntary export restraint" agreements and a joint decision to allow the yen to rise dramatically against the dollar (the Plaza Accord of 1985). These steps did little to temper American consumers' demand for Japanese brand name autos and electronics, but Japan's overheated economy began to implode on its own in the early 1990s.

Modern Japan (1989-Today)

When **Emperor Akihito** began his reign in 1989 as the **Heisei Emperor**, after the death of his father, Japan's economy was at its strongest. Amid mounting worries about inflated stock prices, bad bank loans and over-extended corporate investment overseas, Japan fell into a **recession** in 1992. At the time, most Japanese assumed the economy would bounce back, following a brief contraction. But, in fact, due to a combination of government policy missteps and corporate ennui, the recession only deepened as the decade wore on. The country suffered a further shock in 1995 when a major earthquake hit the city of Kobe near Osaka, killing 6,000 and knocking out a vital port. A deflationary price spiral and the collapse of several major financial institutions further shook Japanese consumers' confidence in the late 1990s. Meanwhile, the LDP briefly lost and then regained its hold on power, but ruled with a series of bland and ineffective leaders.

It wasn't until the early 2000s that Japan began to tackle its structural economic problems in earnest. Unemployment rates soared as Japan Inc. restructured and the government cut wasteful public works spending. But those overdue, if painful, steps set the stage for growth. The Japanese stock market bottomed out in 2003 (at which point it was worth less than 85% of its peak value in 1989). Reforms ushered in by maverick **LDP Prime Minister Junichiro Koizumi**, who led from 2000 to 2006, began to pay off as a full-fledged economic recovery got underway mid-decade. Koizumi also took steps to bolster Japan's global footprint by sending troops to support the U.S. in Afghanistan and Iraq. And his tenure coincided with a "Cool Japan" boom overseas, centering on Japanese animation, comic book culture and video game technology.

Koizumi's successor, **Shinzo Abe**, entered office with record high approval ratings, but dithered on needed reforms and quickly lost the public's confidence. He resigned as premier in September 2007 and was replaced by fellow LDP legislator **Yasuo Fukuda**, who faced a number of daunting tasks. One big issue: fixing Japan's under-funded nationalized medical and pension systems while dealing with sharply falling birthrates and a rapidly aging population. Japan Inc. continued meanwhile to search for ways to thrive amid China's rise as Asia's new growth engine.

JAPANESE RELIGIONS

There's a truism about religion in Japan that 90% of Japanese are Buddhist and 80% practice Shinto. That apparent contradiction comes from the fact that most Japanese practice more than one religion. For example, it's not unusual for a Japanese to be wed in a Christian church, pray regularly at a Shinto shrine and then have a Buddhist funeral. While a Christian minority here believes in only one God, most Japanese are polytheistic, and believe in more than one. The origins of this multi-faceted system of beliefs are complex and deeply intertwined with thousands of years of history during which Japan was influenced by many faiths.

Shintoism

Shinto, which literally means "way of the gods," is an animistic religion built around the idea that all living things—and some non-living—have spirits. The oldest and only native religion to Japan, it is closely linked to the Japanese imperial family, which, until the end of World War II, was itself considered divine. Shinto shrines are located throughout Japan and most Japanese homes have a small shelf in the house that supports a mini-shrine called a *kami-dana*. Perhaps more than any other religion, Shinto links cleanliness with godliness, both literally and figuratively. Shinto is obsessed with various purification rites, such as the ritual of washing one's hands before praying at a shrine or sprinkling salt outside one's doorstop to ward off evil spirits. In the run up to World War II, Japan embraced a fiery, nationalist brand of the religion known as state-sponsored Shintoism. Today, however, Shinto is a gentle and mostly non-political faith. It is common for students, pregnant women and nervous drivers to purchase luck-filled amulets from shrines, which must be returned and burned after the priest-blessed trinkets have served their purpose. Traditionally, weddings in Japan have been performed by Shinto priests, but in recent years more and more couples have chosen to be wed in Christian churches and chapels in Japan or abroad.

Buddhism

The origins of Buddhism are in 5th -century India, but the faith spread to China and Korea before coming to Japan by the 7th century. It quickly caught on among the Japanese ruling classes. They became great patrons of the religion and commissioned lavish Buddhist temples and artwork. As temples grew more and more influential and wealthy, some priests became warlords backed by large and well-armed armies of monks. In time, Buddhism became so ingrained into Japanese society that it was not unusual for members of the nobility—or even the emperor himself—to retire into the Buddhist priesthood. An offshoot of the religion is **Zen Buddhism**, which is unique to Japan. This austere belief is centered on the idea of self-enlightenment through meditation and a strictly disciplined lifestyle. It rose to prominence during the reign of the shoguns, who respected the strict and simple (as well as the martial) aspects of Zen. Today, Zen and many other forms of Buddhism are alive and well in Japan. Indeed, one of the country's largest political parties is closely linked to a charismatic Buddhist sect. Whether Japanese are devout or not, most funeral rites in the country are conducted by Buddhist priests.

Confucianism

While not actively practiced like Buddhism or Shintoism, Confucianism has left a deep imprint on Japanese society. The principles outlined by the 5th century Chinese scholar Confucius dictated the responsibilities of children toward their elders, teachers toward students and public servants toward the citizenry. Japan's shogunates promoted the Confucian ideal of a rigid hierarchy, something that affects the Japanese psyche to this day. Similarly, concepts such as filial piety and seniority-based promotion are rooted in Confucian ideals and still hold wide sway in Japan, even as modern society chips away at them.

Christianity

Unlike the situation in neighboring South Korea, Christians are still a minority in Japan. The faith was imported by the first Europeans, who arrived during the 16th century. By 1549 the Portuguese missionary St. Francis Xavier landed in southern Japan and began converting Japanese to Catholicism. At first, Christianity spread quickly as local warlords initially tolerated, and then eventually joined, the faith. But the shogunate central government grew wary of the ambitions of these warlords and their foreign missionaries. Fearing the expansionist policies of Europeans nations in other parts of Asia, shogun Toyotomi Hideyoshi banned Christianity in the late 1500s.

In 1597, 26 Japanese and European Christians were crucified in Nagasaki, the southern port closely associated with European merchants and missionaries. By 1639, Japan had closed itself off from almost all contact with the outside world and Christianity withered under constant government harassment. But some true believers formed underground churches and eluded detections for hundreds of years, finally emerging in the late 19th-and early 20th centuries. Today, most Japanese Christians are centered in southwestern Japan, where the faith first planted roots.

AN INTRODUCTION TO JAPANESE CULTURE

Acupuncture & Shiatsu

Although most Westerners have heard of acupuncture, they may not be familiar with shiatsu (Japanese pressure-point massage). Most first-class hotels in Japan offer shiatsu in the privacy of your room. There are acupuncture clinics everywhere in Tokyo, and the staff at your hotel should be able to tell you of one nearby. As it's not likely the clinic's staff will speak English, it might be a good idea to have your concierge not only make the reservation but specify the treatment you want. Otherwise, English is spoken at **Yamate Acupuncture Clinic**, second floor of the ULS Nakameguro Building, 1-3-3 Higashiyama, Meguro-ku (**© 03/3792-8989**). English is also spoken at **Tani Clinic**, third floor of the Taishoseimei Hibiya Building, 1-9-1 Yurakucho, Chiyoda-ku (**© 03/3201-5675**).

Ikebana

Japanese flower arranging, or *ikebana*, was first popularized among aristocrats during the Heian Period (A.D. 794–1192). Instruction is available at several schools in Tokyo, a few of which offer classes in English on a regular basis. Call ahead to enroll. **Sogetsu Ikebana School**, 7-2-21 Akasaka (© **03/3408-1151**; www.sogetsu.or.jp), offers instruction in English on Monday from 10am to noon (closed in Aug). The **Ohara Ikebana School**, 5-7-17 Minami Aoyama (© **03/5774-5097**; www.oharary u.or.jp), offers 2-hour instruction in English at 10am on Wednesday and 10am and 1:30pm on Thursday (no classes mid-July – early Sept.).

Pachinko Parlors

Brightly lit and garish, pachinko parlors are packed with upright pinball-like machines, at which row upon row of Japanese businessmen, housewives, and students sit intently immobile. Originating in Nagoya and popular since the 1950s, pachinko is a game in which ball bearings are flung into a kind of vertical pinball machine, one after the other. Humans control the strength with which the ball is released, but otherwise there's very little to do. Some players even wedge a matchstick under the control and just watch the machine with folded arms. Points are amassed according to which holes the ball bearings fall into. If you're good at it, you win ball bearings back, which you can subsequently trade in for food, cigarettes, watches, calculators, and the like.

It's illegal to win money in Japan, but outside many pachinko parlors and along back alleyways, there are slots where you can trade in the watches, calculators, and other prizes for cash. The slots are so small that the person handing over the goods never sees the person who hands back money. Police, meanwhile, look the other way.

Pachinko parlors compete in an ever-escalating war of themes, lights, and noise. Step inside, and you'll wonder how anyone could possibly think; the noise level of thousands of ball bearings clanking is awesome. Perhaps that's the answer to its popularity: You can't think, making it a getaway pastime. Some people seem to be addicted to the mesmerizing game, newspaper articles talk of errant husbands who never come home anymore, and psychologists analyze its popularity. At any rate, every hamlet seems to have a pachinko parlor, and major cities like Tokyo are inundated with them. You'll find them in nightlife districts and clustered around train stations, but with their unmistakable clanging and clanking, you'll hear them long before you notice their brightly lit, gaudy facades.

Tea Ceremony

Brought to Japan from China more than 1,000 years ago, tea first became popular among Buddhist priests as a means of staying awake during long hours of meditation. Gradually, its use filtered down among the upper classes, and in the 16th century, the tea ceremony, *cha-no-yu*, was perfected by a merchant named Sen-no-Rikyu. Using the principles of Zen and the spiritual discipline of the samurai, the tea ceremony became a highly stylized ritual, with detailed rules on how tea should be prepared, served, and drunk. The simplicity of movement and tranquility of setting are meant to free the mind from the banality of everyday life and to allow the spirit to enjoy peace.

Schools that teach the tea ceremony don't accept drop-ins and frown on short-term apprenticeships so it can be hard for visitors to participate. However, several first-class Tokyo hotels hold tea-ceremony demonstrations in special tea-ceremony rooms. Reservations are usually required. **Seisei-an**, on the seventh floor of the **Hotel New Otani**, 4-1 Kioi-cho, Chiyoda-ku (© **03/3265-1111**, ext. 2443), holds 20-minute demonstrations

Thursday through Saturday from 11am to 4pm. **Chosho-an**, on the seventh floor of the **Hotel Okura**, 2-10-4 Toranomon, Minato-ku (© **03/3582-0111**), gives 30-minute demonstrations between 11am and noon and between 1 and 4pm Monday through Saturday except holidays. At **Toko-an**, on the fourth floor of the **Imperial Hotel**, 1-1-1 Uchisaiwaicho, Chiyoda-ku (© **03/3504-1111**), demonstrations are given from 10am to noon and 1 to 4pm Monday through Saturday except holidays.

Zazen

A few temples in the Tokyo vicinity occasionally offer Buddhist zasen ("sitting meditation") with instruction in English. Some 30 minutes east of Akihabara on the Sobu Line is **Ida Ryogoku-do Zazen Dojo** of the Sotoshu Sect, 5-11-20 Minami Yawata, Ichikawa City (© **04/7379-1596**). Zazen is held daily at 5:30 and 10am and at 3 and 8:30pm, generally for 45 minutes (call to confirm times). A **Dogen-Sangha** meeting is held the fourth Saturday of the month from 1 to 2:30pm, with 30 minutes for Zazen followed by a 1-hour English lecture. Participation is free, and if you call from Moto-Yawata Station, someone will come for you.

For more in-depth training in Zen, call Mr. Nishijima at © **03/3435-0701**. The **Young Men's Buddhist Association of Tokyo University**, of the Sotoshu Sect, second floor of the Nippon Shimpan Building, 3-33-5 Hongo (© **03/3235-0701**), holds a Dogen-Sangha meeting the first, third, and fifth Saturday of each month from 1 to 2:30pm.

Higaeri Onsen (Hot Spring Day Trips)

Traditionally, a trip to a hot spring in Japan has meant trekking well outside of major urban areas like Tokyo to remote mountain or seaside spots. While that still holds true for typical weekend getaways, recent innovations in deep drilling technology have allowed hot spring wells to be dug even in central Tokyo. So now Tokyo-ites can enjoy the mineral waters of a hot bath even on a weekday after work. For a unique bathing experience, nothing beats a 3- or 4-hour respite at the **Oedo-Onsen Monogatari**, 2-57 Aomi on Odaiba (✆ **03/5500-1126**; www.ooedo-global.jp/english), which taps mineral-rich hot-spring waters 1,380m (4,600 ft.) below ground to supply this re-created Edo-era bathhouse village. Since as many as 6,500 bathers pour into this facility on weekends, try to come on a weekday; and since signs in English are virtually nonexistent, observe gender before entering bathing areas (a hint: women's baths usually have pink or red curtains, men's blue). Open daily 11am to 9am the next day. Admission is currently under $30 for adults. Reduced rates after 6pm.

Not quite as colorful is the upscale **Spa LaQua**, 1-1-1 Kasuga (✆ **03/3817-4173**; www.tokyo-dome.co.jp/e/laqua), located in the heart of Tokyo at Korakuen's Tokyo Dome City complex. It, too, has hot-spring indoor and outdoor baths, saunas, and massage options, but an adjoining amusement park with roller coasters (and screaming passengers) make this a less relaxing alternative.

DICTIONARY KEY

n	*noun*	*s*	*singular*
v	*verb*	*pl*	*plural*
adj	*adjective*		
prep	*preposition*		
adv	*adverb*		

Japanese verbs are not conjugated. Here, they are listed in their most basic form. To form tenses, see p26.

For food terms, see the Menu Reader (p94) and Grocery section (p102) in Chapter 4, Dining.

A

able, to be able to (can) *v* できる dekiru

above *adj* 上の ue no

accept, to accept *v* 受け入れる uke ireru

Do you accept credit cards? クレジットカードを使えますか? kurejitto kādo o tsukae masu ka.

accident *n* 事故 jiko

I've had an accident. 事故にあいました。jiko ni ai mashita.

account *n* 口座 kōza

I'd like to transfer to / from my checking / savings account. 当座預金/普通預金口座へ/から振り替えたいのですが。tōza-yokin/futsū-yokin e/kara furikaete tai no desuga.

acne *n* にきび nikibi

across *prep* の向こう側 no mukō gawa

across the street この道の向こう側 kono michi no mukō gawa

actual *adj* 実際の jissai no

adapter plug *n* アダプター プラグ adaputā puragu

address *n* 住所 jūsho

What's the address? 住所は何ですか? jūsho wa nan desu ka.

admission fee *n* 入場料 nyūjōryō

in advance 前もって mae motte

African-American *adj* アフリカ系アメリカ人の afurika kei amerika jin no

afternoon *n* 午後 gogo

in the afternoon 午後に gogo ni

age *n* 歳 toshi

What's your age? 何歳ですか? nan sai desu ka.

agency *n* 会社 kaisha

car rental agency レンタ カー会社 rentakā gaisha

agnostic *adj* 不可知論の fukachiron no

air conditioning *n* 冷房 reibō /エアコン eakon

Would you lower / raise the air conditioning? 冷房を下げて/上げていただけませんか? reibō o sagete/agete itadake masen ka.

airport *n* 空港 kūkō

I need a ride to the airport. 空港まで乗って行く必要があります。kūkō made notte iku hitsuyō ga arimasu.

How far is it from the airport? 空港からどのくらいのところにありますか? kūkō kara dono kurai no tokoro ni arimasu ka.

airsickness bag *n* 飛行機酔いの袋 hikōki yoi no fukuro

aisle *n* 通路 tsūro

alarm clock *n* 目覚まし時計 mezamashi tokei

alcohol *n* アルコール arukōru

Do you serve alcohol? アルコールは出していますか? arukōru wa dashite imasu ka.

I'd like nonalcoholic beer. アルコール抜きのビールをください。arukōru nuki no bīru o kudasai.

all *n* すべて subete

all *adj* すべての subete no

all of the time いつも itsumo

That's all, thank you. 以上です。どうもありがとう。ijō desu. dōmo arigatō.

allergic *adj* アレルギー体質の /アレルギー反応の arerugī han nō no

I'm allergic to ____. 私は____にアレルギーがあります。watashi wa ____ ni arerugī ga arimasu. **See p78 and 167 for common allergens.**

altitude *n* 標高 hyōkō

aluminum *n* アルミニウム aruminiumu

ambulance *n* 救急車 kyūkyūsha

American *adj* アメリカの、アメリカ人の amerika no, amerika jin no

amount *n* 量 ryō

angry *adj* 怒った okotta

animal *n* 動物 dōbutsu

another *adj* 別の betsu no

answer *n* 答え kotae

answer, to answer (phone call, question) *v* 答える kotaeru

Answer me, please. 答えてください。kotaete kudasai.

antibiotic *n* 抗生物質 kōsei busshitsu

I need an antibiotic. 抗生物質をください。kōsei busshitsu o kudasai.

antihistamine *n* 抗ヒスタミン剤 kōhisutamin zai

anxious *adj* 心配な shinpai na / 心配している shinpai shiteiru

any *adj* 何か nanika /何も /nanimo

anything *n* 何でも nan demo

anywhere *adv* どこへも doko emo
April *n* 四月 shi gatsu
appointment *n* 予約 yoyaku

Do I need an appointment? 予約が必要ですか？yoyaku ga hitsuyō desu ka.

are *v See* **be, to be.**
Argentinian *adj* アルゼンチンの、アルゼンチン人の aruzenchin no, aruzenchin jin no
arm *n* 腕 ude
arrive, to arrive *v* 到着する tōchaku suru
arrival(s) *n* 到着 tōchaku
animal *n* 動物 dōbutsu

exhibit of art 美術品の展示 bijutsu hin no tenji

art *adj* 芸術の geijutsu no
art museum 美術館 bijutsu kan
artist *n* 美術家 bijutsu ka
Asian *adj* アジアの、アジア人の ajia no, ajia jin no
ask for (request) *v* 頼む tanomu
ask a question *v* 質問する shitsumon suru
aspirin *n* アスピリン asupirin
assist *v* 手伝う tetsudau
assistance *n* 手伝い tetsudai/アシスタンス ashisutansu
asthma *n* 喘息 zensoku

I have asthma. 喘息があります。zensoku ga arimasu./ 喘息を持っています。zensoku o motte imasu.

atheist *n* 無神論者 mushinron sha
ATM *n* ATM 機 ATM ki

I'm looking for an ATM. ATM 機を探しています。ATM ki o sagashite imasu.

attend *v* 参加する sanka suru /出席する shusseki suru
audio *adj* 音声の onsei no
August *n* 八月 hachi gatsu
aunt *n* おば oba / おばさん obasan
Australia *n* オーストラリア ōsutoraria
Australian *adj* オーストラリアの、オーストラリア人の ōsutoraria no, ōsutoraria jin no
autumn *n* 秋 aki
available *adj* 使用可能な shiyō kanō na

B

baby *n* 赤ちゃん aka chan /ベビー bebī
baby *adj* 赤ちゃんの aka chan no

Do you sell baby food? ベビー フードは売っていますか？bebī fūdo wa utte imasu ka.

babysitter *n* ベビーシッター bebī shittā

Do you have babysitters who speak English? 英語を話すベビーシッターはいますか？eigo o hanasu bebī shittā wa imasu ka.

back *n* 背中 senaka

My back hurts. 背中が痛みます。 senaka ga itami masu.

back rub *n* 背中をさする senaka o sasuru

backed up (toilet) *adj* つまっている tsumatte iru

The toilet is backed up. トイレがつまっています。 toire ga tsumatte imasu.

bag *n* 袋

airsickness bag 飛行機酔いの袋 hikōki yoi no fukuro

My bag was stolen. 私のバックが盗まれました。 watashi no baggu ga nusumare mashita.

I lost my bag. 私はバックを失くしました。 watashi wa baggu o nakushi mashita.

bag *v* 袋に入れる fukuro ni ireru

baggage *n* 手荷物 tenimotsu

baggage *adj* 手荷物の tenimotsu no

baggage claim 手荷物引き渡し所 tenimotsu hikiwatashi jo

bait *n* えさ esa

balance (on bank account) *n* 残高 zandaka

balance *v* バランスを取る baransu o toru

balcony *n* バルコニー barukonī

ball (sport) *n* ボール bōru

ballroom dancing *n* 社交ダンス shakō dansu

band (musical ensemble) *n* 演奏 ensō

band-aid *n* vendaje *m,* バンドエイド bando eido

bank *n* 銀行 ginkō

Can you help me find a bank? 銀行はどこにあるか教えていただけますか? ginkō wa doko ni aruka oshiete itadake masu ka.

bar *n* バー bā

barber *n* 理髪店 rihatsu ten

bass (instrument) *n* バス basu

bath *n* お風呂 ofuro

bathroom (restroom) *n* トイレ toire

Where is the nearest public bathroom? ここから一番近い公衆トイレはどこにありますか? koko kara ichiban chikai kōshū toire wa doko ni arimasu ka.

bathtub *n* 浴槽 yokusō

bathe, to bathe oneself *v* お風呂に入る ofuro ni hairu

battery (for flashlight) *n* 電池 denchi

battery (for car) *n* バッテリー batterī

bee *n* ハチ hachi

I was stung by a bee. ハチに刺されました。 hachi ni sasare mashita.

be, to be (temporary state, condition, mood) *v* である de aru

be, to be (permanent quality) *v* である de aru

beach *n* ビーチ bīchi

beach *v* ビーチに乗り上げる bīchi ni noriageru

beard *n* ひげ hige
beautiful *adj* きれいな kireina
bed *n* ベッド beddo
beer *n* ビール bīru
beer on tap 生ビール nama bīru
begin *v* 始まる hajimaru
behave *v* 振る舞う furumau
behind *adv* 後ろの ushiro no
below *adv* 下の shita no
belt *n* ベルト beruto
conveyor belt ベルトコンベヤー beruto konbeyā
berth *n* 寝台 shindai
best 最高の saikō no
bet, to bet *v* かける kakeru
better より良い yori yoi
big *adj* 大きい ōkii
bilingual *adj* 二ヶ国語を話す ni kakoku go o hanasu
bill (currency) *n* 紙幣 shihei
bill *v* 請求する seikyū suru
biography *n* 伝記 denki
biracial *adj* 人種の混じった jinshu no majitta
bird *n* 鳥 tori
birth control *n* 避妊 hinin
I'm out of birth control pills. 避妊薬がなくなりました。hinin yaku ga nakunari mashita.
I need more birth control pills. もっと避妊薬が必要です。motto hinin yaku ga hitsuyō desu.
bit (small amount) *n* 少し sukoshi
black *adj* 黒い kuroi /黒人 koku jin
blanket *n* 毛布 mōfu
bleach *n* ブリーチ burīchi
blind *adj* 目の見えない me no mienai
block *n* 角 kado /ブロック burokku
blond(e) *adj* 金髪の kinpatsu no
blouse *n* ブラウス burausu
blue *adj* 青い aoi
blurry *adj* ぼやけた boyaketa
board *n* 搭乗 tōjō
on board 搭乗して tōjō shite
board *v* 入港する nyūkō suru
boarding pass *n* 搭乗券 tōjō ken
boat *n* ボート bōto
Bolivian *adj* ボリビアの、ボリビア人の boribia no, boribia jin no
bomb *n* 爆弾 bakudan
book *n* 本 hon
bookstore *n* 本屋 hon ya
boss *n* 上司 jōshi
bottle *n* ビン bin
May I heat this (baby) bottle someplace? どこかでこのビンを温めることができますか? dokoka de kono bin o atatameru koto ga deki masu ka.
box (seat) *n* ボックス席 bokkusu seki /ボックスシート bokkusu sīto
box office *n* チケット売り場 chiketto uriba
boy *n* 男の子 otoko no ko
boyfriend *n* ボーイフレンド bōi furendo

braid *n* 編んだ髪 anda kami
braille, American *n* 点字、アメリカの tenji, amerika no
brake *n* ブレーキ burēki
emergency brake 非常ブレーキ hijō burēki
brake *v* ブレーキをかける burēki o kakeru
brandy *n* ブランデー burandē
bread *n* パン pan
break *v* 壊れる kowareru
breakfast *n* 朝食 chōshoku
What time is breakfast? 朝食は何時ですか? chōshoku wa nan ji desu ka.
bridge (across a river, dental) *n* 橋 hashi /歯の矯正ブリッジ ha no kyōsei burijji
briefcase *n* ブリーフケース burīfu kēsu
bright *adj* 明るい akarui
broadband *n* ブロードバンド burōdo bando
bronze *adj* ブロンズ製の buronzu sei no
brother *n* 兄弟 kyōdai / ご兄弟 go kyōdai
brown *adj* 茶色の cha iro no
brunette *n* ブルネット burunetto
Buddhist *n* 仏教徒 bukkyōto
budget *n* 予算 yosan
buffet *n* バイキング baikingu
bug *n* 虫 mushi
bull *n* 雄牛 oushi
bullfight *n* 闘牛 tōgyū
bullfighter *n* 闘牛士 tōgyū shi
burn *v* 焼く yaku/焼きつける yaki tsukeru
Can I burn a CD here? ここでCDに焼きつけ(書込み)できますか? koko de CD ni yakitsuke (kakikomi) deki masu ka.
bus *n* バス basu
Where is the bus stop? バス停はどこにありますか? basu tei wa doko ni arimasu ka.
Which bus goes to ____? ____行きのバスはどれですか。 ____ yuki no basu wa dore desu ka.
business *n* ビジネス bijinesu
business *adj* 商用で shōyō de
business center ビジネス センター bijinesu sentā
busy *adj* 客の多い kyaku no ōi **(restaurant),** 話し中で hanashi chū de **(phone)**
butter *n* バター batā
buy, to buy *v* 買う kau

C

café *n* 喫茶店 kissa ten
Internet café インターネットカフェ intānetto kafe
call, to call *v* 呼ぶ yobu **(shout)** 電話をかける denwa o kakeru **(phone)**
camp, to camp *v* キャンプをする kyanpu o suru
camper *n* キャンパー kyanpā
camping *adj* キャンプの kyanpu no

Do we need a camping permit? キャンプをする許可が必要ですか? kyanpu o suru kyoka ga hitsuyō desu ka.

campsite *n* キャンプサイト kyanpu saito

can *n* 缶詰 kanzume

can (able to) *v* できる dekiru

Canada *n* カナダ kanada

Canadian *adj* カナダの、カナダ人の kanada no, kanada jin no

cancel, to cancel *v* 取り消す tori kesu

My flight was canceled. 私のフライトはキャンセルされました。watashi no furaito wa kyanseru saremashita.

canvas *n* キャンバス kyanbasu **(for painting)** / キャンバス地 kyanbasu ji **(material)**

cappuccino *n* カプチーノ kapuchīno

car *n* 車 kuruma

car rental agency レンタ カー会社 rentakā gaisha

I need a rental car. レンタカーが必要です。rentakā ga hitsuyō desu.

card *n* カード kādo

Do you accept credit cards? クレジットカードを使えますか? kurejitto kādo o tsukae masu ka.

May I have your business card? あなたの名刺をいただけますか? anata no meishi o itadake masu ka.

car seat (child's safety seat) *n* チャイルドシート chairudo shīto

Do you rent car seats for children? チャイルドシートをレンタルしていますか? chairudo shīto o rentaru shite imasu ka.

carsickness *n* 車酔い kuruma yoi

cash *n* 現金 genkin

cash only 現金のみ genkin nomi

cash, to cash *v* 現金に換える genkin ni kaeru

to cash out (gambling) 清算する seisan suru

cashmere *n* カシミヤ kashimiya

casino *n* カジノ kajino

cat *n* ねこ neko

Catholic *adj* カトリック教の katorikku kyō no

cavity (tooth cavity) *n* 虫歯 mushiba

I think I have a cavity. 虫歯があるようなんです。mushiba ga aru yō nandesu.

CD *n* CD

CD player *n* CD プレーヤー CD purēyā

celebrate, to celebrate *v* 祝う iwau

cell phone *n* 携帯電話 keitai denwa

centimeter *n* センチメートル senchi mētoru

chamber music *n* 室内楽 shitsunai gaku

change (money) *n* おつり otsuri

I'd like change, please. おつりをください。otsuri o kudasai.

This isn't the correct change. このおつりは正しくありません。kono otsuri wa tadashiku arimasen.

change (to change money, clothes) *v* 交換する kōkan suru

changing room *n* 更衣室 kōi shitsu

charge, to charge (money) *v* 請求する seikyū suru

charge, to charge (a battery) *v* 充電する jūden suru

charmed *adj* 魅了された miryō sareta

charred (meat) *adj* ベリーウェルで berī weru de

charter, to charter *v* チャーターする chātā suru

cheap *adj* 安い yasui

check *n* 小切手 kogitte / チェックchekku

Do you accept travelers' checks? トラベラーズ チェックを使えますか？toraberāzu chekku o tsukae masu ka.

check, to check *v* 調べる shiraberu

checked (pattern) *adj* チェックの chekku no

check-in *n* チェックイン chekku in

What time is check-in? チェックインは何時ですか？chekku in wa nan ji desu ka.

check-out *n* チェックアウト chekku auto

check-out time チェックアウトの時間 chekku auto no jikan

What time is check-out? チェックアウトは何時ですか？chekku auto wa nan ji desu ka.

check out, to check out *v* チェックアウトする chekku auto suru

cheese *n* チーズ chīzu

chicken *n* チキン chikin

child *n* 子供 kodomo

children *n* 子供たち kodomo tachi

Are children allowed? 子供もいいですか？kodomo mo ii desu ka.

Do you have children's programs? 子供用のプログラムはありますか？kodomo yō no puroguramu wa arimasu ka.

Do you have a children's menu? 子供用のメニューはありますか？kodomo yō no menyū wa arimasu ka.

Chinese *adj* 中国の、中国人の chūgoku no, chūgoku jin no

chiropractor *n* カイロプラクター kairo purakutā

church *n* 教会 kyōkai

cigar *n* 葉巻 hamaki

cigarette *n* タバコ tabako

a pack of cigarettes タバコ1箱 tabako hito hako

cinema *n* 映画館 eiga kan

city *n* 市 shi/ 街machi
claim *n* 請求 seikyū
I'd like to file a claim. 賠償を請求します。baishō o seikyū shimasu.
clarinet *n* クラリネット kurarinetto
class *n* クラス kurasu
business class ビジネス クラス bijinesu kurasu
economy class エコノミークラス ekonomī kurasu
first class ファースト クラス fāsuto kurasu
classical (music) *adj* クラシックの kurasshikku no
clean *adj* 清潔な seiketsu na
clean, to clean *v* 掃除する sōji suru
Please clean the room today. 今日、部屋を掃除してください。kyō, heya o sōji shite kudasai.
clear *v* 明らかにする akiraka ni suru
clear *adj* 透明な tōmei na
climbing *n* 登山 tozan
climb, to climb *v* 登る noboru
to climb a mountain 山に登る yama ni noboru
to climb stairs 階段を昇る kaidan o noboru
close, to close *v* 閉じる tojiru
close (near) 近い chikai
closed *adj* 閉じた tojita
cloudy *adj* 曇った kumotta
clover *n* クローバー kurōbā
go clubbing, to go clubbing *v* クラブに踊りに行く kurabu ni odori ni iku
coat *n* コート kōto
cockfight *n* 闘鶏 tōkei
coffee *n* コーヒー kōhī
iced coffee アイス コーヒー aisu kōhī
cognac *n* コニャック konyakku
coin *n* 硬貨 kōka
cold *n* カゼ kaze
I have a cold. カゼを引きました。kaze o hiki mashita.
cold *adj* 寒い samui
I'm cold. 寒いです。samui desu.
It's cold out. 外は寒いです。soto wa samui desu.
coliseum *n* 大劇場 daigeki jō
collect *adj* 受信人払いの jushin nin barai no
I'd like to place a collect call. コレクト コールをお願いします。korekuto kōru o onegai shimasu.
collect, to collect *v* 集める atsumeru
college *n* 大学 daigaku
Colombian *adj* コロンビアの、コロンビア人の koronbia no, koronbia jin no
color *n* 色 iro
color *v* 色をぬる iro o nuru
computer *n* コンピューター konpyūtā
concert *n* コンサート konsāto

ENGLISH—JAPANESE

condition *n* 状態 jōtai

in good / bad condition 良い/悪い状態 yoi/warui jōtai

condom *n* コンドーム kondōmu

condor *n* コンドル kondoru

confirm, to confirm *v* 確認する kakunin suru

I'd like to confirm my reservation. 予約を確認したいのですが。yoyaku o kakunin shitai no desuga.

confused *adj* 混乱した konran shita

congested *adj* 混雑した konzatsu shita

connection speed *n* 回線速度 kaisen sokudo

constipated *adj* 便秘した benpi shita

I'm constipated. 便秘しています。benpi shite imasu.

contact lens *n* コンタクト レンズ kontakuto renzu *m*

I lost my contact lens. コンタクト レンズをなくしました。kontakuto renzu o nakushi mashita.

continue, to continue *v* 続ける tsuzukeru

convertible *n* オープンカー ōpun kā

cook, to cook *v* 料理する ryōri suru

I'd like a room where I can cook. 料理することができる部屋をお願いします。ryōri suru koto ga dekiru heya o onegai shimasu.

cookie *n* クッキー kukkī

copper *adj* 銅製の dōsei no

corner *n* 隅 sumi

on the corner 隅の

correct *v* 直す naosu

correct *adj* 正しい tadashii

Am I on the correct train? 私は正しい電車に乗っていますか? watashi wa tadashii densha ni notte imasu ka.

cost, to cost *v* 金額がかかる kingaku ga kakaru

How much does it cost? それはいくらしますか? sore wa ikura shimasu ka.

Costa Rican *adj* コスタリカの、コスタリカ人の kosutarika no, kosutarika jin no

costume *n* 衣装 ishō

cotton *n* 綿 men / コットン kotton

cough *n* 咳 seki

cough *v* 咳をする seki o suru

counter (in bar) *n* カウンター kauntā

country-and-western *n* カントリーアンドウェスタン kantorī ando wesutan

court (legal) *n* 裁判所 saiban sho

court (sport) *n* コート kōto

courteous *adj* ていねいな teinei na / 親切な shinsetsuna

cousin *n* いとこ itoko

cover charge (in bar) *n* カバーチャージ kabā chāji

cow *n* 牛 ushi

crack (in glass object) *n* ヒビ割れ hibi ware
craftsperson *n* 職人 shoku nin 工芸家 kōgeika
cream *n* クリーム kurīmu
credit card *n* クレジット カード kurejitto kādo

> **Do you accept credit cards?** クレジットカードを使えますか? kurejitto kādo o tsukae masu ka.

crib *n* ベビーベッド bebī beddo
crown (dental) *n* 歯にかぶせているもの ha ni kabusete iru mono
curb *n* 縁石 enseki
curl *n* カール kāru
curly *adj* カールした kāru shita
currency exchange *n* 両替 ryōgae

> **Where is the nearest currency exchange?** ここから一番近い両替所はどこにありますか? koko kara ichiban chikai ryōgae jo wa doko ni arimasu ka.

current (water) *n* 潮の流れ shio no nagare
customs *n* 税関 zeikan 関税 kanzei
cut (wound) *n* 切り傷 kiri kizu

> **I have a bad cut.** 私はひどい切り傷があります。watashi wa hidoi kirikizu ga arimasu.

cut, to cut *v* 切る kiru
cybercafé *n* サイバー カフェ saibā kafe

> **Where can I find a cybercafé?** サイバー カフェはどこにありますか? saibā kafe wa doko ni arimasu ka.

D

damaged *adj* 損傷した sonshō shita
Damn! *expletive* しまった! shimatta / 残念! zan nen
dance *v* 踊る odoru / ダンスをする dansu o suru
danger *n* 危険 kiken
dark *n* 暗がり kuragari
dark *adj* 暗い kurai
daughter *n* 娘 musume / お嬢さん ojōsan
day *n* 日 hi

> **the day before yesterday** おととい ototoi
> **these last few days** ここ2・3日 koko nisan nichi

dawn *n* 夜明け yoake

> **at dawn** 夜明けに yoake ni

deaf *adj* 耳が聞こえない mimi ga kikoenai
deal (bargain) *n* 取引き torihiki

> **What a great deal!** なんてすばらしい取引だ! nante subarashii torihiki da.

deal (cards) *v* 配る kubaru

> **Deal me in.** 私も入れてください。watashi mo irete kudasai.

December *n* 十二月 jū ni gatsu
declined *adj* 拒否された kyohi sareta

ENGLISH—JAPANESE

Was my credit card declined? 私のクレジットカードが拒否されたのですか? watashi no kurejitto kādo ga kyohi saretano desu ka.

declare *v* 申告する shinkoku suru

I have nothing to declare. 申告するものはありません。shinkoku suru mono wa arimasen.

deep *adj* 深い fukai

delay *n* 遅れ okure

How long is the delay? どのくらいの遅れですか? dono kurai no okure desuka.

delighted *adj* 嬉しい ureshii

democracy *n* 民主主義 minshu shugi

dent *v* へこむ hekomu

He / She dented the car. 彼 / 彼女が車をへこませました。kare / kanojo ga kuruma o hekomase mashita.

dentist *n* 歯医者 haisha

denture *n* 義歯 gishi

denture plate 義歯 gishi

departure *n* 出発 shuppatsu

designer *n* デザイナー dezainā

dessert *n* デザート dezāto

dessert menu デザートのメニュー dezāto no menyū

destination *n* 行き先 yuki saki

diabetic *adj* 糖尿病の tōnyōbyō no

dial (a phone) *v* 電話をかける denwa o kakeru / ダイヤル daiyaru suru

dial direct 直通番号にかける chokutsū bangō ni kakeru

diaper *n* おむつ omutsu

Where can I change a diaper? おむつはどこで替えられますか? omutsu wa doko de kaerare masu ka.

diarrhea *n* 下痢 geri

dictionary *n* 辞書 jisho

different (other) *adj* 異なる kotonaru / 違う chigau / 別の betsuno

difficult *adj* 困難な konnan na / 難しい muzukashii

dinner *n* 夕食 yūshoku

directory assistance (phone) *n* 番号案内 bangō annai

disability *n* 障害 shōgai

disappear *v* 消える kieru

disco *n* ディスコ disuco

disconnected *adj* 切断された setsudan sareta

Operator, I was disconnected. オペレータさん、電話が切れてしまいました。opēretā san, denwa ga kirete shimai mashita.

discount *n* 値引き nebiki

Do I qualify for a discount? 私は値引きの対象になりますか? watashi wa nebiki no taishō ni narimasuka.

dish *n* 料理 ryōri

dive *v* もぐる moguru

scuba dive スキューバダイブ sukyūba daibu

divorced *adj* 離婚した rikon shita

dizzy *adj* めまいがする memai ga suru

do, to do *v* する suru

doctor *n* 医者 isha **doctor's office** *n* 医院 iin

dog *n* 犬 inu

service dog 介護犬 kaigo ken

dollar *n* ドル doru

door *n* ドア doa

double *adj* ダブルの daburu no

double bed ダブル ベッド daburu beddo

double vision 二重映像 nijū eizō

down *adj* 下に shita ni

download *v* ダウンロードする daunrōdo suru

downtown *n* 繁華街 hanka gai

dozen *n* ダース dāsu

drain *n* 排水 haisui

drama *n* 劇の脚本 geki no kyakuhon

drawing (work of art) *n* 絵 e

dress (garment) *n* ドレス doresu

dress (general attire) *n* 服装 fukusō

What's the dress code? 服装の規則は何ですか？fukusō no kisoku wa nan desu ka.

dress *v* 着る kiru

Should I dress up for that affair. そこでは正装しなければなりませんか？soko dewa seisō shinakereba nari masen ka.

dressing (salad) *n* ドレッシング doressingu

dried *adj* 乾燥した kansō shita

drink *n* 飲み物 nomi mono

I'd like a drink. 飲み物をください。nomi mono o kudasai.

drink, to drink *v* 飲む nomu

drip *v* 滴る shitataru

drive *v* 運転する unten suru

driver *n* 運転手 unten shu

driving range *n* ゴルフ練習場 gorufu renshū jō

drum *n* ドラム doramu

dry 乾いた kawaita

This towel isn't dry. このタオルは乾いていません。kono taoru wa kawaite imasen.

dry, to dry *v* 乾かす kawakasu

I need to dry my clothes. 私の服を乾かす必要があります。watashi no fuku o kawakasu hitsuyō ga arimasu.

dry cleaner *n* ドライ クリーナー dorai kurīnā

dry cleaning *n* ドライ クリーニング dorai kurīningu

duck *n* アヒル ahiru

duty-free *adj* 免税の menzei no

duty-free shop *n* 免税店 menzei ten

DVD *n* DVD

Do the rooms have DVD players? その部屋にはDVDプレーヤーがありますか？sono heya niwa DVD purēyā ga arimasu ka.

Where can I rent DVDs or videos? DVDまたはビデオはどこで借りられますか？DVD matawa bideo wa doko de karirare masu ka.

E

early *adj* 早い hayai

It's early. 早いです。hayai desu.

eat *v* 食べる taberu

to eat out 外食する gaishoku suru

economy *n* エコノミー ekonomī

Ecuadorian *adj* エクアドルの、エクアドル人の ekuadoru no, ekuadoru jin no

editor *n* 編集者 henshū sha

educator *n* 教育者 kyōiku sha

eight *n* 八 hachi

eighteen *n* 十八 jū hachi

eighth *n* 8 番目の hachi banme no

eighty *n* 八十 hachi jū

election *n* 選挙 senkyo

electrical hookup *n* 電気接続部 denki setsuzoku bu

elevator *n* エレベーター erebētā

eleven *n* 十一 jū ichi

e-mail *n* Eメール E mēru

May I have your e-mail address? あなたのEメールアドレスをいただけますか? anata no E mēru adoresu o itadake masu ka.

e-mail message Eメール メッセージ E mēru messēji

e-mail, to send e-mail *v* Eメールする ii-mēru suru

embarrassed *adj* 恥ずかしい hazukashii

embassy *n* 大使館 taishi kan

emergency *n* 緊急 kinkyū

emergency brake *n* 非常ブレーキ hijō burēki

emergency exit *n* 非常出口 hijō deguchi

employee *n* 従業員 jūgyō in

employer *n* 雇い主 yatoi nushi

engine *n* エンジン enjin

engineer *n* エンジニア enjinia

England *n* イギリス igirisu

English *adj* イギリス(の)、イギリス人(の) igirisu no, igirisu jin no

Do you speak English? 英語を話しますか? eigo o hanashi masu ka.

enjoy, to enjoy *v* 楽しむ tanoshimu

enter, to enter *v*入る hairu

Do not enter. 進入禁止 shinyū kinshi

enthusiastic *adj* 熱心な nesshin na

entrance *n* 入口 iriguchi

envelope *n* 封筒 fūtō

environment *n* 環境 kankyō

escalator *n* エスカレーター esukarētā

espresso *n* エスプレッソ esupuresso

exchange rate *n* 交換レート kōkan rēto

What is the exchange rate for US / Canadian dollars? アメリカドル/カナダドルの交換レートは何ですか? amerika doru/kanada doru no kōkan rēto wa nan desu ka.

xcuse (pardon) *v* すみません sumi masen

Excuse me. すみません sumi masen

xhausted *adj* 疲れた tsukareta

xhibit *n* 展示 tenji

xit *n* 出口 deguchi

not an exit 出口なし deguchi nashi

xit *v* 出る deru

xpensive *adj* 高い takai

xplain *v* 説明する setsumei suru

xpress *adj* 特急の tokkyū no

express check-in 特別優先チェックイン tokubetsu yūsen chekku in

xtra (additional) *adj* 余分の yobun no

xtra-large *adj* 特大の tokudai no

ye *n* 目 me

yebrow *n* まゆ毛 mayu ge

yeglasses *n* 眼鏡 megane

yelash *n* まつ毛 matsu ge

bric *n* 布 nuno

ce *n* 顔 kao

int *v* 気を失う ki o ushinau

ll (season) *n* 秋 aki

ll *v* 落ちる ochiru

mily *n* 家族 kazoku / ご家族 go kazoku

n *n* 扇風機 senpūki

r 遠くに tōkuni / 遠い tōi

How far is it to ______? ______まではどれだけ遠く離れていますか? ______ made wa doredake tōku hanarete imasu ka.

fare *n* 料金 ryōkin

fast *adj* 速い hayai

fat *adj* 太った futotta

father *n* 父 chichi / お父さん otōsan

faucet *n* 蛇口 jaguchi

fault *n* 落ち度 ochido

I'm at fault. 私に落ち度があります。watashi ni ochido ga arimasu.

It was his fault. それは彼に落ち度があります。sore wa kare ni ochido ga arimasu.

fax *n* ファックス fakkusu

February *n* 二月 ni gatsu

fee *n* 料金 ryōkin

female *adj* 女性の josei no

fiancé(e) *n* 婚約者 konyaku sha

fifteen *adj* 十五の jūgo no

fifth *adj* 五番目の go banme no

fifty *adj* 五十の gojū no

find *v* 見つける mitsukeru

fine (for traffic violation) *n* 罰金 bakkin

fine 元気な genki na

I'm fine. 私は元気です。watashi wa genki desu.

fire! *n* 火事だ! kaji da.

first *adj* 最初の saisho no

fishing pole *n* 釣竿 tsuri zao

fitness center *n* フィットネスセンター fittonesu sentā / ジム jimu

fit (clothes) *v* ぴったり合う pittari au

Does this look like it fits? ぴったり合っているように見えますか? pittari atte iru yō ni miemasu ka.

fitting room *n* 試着室 shichaku shitsu

five *adj* 五つの itsutsu no

flight *n* フライト furaito / __便 __bin

Where do domestic flights arrive / depart? 国内線の出発/到着場所はどこですか? kokunai sen no shuppatsu / tōchaku basho wa doko desu ka.

Where do international flights arrive / depart? 国際線の出発 / 到着場所はどこですか? kokusai sen no shuppatsu / tōchaku basho wa doko desu ka.

What time does this flight leave? このフライトは何時に出発しますか? kono furaito wa nan ji ni shuppatsu shimasu ka.

flight attendant 飛行機の乗務員 hikōki no jōmuin

floor *n* 階 kai

ground floor 1 階 ikkai

second floor 2 階 ni kai

flower *n* 花 hana

flush (gambling) *n* フラッシュ furasshu

flush, to flush *v* 流れる、流す nagareru, nagasu

This toilet won't flush. このトイレは流れません。kono toire wa nagare masen.

flute *n* フルート furūto

food *n* 食べ物 tabe mono

foot (body part, measurement) *n* 足、フット ashi, futto

forehead *n* 額 hitai

formula *n* 粉ミルク kona miruku

Do you sell infants' formula? ベビー用粉ミルクは売っていますか? bebī yō kona miruku wa utte imasu ka.

forty *adj* 四十の yonjū no

forward *adj* 先へ saki e / 前へ mae e

four *adj* 四つの yottsu no

fourteen *adj* 十四の jūyon no / 十四の jū shi no

fourth *adj* 四番目の yon banme no

one-fourth 四分の一 yon bun no ichi

fragile *adj* 割れやすい ware yasui /「割れ物注意」「waremono chūi」

freckle *n* そばかす sobakasu

French *adj* フランスの、フランス人の furansu no, furansu jin no

fresh *adj* 新鮮な shinsen na

Friday *n* 金曜日 kin yō bi

friend *n* 友人 yūjin / 友達 tomodachi

front *adj* 前方の zenpō no

front desk フロント デスク furonto desuku

front door フロントドア furonto doa

fruit *n* 果物 kuda mono

fruit juice *n* フルーツ ジュース furūtsu jūsu

full, to be full (after a meal) *adj* 満腹になった manpuku ni natta

Full house! *n* フル ハウス! furu hausu.

fuse *n* ヒューズ hyūzu

G

gallon *n* ガロン garon

garlic *n* にんにく nin niku

gas *n* ガソリン gasorin

gas gauge 燃料計 nenryō kei

out of gas ガソリンが入っていない gasorin ga haitte inai

gate (at airport) *n* ゲート gēto

German *adj* ドイツの、ドイツ人の doitsu no, doitsu jin no

gift *n* 贈り物 okuri mono

gin *n* ジン jin

girl *n* 女の子 onna no ko

girlfriend *n* ガールフレンド gāru furendo

give, to give *v* あげる ageru

glass *n* グラス gurasu

Do you have it by the glass? グラスでありますか? gurasu de arimasuka.

I'd like a glass please. グラスで一つお願いします。gurasu de hitotsu onegai shimasu.

glasses (eye) *n* 眼鏡 megane

I need new glasses. 新しい眼鏡が必要です。atarashii megane ga hitsuyō desu.

glove *n* 手袋 tebukuro

go, to go *v* 行く iku

goal (sport) *n* ゴール gōru

goalie *n* ゴールキーパー gōru kīpā

gold *adj* 金製の kin sei no

golf *n* ゴルフ gorufu

golf, to go golfing *v* ゴルフをする gorufu o suru

good *adj* よい yoi

goodbye *n* さようなら sayōnara

grade (school) *n* 学年 gakunen

gram *n* グラム guramu

grandfather *n* 祖父 sofu / お祖父さん ojīsan

grandmother *n* 祖母 sobo /お祖母さん obāsan

grandparent *n* 祖父母 sofubo

grape *n* ぶどう budō

gray *adj* 灰色の hai iro no

great *adj* 立派な rippa na

Greek *adj* ギリシャの、ギリシャ人の girisha no, girisha jin no

Greek Orthodox *adj* ギリシャ正教の girisha seikyō no

green *adj* 緑色の midori iro no

groceries *n* 食料品 shokuryō hin

group *n* グループ gurūpu

grow, to grow (get larger) *v* 育つ sodatsu

Where did you grow up? どこで育ちましたか? doko de sodachi mashita ka.

guard *n* ガード gādo

security guard セキュリティガード sekyuritī gādo / 警備員 keibi in

Guatemalan *adj* グアテマラの、グアテマラ人の guatemara no, guatemara jin no

guest *n* お客 okyaku

guide (of tours) *n* ガイド gaido

guide (publication) *n* ガイドブック gaido bukku

guide, to guide *v* 案内する an nai suru

guided tour *n* ガイド付きツアー gaido tsuki tuā

guitar *n* ギター gitā

gym *n* ジム jimu

gynecologist *n* 婦人科医 fujinka i

H

hair *n* 髪の毛 kami no ke

haircut *n* ヘアーカット heā katto

I need a haircut. 髪の毛を切りたいのですが。kami no ke o kiri tai no desuga.

How much is a haircut? カットはいくらですか？ katto wa ikura desuka.

hairdresser *n* ヘアードレッサー heā doressā

hair dryer *n* ヘアードライヤー heā doraiyā

half *n* 半分 hanbun

one-half 二分の一 ni bun no ichi

hallway *n* 廊下 rōka

hand *n* 手 te

handicapped-accessible *adj* 障害者に対応した shōgai sha ni taiō shita

handle, to handle *v* 扱う atsukau

handsome *adj* ハンサムな hansamu na

hangout (hot spot) *n* 溜まり場 tamari ba

hang out (to relax) *v* よく出入りする yoku deiri suru

hang up (to end a phone call) *v* 切る kiru

hanger *n* ハンガー hangā

happy *adj* 幸せな shiawase na / 嬉しい ureshii

hard *adj* 難しい muzukashii **(difficult)** / 堅い katai **(firm)**

hat *n* 帽子 bōshi

have *v* 持つ motsu

hazel *adj* 薄茶色の usu chairo no

headache *n* 頭痛 zutsu

headlight *n* ヘッドライト heddo raito

headphones *n* ヘッドホーン heddo hōn

hear *v* 聞く kiku

hearing-impaired *adj* 聴覚障害の chōkaku shōgai no

heart *n* 心臓 shinzō

heart attack *n* 心臓発作 shinzō hossa

hectare *n* ヘクタール hekutāru

hello *n* こんにちは kon nichi wa

Help! *n* 助けて！ tasukete.

help, to help *v* 助ける tasukeru

hen *n* 雌鶏 mendori
her *adj* 彼女の kanojo no
herb *n* ハーブ hābu
here *n* ここ koko
high *adj* 高い takai
highlights (hair) *n* ハイライト hairaito
highway *n* 高速道路 kōsoku dōro
hike, to hike *v* ハイキングをする haikingu o suru
him *pron* 彼を kare o
Hindu *adj* ヒンズー教の、ヒンズー人の hinzū kyō no, hinzū jin no
hip-hop *n* ヒップホップ hippu hoppu
his *adj* 彼の kare no
historical *adj* 歴史的な rekishi teki na
history *n* 歴史 rekishi
hobby *n* 趣味 shumi
hold, to hold *v* 抱く daku

> **to hold hands** 手を握る te o nigiru
> **Would you hold this for me?** これを持っていただけませんか? kore o motte itadake masen ka.

hold, to hold (to pause) *v* 待つ matsu

> **Hold on a minute!** ちょっと待って! chotto matte.
> **I'll hold.** パスします。pasu shimasu.

hold, to hold (gambling) *v* パスする pasu suru
holiday *n* 休日 kyūjitsu
home *n* 家 ie
homemaker *n* 主婦 shufu
Honduran *adj* ホンジュラスの、ホンジュラス人の honjurasu no, honjurasu jin no
horn *n* 角 tsuno
horse *n* 馬 uma
hostel *n* ホステル hosuteru
hot *adj* 熱い atsui
hot chocolate *n* ホット チョコレート hotto chokorēto
hotel *n* ホテル hoteru

> **Do you have a list of local hotels?** 地元のホテルの一覧表はありますか? jimoto no hoteru no ichiran hyō wa arimasu ka.

hour *n* 時間 jikan
hours (at museum) *n* 時間 jikan
how *adv* いくら ikura ***(how much),*** いくつ ikutsu ***(how many)***
humid *adj* 湿気のある shikke no aru
hundred *n* 百 hyaku
hurry *v* 急ぐ isoide

> **I'm in a hurry.** 私は急いでいます。watashi wa isoide imasu.
> **Hurry, please!** 急いでください! isoide kudasai.

hurt, to hurt *v* 痛む itamu

> **Ouch!That hurts!** 痛い!itai. 痛いです! itai desu.

husband *n* 夫 otto / 主人 shujin/ ご主人 go shujin

I

I *pron* 私は watashi wa
ice *n* 氷 kōri
identification *n* 身分証明書 mibun shōmei sho
inch *n* インチ inchi
indigestion *n* 消化不良 shōka furyō
inexpensive *adj* 高くない takaku nai
infant *n* 赤ちゃん akachan

> **Are infants allowed?** 赤ちゃんもいいですか? Akachan mo ii desu ka.

information *n* 情報 jōhō
information booth *n* 案内所 an nai jo
injury *n* けが kega
insect repellent *n* 虫除け mushi yoke
inside 内部 naibu / 中 naka
insult *v* 侮辱する bujoku suru
insurance *n* 保険 hoken
iinterest rate *n* 金利 kinri
intermission *n* 休憩 kyūkei
Internet *n* インターネット intānetto

> **High-speed Internet** 高速インターネット kōsoku intānetto
> **Do you have Internet access?** インターネットに接続できますか? intānetto ni setsuzoku deki masu ka.
> **Where can I find an Internet café?** インターネットカフェはどこにありますか? intā netto kafe wa doko ni arimasu ka.

interpreter *n* 通訳 tsūyaku

> **I need an interpreter.** 通訳が必要です。tsūyaku ga hitsuyō desu.

introduce, to introduce *v* 紹介する shōkai suru

> **I'd like to introduce you to ____.** あなたを____に紹介します。anata o ____ ni shōkai shimasu.

Ireland *n* アイルランド airurando
Irish *adj* アイルランドの、アイルランド人の airurando no, airurando jin no
is *v See* **be (to be).**
Italian *adj* イタリアの、イタリア人の itaria no, itaria jin no

J

jacket *n* 上着 uwagi
January *n* 一月 ichi gatsu
Japanese *adj* 日本の、日本人の nihon no, nihon jin no
jazz *n* ジャズ jazu
Jewish *adj* ユダヤ教の、ユダヤ人の yudaya kyō no, yudaya jin no
jog, to run *v* ジョギングをする joggingu o suru
juice *n* ジュース jūsu
June *n* 六月 roku gatsu
July *n* 七月 shichi gatsu

K

keep, to keep *v* 保つ tamotsu
kid *n* 子供 kodomo

Are kids allowed? 子供もいいですか? kodomo mo ii desu ka.

Do you have kids' programs? 子供用のプログラムはありますか? kodomo yō no puroguramu wa arimasu ka.

Do you have a kids' menu? 子供用のメニューはありますか? kodomo yō no menyū wa arimasu ka.

kilo *n* キログラム kiro guramu

kilometer *n* キロメートル kiro mētoru

kind *n* 種類 shurui **(type)**

What kind is it? それはどんな種類ですか? sore wa donna shurui desu ka.

kiss *n* キス kisu

kitchen *n* キッチン kicchin

know, to know (something) *v* 知っている shitte iru

know, to know (someone) *v* 知っている shitte iru

L

land, to land *v* 着陸する chakuriku suru / 着く tsuku

landscape *n* 景色 keshiki

language *n* 言語 gengo

laptop *n* ラップトップ rappu toppu

large *adj* 大きい ōkii

last, to last *v* 続く tsuzuku

last *adv* 最後に saigo ni

late *adj* 遅い osoi

Please don't be late. どうか遅れないでください。dōka okure naide kudasai.

later *adv* あとで ato de

See you later. それじゃ、また後で。soreja, mata ato de.

laundry *n* 洗濯 sentaku / randorī

lavender *adj* ラベンダー色の rabendā iro no

law *n* 法律 hōritsu

lawyer *n* 弁護士 bengo shi

least *n* 最小 saishō

least *adj* 最も小さい、最も少ない mottomo chiisai, mottomo sukunai

leather *n* 皮 kawa

leave, to leave (depart) *v* 出発する shuppatsu suru

left *adj* 左の hidari no

on the left 左に hidari ni

leg *n* 脚 ashi

lemonade *n* レモネード remonēdo

less *adj* もっと少ない motto sukunia

lesson *n* レッスン ressun

license *n* 免許証 menkyo shō

driver's license 運転免許証 unten menkyo shō

life preserver *n* 救命用具 kyūmei yōgu

light (lamp) *n* ランプ ranpu

light (for cigarette) *n* 火 hi

May I offer you a light? 火を貸しましょうか? hi o kashima shō ka. **lighter (cigarette)** *n* ライター raitā

like, desire *v* 望む, nozomu

I would like ____. ____が好きです。____ ga suki desu.

like, to like *v* 好きである suki de aru

I like this place. 私はここが好きです。watashi wa koko ga suki desu.

limo *n* リムジン rimujin

liquor *n* 酒 sake

liter *n* リットル rittoru

little *adj* 小さい chiisai **(size)**, 少し sukoshi **(amount)**

live, to live *v* 住む sumu

Where do you live? あなたはどこに住んでいますか？ anata wa doko ni sunde imasu ka.

living *n* 生活 seikatsu

What do you do for a living? 何をして生活していますか？ nani o shite seikatsu shite imasu ka.

local *adj* 地方の chihō no

lock *n* 鍵 kagi

lock, to lock *v* 鍵をかける kagi o kakeru

I can't lock the door. ドアに鍵をかけることができません。doa ni kagi o kakeru koto ga dekima sen.

I'm locked out. ドアに鍵がかかってしまい部屋に入ることができません。doa ni kagi ga kakatte shimai heya ni hairu koto ga deki masen.

locker *n* ロッカー rokkā

storage locker 保管ロッカー hokan rokkā

locker room ロッカールーム rokkā rūmu

long *adv* 長く nagaku

For how long? どれくらい長く？ dore kurai nagaku.

long *adj* 長い nagai

look, to look *v* **(to observe)** 見る miru

I'm just looking. ただ見ているだけです。tada miteiru dake desu.

Look here! ここを見て！ koko o mite.

look, to look *v* **(to appear)** のように見える no yō ni mieru

How does this look? これはどう見えますか？ kore wa dō mie masu ka.

look for, to look for (to search) *v* 探す sagasu

I'm looking for a porter. ポーターを探しています。pōtā o sagashite imasu.

loose *adj* ゆるい yurui

lose, to lose *v* 失くす nakusu

I lost my passport. 私はパスポートを失くしました。watashi wa pasupōto o nakushi mashita.

I lost my wallet. 私は財布を失くしました。watashi wa saifu o nakushi mashita.

I'm lost. 私は迷ってしまいました。watashi wa mayotte shimai mashita.

loud *adj* うるさい urusai
loudly *adv* うるさく urusaku
lounge *n* ラウンジ raunji
lounge, to lounge *v* くつろぐ kutsurogu
love *n* 愛 ai
love, to love *v* 愛する ai suru
to love (family) 愛する ai suru
to love (a friend) 愛する ai suru
to love (a lover) 愛する ai suru
low *adj* 低い hikui
lunch *n* 昼食 chūshoku/ランチranchi
luggage *n* 荷物 nimotsu / 旅行カバン ryokō kaban
Where do I report lost luggage? 旅行カバンの紛失はどこに報告しますか? ryokō kaban no funshitsu wa doko ni hōkoku shimasu ka.
Where is the lost luggage claim? 紛失した旅行カバンを受け取る場所はどこですか? funshitsu shita ryokō kaban o uketoru basho wa doko desu ka.

M

machine *n* 機械 kikai
made of *adj* から作られた kara tsuku rareta
magazine *n* 雑誌 zasshi
maid (hotel) *n* メード mēdo
maiden *adj* 未婚の mikon no
That's my maiden name. それは私の旧姓です。sore wa watashi no kyūsei desu.
mail *n* 郵便 yūbin / 手紙 tegami
air mail 航空便 kōkūbin
registered mail 書留 kakitome
mail *v* 郵便で出す yūbin de dasu
make, to make *v* 作る tsukuru
makeup *n* 化粧 keshō
make up, to make up (apologize) *v* 埋め合せをする ume awase o suru
make up, to make up (apply cosmetics) *v* 化粧をする keshō o suru
male *n* 男性 dansei
male *adj* 男性の dansei no
mall *n* ショッピングセンター shoppingu sentā
man *n* 男 otoko
manager *n* マネージャー manējā
manual (instruction booklet) *n* マニュアル manyuaru
many *adj* 多い ōi / 沢山の takusan no
map *n* 地図 chizu
March (month) *n* 三月 san gatsu
market *n* マーケット māketto / 市場 ichiba
flea market フリーマーケット furii māketto
open-air market 青空市場 aozora ichiba
married *adj* 既婚の kikon no / 結婚している kekkon shite iru

marry, to marry *v* 結婚する kekkon suru

massage *n* マッサージ massāji

match (sport) *n* 試合 shiai

match *n* マッチ macchi *n*

book of matches マッチ macchi

match, to match *v* 調和する chōwa suru

Does this ____ match my outfit? この____は私の服と合いますか kono ____ wa watashi no fuku to aimasu ka?

May (month) *n* 五月 go gatsu

may *v aux* してよい shite yoi

May I ____? ____してもよいですか? ____ shitemo yoi desu ka.

meal *n* 食事 shokuji

meat *n* 肉 niku

meatball *n* ミートボール mīto bōru

medication *n* 薬物治療 yakubutsu chiryō

medium (size) *adj* ミディアム midiamu

medium rare (meat) *adj* ミディアム レア midiamu rea

medium well (meat) *adj* ミディアム ウェル midiamu weru

member *n* 会員 kai in

menu *n* メニュー menyū

May I see a menu? メニューを見せていただけませんか? menyū o misete itadake masen ka.

children's menu 子供用のメニュー kodomo yō no menyū

diabetic menu 糖尿病患者用の tōnyōbyō kanja yō no menyū

kosher menu コーシャ料理の kōsha ryōri no menyū

metal detector *n* 金属探知機 kinzoku tanchi ki

meter *n* メートル mētoru

Mexican *adj* メキシコの、メキシコ人の mekishiko no, mekishiko jin no

middle *adj* 中間の chūkan no

midnight *n* 真夜中 mayonaka

mile *n* マイル mairu

military *n* 軍 gun

milk *n* 牛乳 gyūnyū / ミルク miruku

milk shake ミルクセーキ miruku sēki

milliliter *n* ミリリットル miri rittoru

millimeter *n* ミリメートル miri mētoru

minute *n* 分 fun

in a minute すぐに sugu ni

miss, to miss (a flight) *v* 乗りそこなう nori sokonau

missing *adj* 見つからない mitsukara nai

mistake *n* 間違い machigai

moderately priced *adj* 手頃な値段の tegoro na nedan no

mole (facial feature) *n* ほくろ hokuro

Monday *n* 月曜日 getsu yō bi

money *n* お金 okane

money transfer 振込 furikomi

month *n* see months of the year
morning *n* 朝 asa / 午前 gozen
in the morning 午前 gozen
mosque *n* モスク mosuku
mother *n* 母 haha/ お母さん okāsan
mother, to mother *v* 世話をする sewa o suru
motorcycle *n* バイク baiku
mountain *n* 山 yama
mountain climbing 登山 tozan
mouse *n* ねずみ nezumi
mouth *n* 口 kuchi
move, to move *v* 動く ugoku
movie *n* 映画 eiga
much *n* 多量 taryō / 沢山の takusan no
mug, to mug (someone) *v* 襲う osou
mugged *adj* 襲われた osowareta
museum *n* 美術館 bijutsu kan
music *n* 音楽 ongaku
live music 生演奏 nama ensō
musician *n* ミュージシャン myūjishan
muslim *adj* イスラム教の isuramu kyō no
mustache *n* 口ひげ kuchi hige
mystery (novel) *n* ミステリー misuterī

N

name *n* 名前 namae
My name is ___. 私は___と申します。watashi wa ___ to mōshimasu.
What's your name? あなたの名前は何ですか? anata no namae wa nan desu ka.
napkin *n* ナプキン napukin
narrow *adj* 狭い semai
nationality *n* 国籍 kokuseki
nausea *n* 吐き気 hakike
near *adj* 近い chikai
nearby *adj* 近くに chikaku ni
neat (tidy) *adj* きちんとした kichin to shita
need, to need *v* 欲しい hoshii
neighbor *n* 近所の人 kinjo no hito / ご近所の方 kinjo no kata
nephew *n* おい oi / 甥御さん oigo san
network *n* ネットワーク nettowāku
new *adj* 新しい atarashii
newspaper *n* 新聞 shinbun
newsstand *n* 新聞売り場 shinbun uriba
New Zealand *n* ニュージーランド nyūjīrando
New Zealander *adj* ニュージーランドの、ニュージーランド人の nyūjīrando no, nyūjīrando jin no
next *prep* 次 tsugi
next to の次 no tsugi
the next station 次の駅 tsugi no eki
Nicaraguan *adj* ニカラグアの、ニカラグア人の nikaragua no, nikaragua jin no
nice *adj* すてきな suteki na
niece *n* めい mei / 姪御さん meigo san

night *n* 夜 yoru
at night 夜に yoru ni
per night 一泊当たり ippaku atari
nightclub *n* ナイトクラブ naito kurabu
nine *adj* 九つの kokonotsu no
nineteen *adj* 十九の jūkyū no
ninety *adj* 九十の kyūjū no
ninth *adj* 九番目の kyū banme no
no *adv* でない de nai
noisy *adj* 音がうるさい oto ga urusai
none *n* 何もない nanimo nai / 少しもない sukoshi mo nai、全くない mattaku nai
nonsmoking *adj* 禁煙 kin en
nonsmoking area 禁煙場所 kin en basho
nonsmoking room 禁煙室 kin en shitsu
noon *n* 正午 shōgo
nose *n* 鼻 hana
novel *n* 小説 shōsetsu
November *n* 十一月 jū ichi gatsu
now *adv* 今 ima
number *n* 数字 sūji / 番号 bangō
Which room number? 部屋は何番?heya wa nan ban.
May I have your phone number?あなたの電話番号を教えていただけますか? anata no denwa bangō o oshiete itadake masu ka.
nurse *n* 看護師 kango shi
nurse *v* 授乳する junyū suru
Do you have a place where I can nurse? 授乳できる場所はありますか?junyū dekiru basho wa arimasu ka.
nursery *n* 託児所 takuji sho
Do you have a nursery? 託児所はありますか? takuji sho wa arimasu ka.
nut *n* クルミ kurumi

O

o'clock *adv* 時 ji
two o'clock 2時 ni ji
October *n* 十月 jū gatsu
offer, to offer *v* 提供する teikyō suru
officer *n* 係員 kakari in
oil *n* 油 abura
okay *adv* オッケー okkē
old *adj* 古い furui / _歳の _ sai no
olive *n* オリーブ orību
one *adj* 一つの hitotsu no
one way (traffic sign) *adj* 一方通行 ippō tsūkō
open (business) *adj* 営業中 eigyō chū
Are you open? 営業していますか? eigyō shite imasu ka.
opera *n* オペラ opera
operator (phone) *n* オペレーター operētā
optometrist *n* 検眼師 kengan shi
orange (color) *adj* オレンジ色の orenji iro no

orange juice *n* オレンジ ジュース orenji jūsu

order, to order (demand) *v* 注文する chūmon suru

order, to order (request) *v* 頼む tanomu

organic *adj* 有機の yūki no

Ouch! 痛い! itai.

outside *n* 外 soto

overcooked *adj* 焼き(煮)すぎた yaki (ni) sugita

overheat, to overheat *v* オーバーヒートする ōbāhīto suru

The car overheated. 車がオーバーヒートしました。 kuruma ga ōbāhīto shimashita.

overflowing *adv* あふれて afurete

oxygen tank *n* 酸素タンク sanso tanku

P

package *n* 小包み kozutsumi

pacifier *n* おしゃぶり oshaburi

page, to page (someone) *v* 呼び出す yobidasu

paint, to paint *v* 塗る nuru

painting *n* 絵 e

pale *adj* 青白い ao jiroi

Panamanian *adj* パナマの、パナマ人の panama no, panama jin no

paper *n* 紙 kami

parade *n* パレード parēdo

Paraguayan *adj* パラグアイの、パラグアイ人の paraguai no, paraguai jin no

parent *n* 親 oya

park *n* 公園 kōen

park, to park *v* 駐車する chūsha suru

no parking 駐車禁止 chūsha kinshi

parking fee 駐車料金 chūsha ryōkin

parking garage 車庫 shako

partner *n* パートナー pātonā

party *n* 団体 dantai

party *n* パーティー pātī

political party 政党 seitō

pass, to pass *v* パスする pasu suru

I'll pass. パスします。pasu shimasu.

passenger *n* 乗客 jōkyaku

passport *n* パスポート pasupōto

I've lost my passport. 私はパスポートを失くしました。watashi wa pasupōto o nakushi mashita.

pay, to pay *v* 支払う shiharau

peanut *n* ピーナッツ pīnattsu

pedestrian *adj* 歩行者用の hokōsha yō no

pediatrician *n* 小児科医 shōnika i

Can you recommend a pediatrician? お勧めの小児科医はいますか? osusume no shōnika i wa imasu ka.

permit *n* 許可 kyoka

Do we need a camping permit? キャンプをする許可が必要ですか? kyanpu o suru kyoka ga hitsuyō desu ka.

permit, to permit *v* 許可する kyoka suru

Peruvian *adj* ペルーの、ペルー人の perū no, perū jin no

phone *n* 電話 denwa

May I have your phone number? あなたの電話番号を教えていただけますか? anata no denwa bangō o oshiete itadake masu ka.

Where can I find a public phone? 公衆電話はどこにありますか? kōshū denwa wa doko ni arimasu ka.

phone operator 電話オペレーター denwa operētā

Do you sell prepaid phones? プリペイド電話を売っていますか? puripeido denwa o utte imasu ka.

phone *adj* 電話の denwa no

Do you have a phone directory? 電話帳はありますか?denwa chō wa arimasu ka.

phone call *n* 電話 denwa

I need to make a collect phone call. コレクトコールをしたいのですが。korekuto kōru o shitai no desuga.

an international phone call 国際電話 kokusai denwa

photocopy, to photocopy *v* コピーを取る kopī o toru / コピーする kopī suru

piano *n* ピアノ piano

pillow *n* 枕 makura

down pillow 羽毛の枕 umō no makura

pink *adj* ピンクの pinku no

pint *n* パイント painto

pizza *n* ピザ piza

place, to place *v* 置く oku

plastic *n* プラスチック purasuchikku

play *n* プレイ purei

play, to play (a game) *v* プレイする purei suru

play, to play (an instrument) *v* 演奏する ensō suru / 弾く hiku

playground *n* 遊び場 asobi ba

Do you have a playground? 遊び場はありますか? asobi ba wa arimasu ka.

please (polite entreaty) *adv* どうぞ dōzo

please, to be pleasing to *v* 喜ばせる yorokobaseru

pleasure *n* 喜び yorokobi

It's a pleasure. 嬉しいです。ureshii desu.

plug *n* コンセント konsento

plug, to plug *v* 差し込む sashi komu

point, to point *v* 指す sasu

Would you point me in the direction of____? _____の方向に指し示していただけませんか?_____ no hōkō ni sashi shimeshite itadake masen ka.

police *n* 警察 keisatsu

police station *n* 警察署 keisatsu sho / 警察の派出所 keisatsu no hashutsu sho

pool *n* プール pūru
pool (the game) *n* ビリヤード biriyādo
pop music *n* ポップ ミュージック poppu myūjikku
popular *adj* 人気がある ninki ga aru
port (beverage) *n* ポートワイン pōto wain
port (for ship) *n* 港 minato
porter *n* ポーター pōtā
portion *n* 部分 bubun
portrait *n* 肖像画 shōzō ga
postcard *n* ポストカード posuto kādo
post office *n* 郵便局 yūbin kyoku

Where is the post office? 郵便局はどこにありますか? yūbin kyoku wa doko ni arimasu ka.

poultry *n* 家禽 kakin
pound *n* ポンド pondo
prefer, to prefer *v* の方を好む no hō o konomu
pregnant *adj* 妊娠した ninshin shita
prepared *adj* 準備された junbi sareta
prescription *n* 処方箋 shohōsen / 処方薬 shohōyaku
price *n* 価格 kakaku
print, to print *v* 印刷する insatsu suru
private berth / cabin *n* 個人客室 kojin kyakushitsu/キャビンkyabin
problem *n* 問題 mondai
process, to process *v* 処理する shori suru
product *n* 製品 seihin
professional *adj* プロフェッショナルな purofesshionaru na
program *n* プログラム puroguramu

May I have a program? プログラムをいただけますか? puroguramu o itadake masu ka.

Protestant *n* プロテスタント purotesutanto
publisher *n* 出版社 shuppansha
Puerto Rican *adj* プエルトリコの、プエルトリコ人の puerutoriko no, puerutoriko jin no
pull, to pull *v* 引く hiku
pump *n* ポンプ ponpu
purple *adj* 紫の murasaki no
purse *n* 財布 saifu
push, to push *v* 押す osu
put, to put *v* 置く oku

Q

quarter *adj* 四分の一 yonbun no ichi

one-quarter 四分の一 yon bun no ichi

quiet *adj* 静かな shizuka na

R

rabbit *n* うさぎ usagi
radio *n* ラジオ rajio

satellite radio 衛星ラジオ eisei rajio

rain, to rain *v* 雨が降る ame ga furu

Is it supposed to rain? 雨が降る予定ですか? ame ga furu yotei desuka.

rainy *adj* 雨の ame no

It's rainy. 雨です。ame desu.

ramp, wheelchair *n* スロープ、車椅子 surōpu, kuruma isu

rare (meat) *adj* レアの rea no

rate (for car rental, hotel) *n* 料金 ryōkin

What's the rate per day? 一日当たりの料金はいくらですか? ichi nichi atari no ryōkin wa ikura desu ka.

What's the rate per week? 一週間当たりの料金はいくらですか? isshūkan atari no ryōkin wa ikura desu ka.

rate plan (cell phone) *n* 料金プラン ryōkin puran

rather *adv* むしろ mushiro

read, to read *v* 読む yomu

really *adv* 本当に hontō ni

receipt *n* レシート reshīto

receive, to receive *v* 受け取る uketoru

recommend, to recommend *v* 勧める susumeru

red *adj* 赤の aka no

redhead *n* 赤毛 akage

reef *n* さんご礁 sango shō

refill (of beverage) *n el* お替わり okawari

refill (of prescription) *n* 補充 hojū

reggae *adj* レゲー regē

relative (family) *n* 親戚 shinseki

remove, to remove *v* 取り除く torinozoku / 脱ぐ nugu

rent, to rent *v* 借りる kariru

I'd like to rent a car. 車を借りたいのですが。kuruma o karitai no desuga.

repeat, to repeat *v* 繰り返す kuri kaesu

Would you please repeat that? もう一度繰り返していただけますか? mō ichido kuri kaeshite itadake masu ka.

reservation *n* 予約 yoyaku

I'd like to make a reservation for ____. ____の予約をしたいのですが。____ no yoyaku o shitai no desuga. **See p6 for numbers.**

restaurant *n* レストラン resutoran

Where can I find a good restaurant? よいレストランはどこにありますか? yoi resutoran wa doko ni arimasu ka.

restroom *n* トイレ toire

Do you have a public restroom? 公衆トイレはありますか? kōshū toire wa arimasu ka.

return, to return (to a place) *v* 戻る modoru

return, to return (something to a store) *v* 返品する henpin suru

ride, to ride *v* 乗っていく notte iku

right *adj* 右の migi no

It is on the right. 右側にあります。migi gawa ni arimasu.

Turn right at the corner. 角を右に曲がります。kado o migi ni magari masu.

rights *n pl* 権利 kenri

civil rights 市民の権利 shimin no kenri

river *n* 川 kawa

road *n* 道路 dōro

road closed sign *n* 道路閉鎖中 dōro heisa chū

rob, to rob *v* 奪う ubau

I've been robbed. 強盗に遭いました。gōtō ni aimashita.

rock and roll *n* ロックンロール rokkun rōru

rock climbing *n* ロッククライミング rokku kuraimingu

rocks (ice) *n* ロック rokku

I'd like it on the rocks.ロックでお願いします。rokku de onegai shimasu.

romance (novel) *n* 恋愛小説 ren ai shōsetsu

romantic *adj* ロマンチックな romanchikku na

room (hotel) *n* 部屋 heya

room for one / two 1人 / 2 人部屋 hitori /futari beya

room service ルーム サービス rūmu sābisu

rope *n* ロープ rōpu

rose *n* バラ bara

royal flush *n* ロイヤル フラッシュ roiyaru furasshu

rum *n* ラム酒 ramu shu

run, to run *v* 走る hashiru

S

sad *adj* 悲しい kanashii

safe (for storing valuables) *n* 金庫 kinko

Do the rooms have safes? 室内には金庫がありますか? shitsu nai niwa kinko ga arimasu ka.

safe (secure) *adj* 安全な anzen na

Is this area safe? この地域は安全ですか? kono chiiki wa anzen desu ka.

sail *n* 航海 kōkai

sail, to sail *v* 航海する kōkai suru

When do we sail? いつ出航しますか? itsu shukkō shimasu ka.

salad *n* サラダ sarada

salesperson *n* 販売員 hanbai in

salt *n* 塩 shio

Is that low-salt? それは減塩ですか? sore wa gen en desu ka.

Salvadorian *adj* サルバドルの、サルバドル人の sarubadoru no, sarubadoru jin no

satellite *n* 衛星 eisei

satellite radio 衛星ラジオ eisei rajio

satellite tracking 衛星追跡 eisei tsuiseki

Saturday *n* 土曜日 do yō bi

sauce *n* ソース sōsu

say, to say *v* 言う iu
scan, to scan *v* **(document)** スキャンする sukyan suru
schedule *n* スケジュール sukejūru
school *n* 学校 gakkō
scooter *n* スクーター sukūtā
score *n* 得点 tokuten
Scottish *adj* スコットランドの、スコットランド人の sukottorando no, sukottorando jin no
scratched *adj* 傷のある kizu no aru
scratched surface 擦り傷のある表面 suri kizu no aru hyōmen
scuba dive, to scuba dive *v* スキューバダイブをする sukyūba daibingu o suru
sculpture *n* 彫刻 chōkoku
seafood *n* シーフード shīfūdo 魚介類 gyokai rui
search *n* 検査 kensa
hand search 手で検査する te de kensa suru
search, to search *v* 調べる shiraberu
seasick *adj* 船酔い funa yoi
I am seasick. 船酔いしました。funa yoi shimashita.
seasickness pill *n* 船酔いに効く薬 funa yoi ni kiku kusuri
seat *n* 座席 zaseki / 席 seki
child seat チャイルドシート chairudo shiito
second *adj* 二番目の niban me no
security checkpoint セキュリティチェックポイント sekyuritī chekku pointo
security guard セキュリティガード sekyuritī gādo / 警備員 keibi in
sedan *n* セダン sedan
see, to see *v* 見る miru
May I see it? 見せていただけますか? misete itadake masu ka.
self-serve *adj* セルフサービスの serufu sābisu no
sell, to sell *v* 売る uru
seltzer *n* ソーダ水 sōda sui
send, to send *v* 送る okuru
separated (marital status) *adj* 別れた wakareta / 別居している bekkyo shite iru
September *n* 九月 ku gatsu
serve, to serve *v* 出す dasu
service *n* サービス sābisu
out of service 回送 kaisō
services (religious) *n* 奉仕 hōshi / 礼拝 reihai
service charge *n* サービス料 sābisu ryō
seven *adj* 七つの nanatsu no
seventy *adj* 七十の nana jū no
seventeen *adj* 十七の jūshichi no
seventh *adj* 七番目の nana ban me no
sew, to sew *v* 縫う nuu / 裁縫をする saihō o suru
sex (gender) *n* 性別 seibetsu
shallow *adj* 浅い asai
sheet (bed linen) *n* シーツ shītsu

shellfish *n* 貝類 kai rui

ship *n* 船 fune

ship, to ship *v* 船で運ぶ fune de hakobu

How much to ship this to ____? これを____まで船で送るにはいくらかかりますか? kore o ____ made fune de okuru niwa ikura kakari masu ka.

shipwreck *n* 難破船 nanpa sen

shirt *n* シャツ shatsu

shoe *n* 靴 kutsu

shop *n* 店 mise

shop *v* 買い物をする kaimono o suru

I'm shopping for mens' clothes. 紳士服を買いに来ました。shinshi fuku o kai ni kimashita.

I'm shopping for womens' clothes. 婦人服を買いに来ました。fujin fuku o kai ni kimashita.

I'm shopping for childrens' clothes. 子供服を買いに来ました。kodomo fuku o kai ni kimashita.

short *adj* 短い mijikai

shorts *n* 半ズボン han zubon

shot (liquor) *n* 一杯 ippai

shout *v* 大声で呼ぶ ōgoe de yobu

show (performance) *n* ショー shō

What time is the show? ショーは何時ですか? shō wa nanji desuka?

show, to show *v* 見せる miseru

Would you show me? 見せていただけませんか? misete itadake masen ka.

shower *n* シャワー shawā

Does it have a shower? それにはシャワーが付いていますか? sore niwa shawā ga tsuite imasu ka.

shower, to shower *v* シャワーを浴びる shawā o abiru

shrimp *n* 海老 ebi

shuttle bus *n* シャトル バス shatoru basu

sick *adj* 病気の byōki no

I feel sick. 気分が悪いです。kibun ga warui desu.

side *n* 添え物 soe mono

on the side (e.g., salad dressing) 横に添えて yoko ni soete

sidewalk *n* 歩道 hodō

sightseeing *n* 観光 kankō

sightseeing bus *n* 観光バス kankō basu

sign, to sign *v* 署名 shomei

Where do I sign? どこに署名すればいいですか? doko ni shomei sureba ii desu ka.

silk *n* シルク shiruku

silver *adj* 銀製の gin sei no

sing, to sing *v* 歌う utau

single (unmarried) *adj* 独身の dokushin no

Are you single? あなたは独身ですか? anata wa dokushin desu ka.

single (one) *adj* 一つの hitotsu no

single bed シングル ベッド shinguru beddo

sink *n* 洗面台 senmen dai

sister *n* 姉妹 shimai / ご姉妹 go shimai

sit, to sit *v* 座る suwaru

six *adj* 六つの muttsu no

sixteen *adj* 十六の jūroku no

sixty *adj* 六十の rokujū no

size (clothing, shoes) *n* サイズ saizu

skin *n* 皮膚 hifu

sleeping berth *n* 寝台 shindai

slow *adj* 遅い osoi

slow, to slow *v* 速度を落とす sokudo o otosu

Slow down! 速度を落としてください! sokudo o otoshite kudasai.

slow(ly) *adv* ゆっくり yukkuri

Speak more slowly. もっとゆっくり話してください。motto yukkuri hanashite kudasai.

slum *n* スラム街 suramu gai

small *adj* 小さい chiisai

smell, to smell *v* 匂いをかぐ nioi o kagu

smoke, to smoke *v* タバコを吸う tabako o suu

smoking *n* 喫煙 kitsu en

smoking area 喫煙所 kitsu en jo

No Smoking 禁煙 kin en

snack *n* 軽食 keishoku

Snake eyes! *n* スネークアイだ! sunēku ai da.

snorkel *n* スノーケル sunōkeru

soap *n* 石鹸 sekken

sock *n* 靴下 kutsu shita

soda *n* ソーダ sōda

diet soda ダイエット ソーダ daietto sôda

soft *adj* 柔らかい yawarakai

software *n* ソフトウェア sofuto uea

sold out *adj* 売り切れ urikire

some *adj* いくつかの ikutsukano

someone *n* 誰か dare ka

something *n* 何か nani ka / 何 nani

son *n* 息子 musuko / 息子さん musuko san

song *n* 歌 uta

sorry *adj* すみません sumi masen.

I'm sorry. すみません。sumi masen.

soup *n* スープ sūpu

spa *n* スパ supa

Spain *n* スペイン supein

Spanish *adj* スペインの、スペイン人の supein no, supein jin no

spare tire *n* スペア タイヤ supea taiya

speak, to speak *v* 話す hanasu

Do you speak English? 英語を話しますか? eigo o hanashi masu ka.

Would you speak louder, please? もっと大きな声で話してください。motto ōkina koe de hanashite kudasai. /もっと大きな声で話していただけませんか。motto ōkina koe de hanashite itadake masen ka.

Would you speak slower, please? もっとゆっくり話してください。motto yukkuri hanashite kudasai. / もっとゆっくり話していただけませんか。motto yukkuri hanashite itadake masen ka.

special (featured meal) *n* スペシャル supesharu

specify, to specify *v* 具体的に述べる gutai teki ni noberu

speed limit *n* 制限速度 seigen sokudo

What's the speed limit? 制限速度は何キロですか? seigen sokudo wa nan kiro desu ka.

speedometer *n* 速度計 sokudo kei

spell, to spell *v* つづる tsuzuru

How do you spell that? つづりを言ってください。tsuzuri o itte kudasai. / つづりを言ってもらえますか。tsuzuri o itte morae masu ka.

spice *n* スパイス supaisu

spill, to spill *v* こぼす kobosu

split (gambling) *n* 分ける wakeru

sports *n* スポーツ supōtsu

spring (season) *n* 春 haru

stadium *n* スタジアム sutajiamu

staff (employees) *n* スタッフ sutaffu

stamp (postage) *n* 切手 kitte

stair *n* 階段 kaidan

Where are the stairs? 階段はどこですか? kaidan wa doko desu ka.

Are there many stairs? 階段の数は多いですか? kaidan no kazu wa ōi desu ka.

stand, to stand *v* 立つ tatsu

start, to start (commence) *v* 始まる hajimaru

start, to start (a car) *v* 発車させる hassha saseru

state *n* 状況 jōkyō

station *n* 駅 eki

Where is the nearest _____? ここから一番近い_____はどこですか? koko kara ichiban chikai _____ wa doko desu ka.

gas station ガソリンスタンド gasorin sutando

bus station バス停 basu tei

subway station 地下鉄の駅 chikatetsu no eki

train station 駅 eki

stay, to stay *v* 泊る tomaru / 滞在する taizai suru

We'll be staying for ____ nights. ____日間滞在する予定です。____ nichi kan taizai suru yotei desu. **See p6 for numbers.**

steakhouse *n* ステーキハウス sutēki hausu

steal, to steal *v* 盗む nusumu
stolen *adj* 盗まれた nusumareta
stop *n* 駅 eki 停車駅 **teisha eki**
Is this my stop? ここは私が降りる駅ですか? koko wa watashi ga oriru eki desu ka.
I missed my stop. 私は乗り過ごしてしまいました。watashi wa nori sugoshite shimai mashita.
stop, to stop *v* 停まる tomaru
Please stop. 停まってください。tomatte kudasai.
STOP (traffic sign) 止まれ tomare
Stop, thief! 止まれ、泥棒! tomare, dorobō.
store *n* 店 mise
straight (hair) *adj* ストレートの sutorēto no / 直毛 chokumō
straight ahead ここをまっすぐ koko o saki massugu
straight (drink) ストレートで sutorēto de
Go straight. (giving directions) まっすぐ行きます。massugu ikimasu.
straight (gambling) *n* ストレート sutorēto
street *n* 道 michi
across the street この道の向こう側 kono michi no mukō gawa
down the street この道(の先) kono michi (no saki)
Which street? どの道? dono michi.
How many more streets? あと何本の道がありますか? ato nan bon no michi ga arimasuka?
stressed *adj* ストレスを感じている sutoresu o kanjite iru
striped *adj* 縞の shima no
stroller *n* ベビーカー bebī kā
Do you rent baby strollers? ベビーカーはレンタルできますか? bebī kā wa rentaru deki masu ka.
substitution *n* 替わりのもの kawari no mono
suburb *n* 郊外 kōgai
subway *n* 地下鉄 chikatetsu
subway line 地下鉄の路線 chikatetsu no rosen
subway station 地下鉄の駅 chikatetsu no eki
Which subway do I take for ____? ____へはどの地下鉄で行けばよいですか? ____ ewa dono chikatetsu de ikeba yoi desu ka.
subtitle *n* 字幕 jimaku
suitcase *n* スーツケース sūtsu kēsu
suite *n* スーツ sūtsu
summer *n* 夏 natsu
sun *n* 太陽 taiyō
sunburn *n* 日焼け hiyake
I have a bad sunburn. 私はひどく日焼けしました。watashi wa hidoku hiyake shimashita.
Sunday *n* 日曜日 nichi yō bi
sunglasses *n* サングラス sangurasu

sunny *adj* 晴れた hareta

It's sunny out. 外は晴れています。soto wa harete imasu.

sunroof *n* サンルーフ san rūfu

sunscreen *n* 日焼け止めクリーム hiyake dome kurīmu

Do you have sunscreen SPF ____? SPF ___の日焼け止めクリームはありますか? SPF ___ no hiyake dome kurīmu wa arimasu ka. **See numbers p6.**

supermarket *n* スーパーマーケット sūpā māketto

surf *v* サーフィンする sāfin suru

surfboard *n* サーフボード sāfu bōdo

suspiciously *adv* 怪しそうに ayashisō ni / 様子が変 yōsu ga hen

swallow, to swallow *v* 飲み込む nomi komu

sweater *n* セーター sētā

swim, to swim *v* 泳ぐ oyogu

Can one swim here? ここでは泳げますか? koko dewa oyoge masu ka.

swimsuit *n* 水着 mizugi

swim trunks *n* 水泳パンツ suiei pantsu

symphony *n* 交響楽団 kōkyō gakudan

T

table *n* テーブル tēburu

table for two 2人用のテーブル futari yō no tēburu

tailor *n* 仕立て屋 shitate ya

Can you recommend a good tailor? よい仕立て屋を勧めていただけませんか?yoi shitate ya o susumete itadake masen ka.

take, to take *v* 連れて行く tsureteiku

Take me to the station. 駅まで連れて行ってください。eki made tsurete itte kudasai.

How much to take me to ____? ____まで行くにはいくらかかりますか? ____ made iku niwa ikura kakari masu ka

takeout menu *n* 持帰り用のメニュー mochi kaeri yō no menyū

talk, to talk *v* 話す hanasu

tall *adj* 高い takai / 背が高い se ga takai

tanned *adj* 日焼けした hiyake shita

taste (flavor) *n* 味 aji

taste *n* **(discernment)** 好み konomi

taste, to taste *v* 味見する ajimi suru

tax *n* 税金 zeikin

value-added tax (VAT) 付加価値税 fuka kachi zei

taxi *n* タクシー takushī

Taxi! タクシー! takushī.

Would you call me a taxi? タクシーを呼んでいただけませんか? takushī o yonde itadake masen ka.

tea *n* お茶 ocha / 茶 cha

team *n* チーム chīmu

Techno *n* テクノ tekuno
television *n* テレビ terebi
temple *n* 寺院 jiin
ten *adj* 十の jū no
tennis *n* テニス tenisu
tennis court テニスコート tenisu kōto
tent *n* テント tento
tenth *adj* 十番目の jū ban me no
terminal *n* **(airport)** ターミナル tāminaru
Thank you. どうもありがとう。 dōmo arigatō
that (near) *adj* その sono
that (far away) *adj* あの ano
theater *n* 劇場 gekijō
them (m/f) 彼ら(に、を) karera (ni, o)
there (demonstrative) *adv* そこに soko ni **(nearby),** あそこに asoko ni **(far)**
Is / Are there ? ありますか? arimasu ka.
over there あそこに asoko ni
these *adj* これらの korera no
thick *adj* 厚い atsui
thin *adj* 薄い usui
third *adj* 3番目の san banme no
thirteen *adj* 十三の jū san no
thirty *adj* 三十の sanjū no
this *adj* この kono
those *adj* それらの sorerano
thousand 千 sen
three 三 san
Thursday *n* 木曜日 moku yō bi
ticket *n* 切符 kippu / チケット chiketto
ticket counter 切符売り場 kippu uriba / チケットカウンター chiketto kauntā
one-way ticket 片道切符 katamichi kippu
round-trip ticket 往復切符 ōfuku kippu
tight *adj* きつい kitsui
time *n* 時間 jikan
Is it on time? それは定刻通りですか? sore wa teikoku dōri desu ka.
At what time? 何時に? nan ji ni.
What time is it? 何時ですか? nan ji desu ka.
timetable *n* **(train)** 時刻表 jikoku hyō
tip (gratuity) チップ chippu
tire *n* タイヤ taiya
I have a flat tire. タイヤがパンクしました。 taiya ga panku shima shita.
tired *adj* 疲れた tsukareta/ 疲れている tsukarete iru
today *n* 今日 kyō
toilet *n* トイレ toire
The toilet is overflowing. トイレの水が溢れているんです。 toire no mizu ga afurete irun desu.
The toilet is backed up. トイレがつまっています。 toire ga tsumatte imasu.
toilet paper *n* トイレットペーパー toiretto pēpā

You're out of toilet paper. トイレット ペーパーがなくなりました。toiretto pēpā ga naku nari mashita.

toiletries *n* 洗面用品 senmen yōhin

toll *n* 使用料 shiyōryō

tomorrow *n* 明日 ashita

ton *n* トン ton

too (excessively) *adv* ～過ぎる ～sugiru

too (also) *adv* ～も ～mo

tooth *n* 歯 ha

I lost my tooth. 歯が 1 本抜けました。ha ga ippon nuke mashita.

toothache *n* 歯痛 haita

I have a toothache. 歯が痛みます。ha ga itami masu.

total *n* 合計 gōkei

What is the total? 合計でいくらですか? gōkei de ikura desu ka.

tour *n* ツアー tsuā

Are guided tours available? ガイド付きツアーはありますか? gaido tsuki tsuā wa arimasu ka.

Are audio tours available? 音声ガイド付きツアーはありますか? onsei gaido tsuki tsuā wa arimasu ka.

towel *n* タオル taoru

May we have more towels? もっとタオルをいただけますか? motto taoru o itadake masu ka.

toy *n* おもちゃ omocha

toy store *n* おもちゃ屋 omocha ya

Do you have any toys for the children? 子供のおもちゃはありますか? kodomo no omocha wa arimasu ka.

traffic *n* 交通 kōtsū

How's traffic? 交通状態はどうですか? kōtsū jōtai wa dō desu ka.

traffic rules 交通規則 kōtsū kisoku

trail *n* 登山道 tozan dō / トレイル toreiru

Are there trails? 登山道はありますか? tozan dō wa arimasuka.

train *n* 列車 ressha / 電車 densha

express train 特急列車 tokkyū ressha

local train 普通列車 futsū ressha

Does the train go to ____? この電車は______へ行きますか? kono densha wa ______ e ikimasu ka.

May I have a train schedule? 電車の時刻表をいただけますか? densha no jikokuhyō o itadake masu ka.

Where is the train station? 駅はどこにありますか? eki wa doko ni arimasuka.

train, to train *v* 訓練する kunren suru

transfer, to transfer *v* 移す utsusu

I need to transfer funds. 振込したいのですが。furikomi shitai no desuga.

transmission *n* 変速機 hensoku ki

automatic transmission オートマチック ōto machikku

standard transmission マニュアル manyuaru

travel, to travel *v* 旅行する ryokō suru

travelers' check *n* トラベラーズチェック toraberāzu chekku

Do you cash travelers' checks? トラベラーズチェックを現金に交換できますか？ toraberāzu chekku o genkin ni kōkan deki masu ka.

trim, to trim (hair) *v* 切りそろえる kiri soroeru / そろえる soroeru

trip *n* 旅行 ryokō

triple *adj* 3 倍の san bai no ***adj*** triple

trumpet *n* トランペット tranpetto

trunk *n* 旅行カバン ryokō kaban **(luggage)** , トランク toranku **(in car)**

try, to try (attempt) *v* 試す tamesu

try, to try on (clothing) *v* 試着する shichaku suru

try, to try (food) *v* 試食する shishoku suru

Tuesday *n* 火曜日 ka yō bi

turkey *n* 七面鳥 shichimenchō

turn, to turn *v* 曲がる magaru

to turn left / right 左 / 右に曲がる hidari / migi ni magaru

to turn off / on 消す / 付ける kesu / tsukeru

twelve *adj* 十二の jūni no

twenty *adj* 二十の nijū no

twine *n* 麻ひも asa himo / ひも himo

two *adj* 二つの futatsu no

U

umbrella *n* 傘 kasa ***f***

uncle *n* おじ oji / おじさん ojisan

undercooked *adj* 完全に煮えていない kanzen ni niete iai

understand, to understand *v* 理解する rikai suru

I don't understand. わかりません。wakari masen.

Do you understand? わかりますか？wakari masu ka.

underwear *n* 下着 shitagi

university *n* 大学 daigaku

up *adv* 上に ue ni

update, to update *v* 更新する kōshin suru

upgrade *n* アップグレード appugurēdo

upload, to upload *v* アップロードする appurōdo suru

upscale *adj* 高級な kōkyūna

Uruguayan *adj* ウルグアイの、ウルグアイ人の uruguai no, uruguai jin no

us *pron* 私達(に、を) watashi tachi (ni, o)

USB port *n* USB ポート USB pōto

use, to use *v* 使う tsukau

V

vacation *n* バケーション bakēshon / 休暇 kyūka

on vacation 休暇で kyūka de

to go on vacation バケーションに出かける bakēshon ni dekakeru

vacancy *n* 空き室 aki shitsu

van *n* バン ban

VCR *n* ビデオデッキ bideo dekki

Do the rooms have VCRs? 部屋にはビデオデッキが置いてありますか? heya niwa bideo dekki ga oite arimasu ka.

vegetable *n* 野菜 yasai

vegetarian *n* ベジタリアン bejitarian

vending machine *n* 自動販売機 jidō hanbai ki

Venezuelan *adj* ベネズエラの、ベネズエラ人の benezuera no, benezuera jin no

version *n* バージョン bājon

very とても totemo

video *n* ビデオ bideo

Where can I rent videos or DVDs? DVD またはビデオはどこで借りられますか? DVD matawa bideo wa doko de karirare masu ka.

view *n* 眺め nagame

beach view ビーチの眺め bīchi no nagame

city view 市街の眺め shigai no nagame

vineyard *n* ぶどう園 budō en

vinyl *n* ビニール binīru

violin *n* バイオリン baiorin

visa *n* ビザ biza

Do I need a visa? ビザが必要ですか? biza ga hitsuyō desu ka.

vision *n* 視力 shiryoku

visit, to visit *v* 訪ねる tazuneru

visually-impaired *adj* 視覚障害の shikaku shōgai no

vodka *n* ウオッカ uokka

voucher *n* 利用券 riyōken

W

wait, to wait *v* 待つ matsu

Please wait. どうかお待ちください。dōka omachi kudasai.

How long is the wait? どのくらい待ちますか? dono kurai machi masu ka.

waiter *n* ウエイター ueitā

waiting area *n* 待合室 machiai shitu

wake-up call *n* ウェークアップコール ueku appu kōru

wallet *n* 財布 saifu

I lost my wallet. 私は財布を失くしました。watashi wa saifu o nakushi mashita.

Someone stole my wallet. 誰かに財布を盗まれました。dareka ni saifu o nusumare mashita.

walk, to walk *v* 歩く aruku
walker (ambulatory device) *n* 歩行器 hokōki
walkway *n* 歩道 hodō
moving walkway 自動移動通路 jidō idō tsūro
want, to want *v* ～欲しい～ hoshii
war *n* 戦争 sensō
warm *adj* 暖かい atatakai
watch, to watch *v* 観察する kansatsu suru
water *n* 水 mizu
Is the water potable? この水は飲めますか? kono mizu wa nome masu ka.
Is there running water? ここに水道水はありますか? koko ni suidōsui wa arimasu ka.
wave, to wave *v* 振る furu
waxing *n* ワックス wakkusu
weapon *n* 武器 buki
wear, to wear *v* 着る kiru
weather forecast *n* 天気予報 tenki yohō
Wednesday *n* 水曜日 sui yō bi
week *n* 週 shū
this week 今週 konshū
last week 先週 senshū
next week 来週 raishū
weigh *v* 重い omoi
I weigh ____. 私は体重が____あります。watashi wa taijyū ga ____ arimasu.
It weighs ____. これは____の重さがあります。kore wa ____ no omosa ga arimasu. **See p6 for numbers.**
weights *n* 重さ omosa
welcome *adv* ようこそ yōkoso
You're welcome. どういたしまして。dō itashi mashite.
well *adv* よく yoku
well done (meat) ウェル ダン weru dan
well done (task) よくやった yoku yatta
I don't feel well. 気分がよくありません。kibun ga yoku arimasen.
western *adj* ウェスタンの uesutan no
whale *n* 鯨 kujira
what *adv* 何の nan no / 何 nani
What sort of ____? どんな種類の____? donna shurui no ____.
What time is ____? ____は何時? ____ wa nan ji.
wheelchair *n* 車椅子 kuruma isu
wheelchair access 車椅子でのアクセス kurumaisu deno akusesu

wheelchair ramp 車椅子用スロープ kuruma isu yō surōpu
power wheelchair 電動車椅子 dendō kuruma isu
wheeled (luggage) *adj* 車輪付き sharin tsuki
when *adv* いつ itsu
See p112 for questions.
where *adv* どこ doko
Where is it? それはどこにありますか? sore wa doko ni arimasu ka.
which *adv* どれ dore
Which one? どっち? docchi
white *adj* 白い shiroi
who *adv* 誰 dare
whose *adj* 誰の dare no
wide *adj* 広い hiroi
widow, widower *n* 未亡人 mibō jin やもめ, yamome
wife *n* 妻 tsuma / 奥さん okusan
wi-fi *n* ワイファイ wai fai
window *n* 窓 mado
windshield *n* フロントガラス furonto garasu
windshield wiper *n* ワイパー waipā
windy *adj* 風が強い kaze ga tsuyoi
wine *n* ワイン wain
winter *n* 冬 fuyu
wiper *n* ワイパー waipā
with *prep* ～と一緒に ～to issho ni
withdraw *v* 引く hiku
I need to withdraw money. お金を引き出したいのですが。okane o hiki dashi tai no desuga.
without *prep* ～なしで ～nashi de
woman *n* 女性 josei
work, to work *v* 機能する kinō suru
This doesn't work. これは機能しません。kore wa kinō shimasen.
workout *n* ワークアウト wāku auto
worse ～よりも悪い ～yori mo warui
worst 最悪 sai aku
write, to write *v* 書く kaku
Would you write that down for me? 紙に書いていただけますか? kami ni kaite itadake masu ka.
writer *n* 作家 sakka

X

x-ray machine *n* レントゲン rentogen

ENGLISH—JAPANESE

Y

yellow *adj* 黄色い kiiroi

Yes. *adv* はい。hai.

yesterday *n* 昨日 kinō

the day before yesterday おととい ototoi

yield sign *n* 優先標識 yūsen hyōshiki

you *pron* あなた、あなた達 anata, anata tachi

your, yours *adj* あなたの、あなた達の anata no, anata tachi no

young *adj* 若い wakai

Z

zoo *n* 動物園 dōbutsu en

A

abura 油 *oil n*
adaputā puragu アダプター プラグ *adapter plug n*
afurete あふれて *overflowing adv*
afurika kei amerika jin no アフリカ系アメリカ人の *African-American adj*
ageru あげる *give, to give v*
ahiru アヒル *duck n*
ai suru 愛する *love, to love v*

> ai suru 愛する *to love (family)*
> ai suru 愛する *to love (a friend)*
> ai suru 愛する *to love (a lover)*

ai 愛 *love n*
airurando no, airurando jin no アイルランドの、アイルランド人の *Irish adj*
airurando アイルランド *Ireland n*
aji 味 *taste (flavor) n*
ajia no, ajia jin no アジアの、アジア人の *Asian adj*
ajimi suru 味見する *taste, to taste v*
aka chan no 赤ちゃんの *baby adj*

> bebī fūdo wa utte imasu ka. ベビー フードは売っていますか? *Do you sell baby food?*

aka chan 赤ちゃん/bebī ベビー baby *n*
aka no 赤の *red adj*
akage 赤毛 *redhead n*
akarui 明るい *bright adj*
aki shitsu 空き室 *vacancy n*
aki 秋 *autumn n*
aki 秋 *fall (season) n*
akiraka ni suru 明らかにする *clear v*
ame ga furu 雨が降る *rain, to rain v*

> ame ga furu yotei desuka. 雨が降る予定ですか? *Is it supposed to rain?*

ame no 雨の *rainy adj*

> ame desu. 雨です。*It's rainy.*

amerika no, amerika jin no アメリカの、アメリカ人の *American adj*
an nai jo 案内所 *information booth n*
an nai suru 案内する *guide, to guide v*
anata no, anata tachi no あなたの、あなた達の *your, yours adj*
anata, anata tachi あなた、あなた達 *you pron*
anda kami 編んだ髪 *braid n*
ano あの *that (far away) adj*
anzen na 安全な *safe (secure) adj*

> kono chiiki wa anzen desu ka. この地域は安全ですか? *Is this area safe?*

ao jiroi 青白い *pale adj*
aoi 青い *blue adj*
appugurēdo アップグレード *upgrade n* p47
appurōdo suru アップロードする *upload, to upload v*
are *v See* **be, to be.**

arerugī han nō no アレルギー体質の / アレルギー反応の *allergic adj*

watashi wa _____ ni arerugī ga arimasu. 私は_____にアレルギーがあります。*I'm allergic to _____.* See p78 and 167 for common allergens.

arukōru アルコール *alcohol n*

arukōru wa dashite imasu ka. アルコールは出していますか? *Do you serve alcohol?*

arukōru nuki no bīru o kudasai. アルコール抜きのビールをください。*I'd like nonalcoholic beer.*

aruku 歩く *walk, to walk v*

aruminiumu アルミニウム *aluminum n*

aruzenchin no, aruzenchin jin no アルゼンチンの、アルゼンチン人の *Argentinian adj*

asa himo 麻ひも / himo ひも *twine n*

asa 朝 / gozen 午前 *morning n*

gozen 午前 *in the morning*

asai 浅い *shallow adj*

ashi 脚 *leg n*

ashi, futto 足、フット *foot (body part, measurement) n*

ashita 明日 *tomorrow n*

asobi ba 遊び場 *playground n*

asobi ba wa arimasu ka. 遊び場はありますか? *Do you have a playground?*

asupirin アスピリン *aspirin n*

atarashii 新しい *new adj*

atatakai 暖かい *warm adj*

ATM ki ATM 機 *ATM n*

ATM ki o sagashite imasu. ATM 機を探しています。*I'm looking for an ATM.*

ato de あとで *later adv*

soreja, mata ato de. それじゃ、また後で。*See you later.*

atsui 厚い *thick adj*

atsui 熱い *hot adj*

atsukau 扱う *handle, to handle v*

atsumeru 集める *collect, to collect v*

ayashisō ni 怪しそうに / yōsu ga hen 様子が変 *suspiciously adv* p44

B

bā バー *bar n*

baikingu バイキング *buffet n*

baiku バイク *motorcycle n*

baiorin バイオリン *violin n*

bājon バージョン *version n*

bakēshon / 休暇 kyūka バケーション *vacation n*

kyūka de 休暇で *on vacation*

bakēshon ni dekakeru バケーションに出かける *to go on vacation*

bakkin 罰金 *fine (for traffic violation) n*

bakudan 爆弾 *bomb n*

ban バン *van n*

bangō annai 番号案内 *directory assistance (phone) n*

bara バラ *rose n*
baransu o toru バランスを取る *balance v*
barukonī バルコニー *balcony n*
basu バス *bass (instrument) n*
basu バス *bus n*

basu tei wa doko ni arimasu ka. バス停はどこにありますか? *Where is the bus stop?*
____ yuki no basu wa dore desu ka. ____行きのバスはどれですか。*Which bus goes to ____?*

batā バター *butter n*
batterī バッテリー *battery (for car) n*
be, to be (permanent quality) v
bebī beddo ベビーベッド *crib n*
bebī kā ベビーカー *stroller n*

bebī kā wa rentaru deki masu ka. ベビーカーはレンタルできますか? *Do you rent baby strollers?*

bebī shittā ベビーシッター *babysitter n*

eigo o hanasu bebī shittā wa imasu ka. 英語を話すベビーシッターはいますか? *Do you have babysitters who speak English?*

beddo ベッド *bed n*
bejitarian ベジタリアン *vegetarian n*
benezuera no, benezuera jin no ベネズエラの、ベネズエラ人の *Venezuelan adj*
bengo shi 弁護士 *lawyer n*
benpi shita 便秘した *constipated adj*

benpi shite imasu. 便秘しています。*I'm constipated.*

berī weru de ベリーウェルで *charred (meat) adj*
beruto ベルト *belt n*

beruto konbeyā ベルトコンベヤー *conveyor belt*

betsu no 別の *another adj*
bīchi ni noriageru ビーチに乗り上げる *beach v*
bīchi ビーチ *beach n*
bideo dekki ビデオデッキ *VCR n*

heya niwa bideo dekki ga oite arimasu ka. 部屋にはビデオデッキが置いてありますか? *Do the rooms have VCRs?*

bideo ビデオ *video n*

DVD matawa bideo wa doko de karirare masu ka. DVDまたはビデオはどこで借りられますか? *Where can I rent videos or DVDs?*

bijinesu ビジネス *business n*
bijutsu ka 美術家 *artist n*
bijutsu kan 美術館 *art museum*
bijutsu kan 美術館 *museum n*
bin ビン *bottle n*

dokoka de kono bin o atatameru koto ga deki masu ka. どこかでこのビンを温めることができますか? *May I heat this (baby) bottle someplace?*

binīru ビニール *vinyl n*

biriyādo ビリヤード *pool (the game) n*
bīru ビール *beer n*
 nama bīru 生ビール *beer on tap*
biza ビザ *visa n*
 biza ga hitsuyō desu ka. ビザが必要ですか? *Do I need a visa?*
bōi furendo ボーイフレンド *boyfriend n*
bokkusu seki ボックス席 / **bokkusu sīto** ボックスシート *box (seat) n*
boribia no, boribia jin no ボリビアの、ボリビア人の *Bolivian adj*
bōru ボール *ball (sport) n*
bōshi 帽子 *hat n*
bōto ボート *boat n*
boyaketa ぼやけた *blurry adj*
bubun 部分 *portion n*
budō en ぶどう園 *vineyard n*
budō ぶどう *grape n*
bujoku suru 侮辱する *insult v*
buki 武器 *weapon n*
bukkyōto 仏教徒 *Buddhist n*
burandē ブランデー *brandy n*
burausu ブラウス *blouse n*
burēki o kakeru ブレーキをかける *brake v*
burēki ブレーキ *brake n*
 hijō burēki 非常ブレーキ *emergency brake*
burīchi ブリーチ *bleach n*
burīfu kēsu ブリーフケース *briefcase n*
burōdo bando ブロードバンド *broadband n*
buronzu sei no ブロンズ製の *bronze adj*
burunetto ブルネット *brunette n*
byōki no 病気の *sick adj*
 kibun ga warui desu. 気分が悪いです。*I feel sick.*

C

CD *CD n*
CD purēyā CDプレーヤー *CD player n*
cha iro no 茶色の *brown adj*
chairudo shīto チャイルドシート *car seat (child's safety seat) n*
 chairudo shīto o rentaru shite imasu ka. チャイルドシートをレンタルしていますか? *Do you rent car seats for children?*
chakuriku suru 着陸する / **tsuku** 着く *land, to land v*
chātā suru チャーターする *charter, to charter v*
chekku auto suru チェックアウトする *check out, to check out v*
chekku auto チェックアウト *check-out n*
 chekku auto no jikan チェックアウトの時間 *check-out time*
 chekku auto wa nan ji desu ka. チェックアウトは何時ですか? *What time is check-out?*
chekku in チェックイン *check-in n*
 chekku in wa nan ji desu ka. チェックインは何時ですか? *What time is check-in?*

chekku no チェックの *checked (pattern) adj*
chichi 父 / otōsan お父さん *father n*
chihō no 地方の *local adj*
chiisai 小さい *little adj* (size) sukoshi、少し *(amount)*
chiisai 小さい *small adj*
chikai 近い *close (near)*
chikai 近い *near adj*
chikaku ni 近くに *nearby adj*
chikatetsu 地下鉄 *subway n*

chikatetsu no rosen 地下鉄の路線 *subway line*
chikatetsu no eki 地下鉄の駅 *subway station*
____ ewa dono chikatetsu de ikeba yoi desu ka. ____へはどの地下鉄で行けばよいですか? *Which subway do I take for ____?*

chiketto uriba チケット売り場 *box office n*
chikin チキン *chicken n*
chīmu チーム *team n*
chippu チップ *tip (gratuity)*
chīzu チーズ *cheese n*
chizu 地図 *map n*
chōkaku shōgai no 聴覚障害の *hearing-impaired adj*
chōkoku 彫刻 *sculpture n*
chōshoku 朝食 *breakfast n*

chōshoku wa nan ji desu ka. 朝食は何時ですか? *What time is breakfast?*

chōwa suru 調和する *match, to match v*

kono ____ wa watashi no fuku to aimasu ka? この____は私の服と合いますか *Does this ____ match my outfit?*

chūgoku no, chūgoku jin no 中国の、中国人の *Chinese adj*
chūishite atsukau 注意して扱う *Handle with care adj*
chūkan no 中間の *middle adj*
chūmon suru 注文する *order, to order (demand) v*
chūsha suru 駐車する *park, to park v*

chūsha kinshi 駐車禁止 *no parking*
chūsha ryōkin 駐車料金 *parking fee*
shako 車庫 *parking garage*

chūshoku 昼食 / ranchi ランチ *lunch n*

D

daburu no ダブルの *double adj*

daburu beddo ダブル ベッド *double bed*
nijū eizō 二重映像 *double vision*

daigaku 大学 *college n*
daigaku 大学 *university n*
daigeki jō 大劇場 *coliseum n*
daku 抱く *hold, to hold v*

te o nigiru 手を握る *to hold hands*
kore o motte itadake masen ka. これを持っていただけませんか? *Would you hold this for me?*

dansei no 男性の *male adj*

dansei 男性 *male n*
dantai 団体 *party n*
dare ka 誰か *someone n*
dare no 誰の *whose adj*
dare 誰 *who adv*
dāsu ダース *dozen n*
dasu 出す *serve, to serve v*
daunrōdo suru ダウンロードする *download v*
de aru である
de aru である *be, to be (temporary state, condition, mood) v*
de nai でない *no adv*
deguchi 出口 *exit n*
deguchi nashi 出口なし *not an exit*
dekiru できる *able, to be able to (can) v*
dekiru できる *can (able to) v*
denchi 電池 *battery (for flashlight) n*
denki setsuzoku bu 電気接続部 *electrical hookup n*
denki 伝記 *biography n*
denwa no 電話の *phone adj*
denwa chō wa arimasu ka. 電話帳はありますか? *Do you have a phone directory?*
denwa o kakeru 電話をかける yaru suru / ダイヤル dai *dial (a phone) v*
chokutsū bangō ni kakeru 直通番号にかける *dial direct*
denwa 電話 *phone call n*
korekuto kōru o shitai no desuga. コレクトコールをしたいのですが。 *I need to make a collect phone call.*
kokusai denwa 国際電話 *an international phone call*
denwa 電話 *phone n*
anata no denwa bangō o oshiete itadake masu ka. あなたの電話番号を教えていただけますか? *May I have your phone number?*
kōshū denwa wa doko ni arimasu ka. 公衆電話はどこにありますか? *Where can I find a public phone?*
denwa operētā 電話オペレーター *phone operator*
puripeido denwa o utte imasu ka. プリペイド電話を売っていますか? *Do you sell prepaid phones?*
deru 出る *exit v*
dezainā デザイナー *designer n*
dezāto デザート *dessert n*
dezāto no menyū デザートのメニュー *dessert menu*
disuco ディスコ *disco n*
do yō bi 土曜日 *Saturday n*
doa ドア *door n*
dōbutsu en 動物園 *zoo n*
dōbutsu 動物 *animal n*
dōbutsu 動物 *animal n*
bijutsu hin no tenji 美術品の展示 *exhibit of art*
doitsu no, doitsu jin no ドイツの、ドイツ人の *German adj*

doko demo どこへも *anywhere adv*

doko どこ *where adv*

> sore wa doko ni arimasu ka. それはどこにありますか? *Where is it?*

dokushin no 独身の *single (unmarried) adj*

> anata wa dokushin desu ka? あなたは独身ですか? *Are you single?*

dōmo arigatō どうもありがとう。 *Thank you.*

dorai kurīnā ドライ クリーナー *dry cleaner n*

dorai kurīningu ドライ クリーニング *dry cleaning n*

doramu ドラム *drum n*

dore どれ *which adv*

> docchi どっち? *Which one?*

doressingu ドレッシング *dressing (salad) n*

doresu ドレス *dress (garment) n*

dōro heisa chū 道路閉鎖中 *road closed sign n*

dōro 道路 *road n*

doru ドル *dollar n*

dōsei no 銅製の *copper adj*

dōzo どうぞ *please (polite entreaty) adv*

DVD *DVD n*

> sono heya niwa DVD purēyā ga arimasu ka. その部屋にはDVD プレーヤーがありますか? *Do the rooms have DVD players?*
>
> DVD matawa bideo wa doko de karirare masu ka. DVD またはビデオはどこで借りられますか? *Where can I rent DVDs or videos?*

E

E mēru Eメール *e-mail n*

> anata no E mēru adoresu o itadake masu ka. あなたのEメールアドレスをいただけますか? *May I have your e-mail address?*
>
> ii mēru messēji Eメール メッセージ *e-mail message*

e 絵 *drawing (work of art) n*

e 絵 *painting n*

ebi 海老 *shrimp n*

eiga kan 映画館 *cinema n*

eiga 映画 *movie n*

eigyō chū 営業中 *open (business) adj*

> eigyō shite imasu ka. 営業していますか? *Are you open?*

eisei 衛星 *satellite n*

> eisei rajio 衛星ラジオ *satellite radio*
>
> eisei tsuiseki 衛星追跡 *satellite tracking*

eki 駅 / teisha eki 停車駅 *stop n*

> koko wa watashi ga oriru eki desu ka. ここは私が降りる駅ですか? *Is this my stop?*
>
> watashi wa nori sugoshite shimai mashita. 私は乗り過ごしてしまいました。 *I missed my stop.*

eki 駅 *station n*

koko kara ichiban chikai _____ wa doko desu ka. ここから一番近い_____はどこですか? *Where is the nearest_____?*
gasorin sutando ガソリン スタンド *gas station*
basu tei バス停 *bus station*
chikatetsu no eki 地下鉄の駅 *subway station*
eki 駅 *train station*

ekonomī エコノミー *economy n*
ekuadoru no, ekuadoru jin no エクアドルの、エクアドル人の *Ecuadorian adj*
enjin エンジン *engine n*
enjinia エンジニア *engineer n*
enseki 縁石 *curb n*
ensō suru 演奏する / hiku 弾く *play, to play (an instrument) v*
ensō 演奏 *band (musical ensemble) n*
erebētā エレベーター *elevator n*
esa えさ *bait n*
esukarētā エスカレーター *escalator n*
esupuresso エスプレッソ *espresso n*

F

fakkusu ファックス *fax n*
fittonesu sentā フィットネス センター / jimu ジム *fitness center n*
fujinka i 婦人科医 *gynecologist n*
fukachiron no 不可知論の *agnostic adj*
fukai 深い *deep adj*
fukuro ni ireru 袋に入れる *bag v*
fukuro 袋 *bag n*

hikōki yoi no fukuro 飛行機酔いの袋 *airsickness bag*
watashi no baggu ga nusumare mashita. 私のバックが盗まれました。*My bag was stolen.*
watashi wa baggu o nakushi mashita. 私はバックを失くしました。*I lost my bag.*

fukusō 服装 *dress (general attire) n*

fukusō no kisoku wa nan desu ka. 服装の規則は何ですか? *What's the dress code?*

fun 分 *minute n*

sugu ni すぐに *in a minute*

funa yoi ni kiku kusuri 船酔いに効く薬 *seasickness pill n*
funa yoi 船酔い *seasick adj*

funa yoi shimashita. 船酔いしました。*I am seasick.*

fune de hakobu 船で運ぶ *ship, to ship v*

kore o ____ made fune de okuru niwa ikura kakari masu ka? これを____まで船で送るにはいくらかかりますか? *How much to ship this to ____?*

fune 船 *ship n*
furaito フライト / ___bin __便 *flight n*

kokunai sen no shuppatsu / tōchaku basho wa doko desu ka. 国内線の出発/到着場所はどこですか? *Where do domestic flights arrive / depart?*

kokusai sen no shuppatsu / tōchaku basho wa doko desu ka. 国際線の出発 / 到着場所はどこですか? *Where do international flights arrive / depart?*

kono furaito wa nan ji ni shuppatsu shimasu ka. このフライトは何時に出発しますか? *What time does this flight leave?*

furansu no, furansu jin no フランスの、フランス人の *French adj*

furasshu フラッシュ *flush (gambling)* n

furikomi 振り込み *money transfer*

furonto garasu フロントガラス *windshield n*

furu hausu. フル ハウス! *Full house! n*

furu 振る *wave, to wave v*

furui 古い / sai no __歳の _ *old adj*

furumau 振る舞う *behave v*

furūto フルート *flute n*

furūtsu jūsu フルーツ ジュース *fruit juice n*

futatsu no 二つの *two adj*

fūtō 封筒 *envelope n*

futotta 太った *fat adj*

fuyu 冬 *winter n*

G

gādo ガード *guard n*

gaido bukku ガイドブック *guide (publication) n*

gaido tsuki tuā ガイド付きツアー *guided tour n*

gaido ガイド *guide (of tours) n*

gakkō 学校 *school n*

gakunen 学年 *grade (school) n*

garon ガロン *gallon n*

gāru furendo ガールフレンド *girlfriend n*

gasorin ガソリン *gas n*

nenryō kei 燃料計 *gas gauge*

gasorin ga haitte inai ガソリンが入っていない *out of gas*

geijutsu no 芸術の *art adj*

geki no kyakuhon 劇の脚本 *drama n*

gekijō 劇場 *theater n*

gengo 言語 *language n*

genki na 元気な *fine*

watashi wa genki desu. 私は元気です。*I'm fine.*

genkin ni kaeru 現金に換える *cash, to cash v*

seisan suru 清算する *to cash out (gambling)*

genkin 現金 *cash n*

genkin nomi 現金のみ *cash only*

geri 下痢 *diarrhea n*

gēto ゲート *gate (at airport) n*

getsu yō bi 月曜日 *Monday n*

gin sei no 銀製の *silver adj*

ginkō 銀行 *bank n*

ginkō wa doko ni aruka oshiete itadake masu ka. 銀行はどこにあるか教えていただけますか? *Can you help me find a bank?*

girisha no, girisha jin no ギリシャの、ギリシャ人の *Greek adj*

girisha seikyō no ギリシャ正教の *Greek Orthodox adj*

gishi 義歯 *denture n*

gishi 義歯 *denture plate*

gitā ギター *guitar n*

go banme no 五番目の *fifth adj*

go gatsu 五月 *May (month) n*

gogo 午後 *afternoon n*

gogo ni 午後に *in the afternoon*

gojū no 五十の *fifty adj*

gōkei 合計 *total n*

合計でいくらですか? gōkei de ikura desu ka. *What is the total?*

gōru kīpā ゴールキーパー *goalie n*

gōru ゴール *goal (sport) n*

gorufu o suru ゴルフをする *golf, to go golfing v*

gorufu renshū jō ゴルフ練習場 *driving range n*

gorufu ゴルフ *golf n*

guatemara no, guatemara jin no グアテマラの、グアテマラ人の *Guatemalan adj*

gun 軍 *military n*

guramu グラム *gram n*

gurasu グラス *glass n*

gurasu de arimasuka. グラスでありますか? *Do you have it by the glass?*

gurasu de hitotsu onegai shimasu. グラスで一つお願いします。*I'd like a glass please.*

gurūpu グループ *group n* p152

gutai teki ni noberu 具体的に述べる *specify, to specify v*

gyūnyū 牛乳 / miruku ミルク *milk n*

miruku sēki ミルクセーキ *milk shake*

H

ha ni kabusete iru mono 歯にかぶせているもの *crown (dental) n*

ha 歯 *tooth n*

ha ga ippon nuke mashita. 歯が 1 本抜けました。*I lost my tooth.*

hābu ハーブ *herb n*

hachi banme no 8 番目の *eighth n*

hachi gatsu 八月 *August n*

hachi jū 八十 *eighty n*

hachi ハチ *bee n*

hachi ni sasare mashita. ハチに刺されました。*I was stung by a bee.*

hachi 八 *eight n*

haha 母 / okāsan お母さん *mother n*

hai iro no 灰色の *gray adj*

hai. はい。*Yes. adv*

haikingu o suru ハイキングをする *hike, to hike v*

hairaito ハイライト *highlights (hair) n*

hairu 入る *enter, to enter v*

shinyū kinshi 進入禁止 *Do not enter.*

haisha 歯医者 *dentist n*

haisui 排水 *drain n*

haita 歯痛 *toothache n*

ha ga itami masu. 歯が痛みます。*I have a toothache.*

hajimaru 始まる *begin v*

hajimaru 始まる *start, to start (commence) v*

hakike 吐き気 *nausea n*

hamaki 葉巻 *cigar n*

han zubon 半ズボン *shorts n*

hana 花 *flower n*

hana 鼻 *nose n*

hanasu 話す *speak, to speak v*

eigo o hanashi masu ka? 英語を話しますか? *Do you speak English?* p2

motto ōkina koe de hanashite kudasai. もっと大きな声で話してください。/ motto ōkina koe de hanashite itadake masen ka. もっと大きな声で話していただけませんか。*Would you speak louder, please?* p2

motto yukkuri hanashite kudasai. もっとゆっくり話してください。/ motto yukkuri hanashite itadake masen ka. もっとゆっくり話していただけませんか。*Would you speak slower, please?*

hanasu 話す *talk, to talk v*

hanbai in 販売員 *salesperson n*

hanbun 半分 *half n*

ni bun no ichi 二分の一 *one-half*

hangā ハンガー *hanger n*

hanka gai 繁華街 *downtown n*

hansamu na ハンサムな *handsome adj*

hareta 晴れた *sunny adj*

soto wa harete imasu. 外は晴れています。*It's sunny out.*

haru 春 *spring (season) n*

hashi 橋 /ha no kyōsei burijji 歯の矯正ブリッジ *bridge (across a river, dental) n*

hashiru 走る *run, to run v*

hassha saseru 発車させる *start, to start (a car) v*

hayai 早い *early adj*

hayai desu. 早いです。*It's early.*

hayai 速い *fast adj*

hazukashii 恥ずかしい *embarrassed adj*

heā doraiyā ヘアードライヤー *hair dryer n*

heā doressā ヘアードレッサー *hairdresser n*

heā katto ヘアーカット *haircut n*

kami no ke o kiri tai no desuga. 髪の毛を切りたいのですが。*I need a haircut.*

katto wa ikura desuka. カットはいくらですか? *How much is a haircut?*

heddo hōn ヘッドホーン *headphones n*

heddo raito ヘッドライト *headlight n*

hekomu へこむ *dent v*

kare / kanojo ga kuruma o hekomase mashita. 彼 / 彼女が車をへこませました。*He / She dented the car.*

hekutāru ヘクタール *hectare n*

henpin suru 返品する *return, to return (something to a store) v*

henshū sha 編集者 *editor n*

hensoku ki 変速機 *transmission n*

ōto machikku オートマチック *automatic transmission*

manyuaru マニュアル *standard transmission*

heya 部屋 *room (hotel) n*

hitori /futari beya 1人 / 2 人部屋 *room for one / two*

rūmu sābisu ルーム サービス *room service*

hi 日 *day n*

ototoi 一おととい *the day before yesterday*

koko nisan nichi ここ2–3日 *these last few days*

hi 火 *light (for cigarette) n*

hi o kashima shō ka. 火を貸しましょうか? *May I offer you a light?* raitā ライター *lighter (cigarette) n*

hibi ware ヒビ割れ *crack (in glass object) n*

hidari no 左の *left adj*

hidari ni 左に *on the left*

hifu 皮膚 *skin n*

hige ひげ *beard n*

hijō burēki 非常ブレーキ *emergency brake n*

hijō deguchi 非常出口 *emergency exit n*

hikōki no jōmuin 飛行機の乗務員 *flight attendant*

hikōki yoi no fukuro 飛行機酔いの袋 *airsickness bag n*

hiku 引く *pull, to pull v*

hiku 引く *withdraw v*

okane o hiki dashi tai no desuga. お金を引き出したいのですが。*I need to withdraw money.*

hikui 低い *low adj*

hinin 避妊 *birth control n*

hinin yaku ga nakunari mashita. 避妊薬がなくなりました。*I'm out of birth control pills.*

motto hinin yaku ga hitsuyō desu. もっと避妊薬が必要です。*I need more birth control pills.*

hinzū kyō no, hinzū jin no ヒンズー教の、ヒンズー人の *Hindu adj*

hippu hoppu ヒップホップ *hip-hop n*

hiroi 広い *wide adj*

hitai 額 *forehead n*

hitotsu no 一つの *one adj*

hitotsu no 一つの *single (one) adj*

shinguru beddo シングル ベッド *single bed*

hiyake dome kurīmu 日焼け止めクリーム *sunscreen n*

SPF ___ no hiyake dome kurīmu wa arimasu ka. SPF ___の日焼け止めクリームはありますか? *Do you have sunscreen SPF ___? See numbers p7.*

hiyake shita 日焼けした *tanned adj*

hiyake 日焼け *sunburn n*

watashi wa hidoku hiyake shimashita. 私はひどく日焼けしました。*I have a bad sunburn.*

hodō 歩道 *sidewalk n*

hodō 歩道 *walkway n*

jidō idō tsūro 自動移動通路 *moving walkway*

hojū 補充 *refill (of prescription) n*

hoken 保険 *insurance n*

hokōki 歩行器 *walker (ambulatory device) n*

hokōsha yō no 歩行者用の *pedestrian adj*

hokuro ほくろ *mole (facial feature) n*

hon ya 本屋 *bookstore n*

hon 本 *book n*

honjurasu no, honjurasu jin no ホンジュラスの、ホンジュラス人の *Honduran adj*

hontō ni 本当に *really adv*

hōritsu 法律 *law n*

hōshi 奉仕 / reihai 礼拝 *services (religious) n*

hoshii ～欲しい ～ *want, to want v*

hoshii 欲しい *need, to need v*

hosuteru ホステル *hostel n*

hoteru ホテル *hotel n*

jimoto no hoteru no ichiran hyō wa arimasu ka. 地元のホテルの一覧表はありますか? *Do you have a list of local hotels?*

hotto chokorēto ホット チョコレート *hot chocolate n*

hyaku 百 *hundred n*

hyōkō 標高 *altitude n*

hyūzu ヒューズ *fuse n*

I

ichi gatsu 一月 *January n*

ie 家 *home n*

igirisu jin, igirisu no, igirisu jin no イギリス(の)、イギリス人(の) *English n, adj*

eigo o hanashi masu ka. 英語を話しますか? *Do you speak English?*

igirisu イギリス *England n*

ii mēru suru Eメールする *e-mail, to send e-mail v*

iin 医院 *doctor's office n*

iku 行く *go, to go v*

ikura いくら *how adv (how much)*, ikutsu いくつ *(how many)*

ikutsukano いくつかの *some adj*

ima 今 *now adv*

inchi インチ *inch n*

insatsu suru 印刷する *print, to print v*
intānetto インターネット *Internet n*
kōsoku intānetto 高速インターネット *High-speed Internet*
intānetto ni setsuzoku deki masu ka. インターネットに接続できますか? *Do you have Internet access?*
intā netto kafe wa doko ni arimasu ka. インターネットカフェはどこにありますか?*Where can I find an Internet café?*
inu 犬 *dog n*
kaigo ken 介護犬 *service dog*
ippai 一杯 *shot (liquor) n*
ippō tsūkō 一方通行 *one way (traffic sign) adj*
iriguchi 入口 *entrance n*
iro o nuru 色をぬる *color v*
iro 色 *color n*
isha 医者 *doctor n*
ishō 衣装 *costume n*
isoide 急ぐ *hurry v*
watashi wa isoide imasu. 私は急いでいます。*I'm in a hurry*
isoide kudasai. 急いでください! *Hurry, please!*
isuramu kyō no イスラム教の *muslim adj*
itai. 痛い! *Ouch!*
itamu 痛む *hurt, to hurt v*
itai desu. 痛い!itai. 痛いです! *Ouch!That hurts!*
itaria no, itaria jin no イタリアの、イタリア人の *Italian adj*
itoko いとこ *cousin n*
itsu いつ *when adv*
See p2 for questions.
itsutsu no 五つの *five adj*
iu 言う *say, to say v*
iwau 祝う *celebrate, to celebrate v*

J

jaguchi 蛇口 *faucet n*
jazu ジャズ *jazz n*
ji 時 *o'clock adv*
ni ji 時 *two o'clock 2*
jidō hanbai ki 自動販売機 *vending machine n*
jiin 寺院 *temple n*
jikan 時間 *hour n*
jikan 時間 *hours (at museum) n*
jikan 時間 *time n*
sore wa teikoku dōri desu ka. それは定刻通りですか? *Is it on time?*
nan ji ni. 何時に? *At what time?*
nan ji desu ka. 何時ですか? *What time is it?*
jiko 事故 *accident n*
jiko ni ai mashita. 事故にあいました。*I've had an accident.*
jikoku hyō 時刻表 *timetable (train) n*
jimaku 字幕 *subtitle n*
jimu ジム *gym n*
jin ジン *gin n*
jinshu no majitta 人種の混じった *biracial adj*
jisho 辞書 *dictionary n*
jissai no 実際の *actual adj*

joggingu o suru ジョギングをする *jog, to run v*
jōhō 情報 *information n*
jōkyaku 乗客 *passenger n*
jōkyō 状況 *state n*
josei no 女性の *female adj*
josei 女性 *woman n*
jōshi 上司 *boss n*
jōtai 状態 *condition n*
yoi/warui jōtai 良い/悪い状態 *in good / bad condition*
jū ban me no 十番目の *tenth adj*
jū gatsu 十月 *October n*
jū hachi 十八 *eighteen n*
jū ichi gatsu 十一月 *November n*
jū ichi 十一 *eleven n*
jū ni gatsu 十二月 *December n*
jū no 十の *ten adj*
jū san no 十三の *thirteen adj*
jūden suru 充電する *charge, to charge (a battery) v*
jūgo no 十五の *fifteen adj*
jūgyō in 従業員 *employee n*
jūkyū no 十九の *nineteen adj*
junbi sareta 準備された *prepared adj*
jūni no 十二の *twelve adj*
junyū suru 授乳する *nurse v*
junyū dekiru basho wa arimasu ka. 授乳できる場所はありますか? *Do you have a place where I can nurse?*
jūroku no 十六の *sixteen adj*
jūshichi no 十七の *seventeen adj*
jushin nin barai no 受信人払いの *collect adj*
korekuto kōru o onegai shimasu. コレクト コールをお願いします。*I'd like to place a collect call.*
jūsho 住所 *address n*
jūsho wa nan desu ka. 住所は何ですか? *What's the address?*
jūsu ジュース *juice n*
jūyon no 十四の / jū shi no 十四の *fourteen adj*

K

ka yō bi 火曜日 *Tuesday n*
kabā chāji カバーチャージ *cover charge (in bar) n*
kādo カード *card n*
kurejitto kādo o tsukae masu ka. クレジットカードを使えますか? *Do you accept credit cards?*
anata no meishi o itadake masu ka. あなたの名刺をいただけますか? *May I have your business card?*
kado 角 /burokku ブロック *block n*
kagi o kakeru 鍵をかける *lock, to lock v*
doa ni kagi o kakeru koto ga dekima sen. ドアに鍵をかけることができません。*I can't lock the door.*
doa ni kagi ga kakatte shimai heya ni hairu koto ga deki masen. ドアに鍵がかかってしまい部屋に入ることができません。*I'm locked out.*

kagi 鍵 *lock n*
kai in 会員 *member n*
kai rui 貝類 *shellfish n*
kai 階 *floor n*
ikkai 1 階 *ground floor*
ni kai 2 階 *second floor*
kaidan 階段 *stair n*
kaidan wa doko desu ka. 階段はどこですか？ *Where are the stairs?*
kaidan no kazu wa ōi desu ka. 階段の数は多いですか？ *Are there many stairs?*
kaimono o suru 買い物をする *shop v*
shinshi fuku o kai ni kimashita. 紳士服を買いに来ました。 *I'm shopping for mens' clothes.*
fujin fuku o kai ni kimashita. 婦人服を買いに来ました。*I'm shopping for womens' clothes.*
kodomo fuku o kai ni kimashita. 子供服を買いに来ました。*I'm shopping for childrens' clothes.*
kairo purakutā カイロプラクター *chiropractor n*
kaisen sokudo 回線速度 *connection speed n*
kaisha 会社 *agency n*
rentakā gaisha レンタ カー会社 *car rental agency*
kaji da. 火事だ! *fire! n*
kajino カジノ *casino n*
kakaku 価格 *price n*
kakari in 係員 *officer n*
kakeru かける *bet, to bet v*
kakin 家禽 *poultry n*
kaku 書く *write, to write v*
kami ni kaite itadake masu ka. 紙に書いていただけますか？ *Would you write that down for me?*
kakunin suru 確認する *confirm, to confirm v*
yoyaku o kakunin shitai no desuga. 予約を確認したいのですが。*I'd like to confirm my reservation.*
kami no ke 髪の毛 *hair n*
kami 紙 *paper n*
kanada no, kanada jin no カナダの、カナダ人の *Canadian adj*
kanada カナダ *Canada n*
kanashii 悲しい *sad adj*
kango shi 看護師 *nurse n*
kankō basu 観光バス *sightseeing bus n*
kankō 観光 *sightseeing n*
kankyō 環境 *environment n*
kanojo no 彼女の *her adj*
kansatsu suru 観察する *watch, to watch v*
kansō shita 乾燥した *dried adj*
kantorī ando wesutan カントリーアンドウェスタン *country-and-western n*
kanzen ni niete iai 完全に煮えていない *undercooked adj*
kanzume 缶詰 *can n*
kao 顔 *face n*

kapuchīno カプチーノ *cappuccino n*

kara tsuku rareta から作られた *made of adj*

kare no 彼の *his adj*

kare o 彼を *him pron*

karera (ni, o) 彼ら（に、を） *them (m/f)*

kariru 借りる *rent, to rent v*

> kuruma o karitai no desuga. 車を借りたいのですが。*I'd like to rent a car.*

kāru shita カールした *curly adj*

kāru カール *curl n*

kasa 傘 *umbrella n*

kashimiya カシミヤ *cashmere n*

katorikku kyō no カトリック教の *Catholic adj*

kau 買う *buy, to buy v*

kauntā カウンター *counter (in bar) n*

kawa 川 *river n*

kawa 皮 *leather n*

kawaita 乾いた *dry*

> kono taoru wa kawaite imasen. このタオルは乾いていません。*This towel isn't dry.*

kawakasu 乾かす *dry, to dry v*

> watashi no fuku o kawakasu hitsuyō ga arimasu. 私の服を乾かす必要があります。*I need to dry my clothes.*

kawari no mono 替わりのもの *substitution n*

kaze ga tsuyoi 風が強い *windy adj*

kaze カゼ *cold n*

> kaze o hiki mashita. カゼを引きました。*I have a cold.*

kazoku 家族 / go kazoku ご家族 *family n*

kega けが *injury n*

keisatsu sho 警察署 / keisatsu no hashutsu sho 警察の派出所 *police station n*

keisatsu 警察 *police n*

keishoku 軽食 *snack n*

keitai denwa 携帯電話 *cell phone n*

kekkon suru 結婚する *marry, to marry v*

kengan shi 検眼師 *optometrist n*

kenri 権利 *rights n pl*

> shimin no kenri 市民の権利 *civil rights*

kensa 検査 *search n*

> te de kensa suru 手で検査する *hand search*

keshiki 景色 *landscape n*

keshō o suru 化粧をする *make up, to make up (apply cosmetics) v*

keshō 化粧 *makeup n*

ki o ushinau 気を失う *faint v*

kicchin キッチン *kitchen n*

kichin to shita きちんとした *neat (tidy) adj*

kieru 消える *disappear v*

kiiroi 黄色い *yellow adj*

kikai 機械 *machine n*

kiken 危険 *danger n*

kikon no 既婚の / kekkon shite iru 結婚している *married adj*

kiku 聞く *hear v*

kin en no 禁煙の *non-smoking adj*

kin en no 禁煙の *no smoking*
kin en no shitsu 禁煙の室 *non-smoking room*

kin sei no 金製の *gold adj*

kin yō bi 金曜日 *Friday n*

kingaku ga kakaru 金額がかかる *cost, to cost v*

sore wa ikura shimasu ka. それはいくらしますか? *How much does it cost?*

kinjo no hito 近所の人 / kinjo no kata ご近所の方 *neighbor n*

kinko 金庫 *safe (for storing valuables) n*

shitsu nai niwa kinko ga arimasu ka. 室内には金庫がありますか? *Do the rooms have safes?*

kinkyū 緊急 *emergency n*

kinō suru 機能する *work, to work v*

kore wa kinō shimasen. これは機能しません。*This doesn't work.*

kinō 昨日 *yesterday n*

ototoi おととい *the day before yesterday*

kinpatsu no 金髪の *blond(e) adj*

kinri 金利 *interest rate n*

kinzoku tanchi ki 金属探知機 *metal detector n*

kippu 切符 / chiketto チケット *ticket n*

kippu uriba 切符売り場 / chiketto kauntā チケットカウンター *ticket counter*
katamichi kippu 片道切符 *one-way ticket*
ōfuku kippu 往復切符 *round-trip ticket*

kireina きれいな *beautiful adj*

kiri kizu 切り傷 *cut (wound) n*

watashi wa hidoi kirikizu ga arimasu. 私はひどい切り傷があります。*I have a bad cut.*

kiri soroeru 切りそろえる / soroeru そろえる *trim, to trim (hair) v*

kiro guramu キログラム *kilo n*

kiro mētoru キロメートル *kilometer n*

kiru 切る *cut, to cut v*

kiru 切る *hang up (to end a phone call) v*

kiru 着る *dress v*

soko dewa seisō shinakereba nari masen ka. そこでは正装しなければなりませんか? *Should I dress up for that affair.*

kiru 着る *wear, to wear v*

kissa ten 喫茶店 *café n*

intānetto kafe インターネットカフェ *Internet café*

kisu キス *kiss n*

kitsu en 喫煙 *smoking n*

kitsu en jo 喫煙所 *smoking area*
kin en 禁煙 *No Smoking*

kitsui きつい *tight adj*
kitte 切手 *stamp (postage) n*
kizu no aru 傷のある *scratched adj*
suri kizu no aru hyōmen 擦り傷のある表面 *scratched surface*
kobosu こぼす *spill, to spill v*
kodomo tachi 子供たち *children n*
kodomo mo ii desu ka. 子供もいいですか? *Are children allowed?*
kodomo yō no puroguramu wa arimasu ka. 子供用のプログラムはありますか? *Do you have children's programs?*
kodomo yō no menyū wa arimasu ka. 子供用のメニューはありますか? *Do you have a children's menu?*
kodomo 子供 *child n*
kodomo 子供 *kid n*
kodomo mo ii desu ka. 子供もいいですか? *Are kids allowed?*
kodomo yō no puroguramu wa arimasu ka. 子供用のプログラムはありますか? *Do you have kids' programs?*
kodomo yō no menyū wa arimasu ka. 子供用のメニューはありますか? *Do you have a kids' menu?*
kōen 公園 *park n*
kōgai 郊外 *suburb n*
kogitte 小切手 / chekku チェック *check n*
toraberāzu chekku o tsukae masu ka. トラベラーズ チェックを使えますか? *Do you accept travelers' checks?*
kōhī コーヒー *coffee n*
aisu kōhī アイス コーヒー *iced coffee*
kōhisutamin zai 抗ヒスタミン剤 *antihistamine n*
kōi shitsu 更衣室 *changing room n*
kojin kyakushitsu 個人客室 / kyabin キャビン *private berth / cabin n*
kōka 硬貨 *coin n*
kōkai suru 航海する sail, to sail v
itsu shukkō shimasu ka. いつ出航しますか? *When do we sail?*
kōkai 航海 *sail n*
kōkan rēto 交換レート *exchange rate n*
amerika doru/kanada doru no kōkan rēto wa nan desu ka. アメリカドル/カナダドルの交換レートは何ですか? *What is the exchange rate for US / Canadian dollars?*
kōkan suru 交換する *change (to change money, clothes) v*
koko ここ *here n*
kokonotsu no 九つの *nine adj*
kokuseki 国籍 *nationality n*
kōkyō gakudan 交響楽団 *symphony n*

kōkyūna 高級な *upscale adj*
kon nichi wa こんにちは *hello n*
kona miruku 粉ミルク *formula n*
bebī yō kona miruku wa utte imasu ka. ベビー用粉ミルクは売っていますか? *Do you sell infants' formula?*
kondoru コンドル *condor n*
konnan na 困難な / muzukashii 難しい *difficult adj*
kono この *this adj*
konomi 好み *taste (discernment) n*
konpyūtā コンピューター *computer n*
konran shita 混乱した *confused adj*
konsāto コンサート *concert n*
konsento コンセント *plug n*
kontakuto renzu コンタクトレンズ *contact lens n*
kontakuto renzu o nakushi mashita. コンタクトレンズをなくしました。*I lost my contact lens.*
konyakku コニャック *cognac n*
konyaku sha 婚約者 *fiancé(e) n*
konzatsu shita 混雑した *congested adj*
kopī o toru コピーを取る / kopī suru コピーする *photocopy, to photocopy v*
korera no これらの *these adj*
kōri 氷 *ice n*
koronbia no, koronbia jin no コロンビアの、コロンビア人の *Colombian adj*
kōsei busshitsu 抗生物質 *antibiotic n*
kōsei busshitsu o kudasai. 抗生物質をください。*I need an antibiotic.*
kōshin suru 更新する *update, to update v*
kōsoku dōro 高速道路 *highway n*
kosutarika no, kosutarika jin no コスタリカの、コスタリカ人の *Costa Rican adj*
kotae 答え *answer n*
kotaeru 答える *answer, to answer (phone call, question) v*
kotaete kudasai. 答えてください。*Answer me, please.*
kōto コート *coat n*
kōto コート *court (sport) n*
kotonaru 異なる / chigau 違う / betsuno 別の *different (other) adj*
kōtsū 交通 *traffic n*
kōtsū jōtai wa dō desu ka. 交通状態はどうですか? *How's traffic?*
kōtsū kisoku 交通規則 *traffic rules*
kowareru 壊れる *break v*
kōza 口座 *account n*
tōza-yokin/futsū-yokin e/kara furikaete tai no desuga. 当座預金/普通預金口座へ/から振り替えたいのですが。*I'd like to transfer to / from my checking / savings account.*

kozutsumi 小包み *package n*
ku gatsu 九月 *September n*
kubaru 配る *deal (cards) v*
watashi mo irete kudasai. 私も入れてください。*Deal me in.*
kuchi hige 口ひげ *mustache n*
kuchi 口 *mouth n*
kuda mono 果物 *fruit n*
kujira 鯨 *whale n*
kukkī クッキー *cookie n*
kūkō 空港 *airport n*
kūkō made notte iku hitsuyō ga arimasu. 空港まで乗って行く必要があります。*I need a ride to the airport.*
kūkō kara dono kurai no tokoro ni arimasu ka. 空港からどのくらいのところにありますか? *How far is it from the airport?*
kumotta 曇った *cloudy adj*
kunren suru 訓練する *train, to train v*
kurabu ni odori ni iku クラブに踊りに行く *go clubbing, to go clubbing v*
kuragari 暗がり *dark n*
kurai 暗い *dark adj*
kurarinetto クラリネット *clarinet n*
kurasshikku no クラシックの *classical (music) adj*
kurasu クラス *class n*
bijinesu kurasu ビジネス クラス *business class*
ekonomī kurasu エコノミークラス *economy class*
fāsuto kurasu ファースト クラス *first class*
kurejitto kādo クレジット カード *credit card n*
kurejitto kādo o tsukae masu ka. クレジットカードを使えますか? *Do you accept credit cards?*
kuri kaesu 繰り返す *repeat, to repeat v*
mō ichido kuri kaeshite itadake masu ka. もう一度繰り返していただけますか? *Would you please repeat that?*
kurīmu クリーム *cream n*
kurōbā クローバー *clover n*
kuroi 黒い /koku jin 黒人 *black adj*
kuruma isu 車椅子 *wheelchair n*
kurumaisu deno akusesu 車椅子でのアクセス *wheelchair access*
kuruma isu yō surōpu 車椅子用スロープ *wheelchair ramp*
dendō kuruma isu 電動車椅子 *power wheelchair*
kuruma yoi 車酔い *carsickness n*
kuruma 車 *car n*
rentakā gaisha レンタ カー会社 *car rental agency*
rentakā ga hitsuyō desu. レンタ カーが必要です。*I need a rental car.*
kurumi クルミ *nut n*
kutsu shita 靴下 *sock n*
kutsu 靴 *shoe n*

kutsurogu くつろぐ *lounge, to lounge v*

kyaku no ōi 客の多い *(restaurant),* **hanashi chū de** 話し中で *(phone) busy adj*

kyanbasu キャンバス *(for painting)/* **kyanbasu ji** キャンバス地 *(material) canvas n*

kyanpā キャンパー *camper n*

kyanpu no キャンプの *camping adj*

> **kyanpu o suru kyoka ga hitsuyō desu ka.** キャンプをする許可が必要ですか? *Do we need a camping permit?*

kyanpu o suru キャンプをする *camp, to camp v*

kyanpu saito キャンプサイト *campsite n*

kyō 今日 *today n*

kyōdai 兄弟/**go kyōdai** ご兄弟 *brother n*

kyohi sareta 拒否された *declined adj*

> **watashi no kurejitto kādo ga kyohi saretano desu ka.** 私のクレジットカードが拒否されたのですか? *Was my credit card declined?*

kyōiku sha 教育者 *educator n*

kyoka suru 許可する *permit, to permit v*

kyoka 許可 *permit n*

> **kyanpu o suru kyoka ga hitsuyō desu ka.** キャンプをする許可が必要ですか? *Do we need a camping permit?*

kyōkai 教会 *church n*

kyū banme no 九番目の *ninth adj*

kyūjitsu 休日 *holiday n*

kyūjū no 九十の *ninety adj*

kyūkei 休憩 *intermission n*

kyūkyūsha 救急車 *ambulance n*

kyūmei yōgu 救命用具 *life preserver n*

M

macchi マッチ *match n*

> **macchi** マッチ *book of matches*

machiai shitu 待合室 *waiting area n*

machigai 間違い *mistake n*

mado 窓 *window n*

mae motte 前もって *in advance*

magaru 曲がる *turn, to turn v*

> **hidari / migi ni magaru** 左 / 右に曲がる *to turn left / right*
> **kesu / tsukeru** 消す / 付ける *to turn off / on*

mairu マイル *mile n*

māketto マーケット / **ichiba** 市場 *market n*

> **furii māketto** フリーマーケット *flea market*
> **aozora ichiba** 青空市場 *open-air market*

makura 枕 *pillow n*

> **umō no makura** 羽毛の枕 *down pillow*

manējā マネージャー *manager n*

manpuku ni natta 満腹になった *full, to be full (after a meal) adj*

manyuaru マニュアル *manual (instruction booklet) n*

massāji マッサージ *massage n*

matsu ge まつ毛 *eyelash n*

matsu 待つ *hold, to hold (to pause) v*

chotto matte. ちょっと待って! *Hold on a minute!*

pasu shimasu. パスします。*I'll hold.*

matsu 待つ *wait, to wait v*

dōka omachi kudasai. どうかお待ちください。*Please wait.*

dono kurai machi masu ka. どのくらい待ちますか? *How long is the wait?*

mayonaka 真夜中 *midnight n*

mayu ge まゆ毛 *eyebrow n*

me no mienai 目の見えない *blind adj*

me 目 *eye n*

mēdo メード *maid (hotel) n*

megane 眼鏡 *eyeglasses n*

megane 眼鏡 *glasses (eye) n*

atarashii megane ga hitsuyō desu. 新しい眼鏡が必要です。*I need new glasses.*

mei めい / meigo san 姪御さん *niece n*

mekishiko no, mekishiko jin no メキシコの、メキシコ人の *Mexican adj*

memai ga suru めまいがする *dizzy adj*

men 綿/kotton コットン *cotton n*

mendori 雌鶏 *hen n*

menkyo shō 免許証 *license n*

unten menkyo shō 運転免許証 *driver's license*

menyū メニュー *menu n*

menyū o misete itadake masen ka. メニューを見せていただけませんか? *May I see a menu?*

kodomo yō no menyū 子供用のメニュー *children's menu*

tōnyōbyō kanja yō no menyū 糖尿病患者用の *diabetic menu*

kōsha ryōri no menyū コーシャ料理の *kosher menu*

menzei no 免税の *duty-free adj*

menzei ten 免税店 *duty-free shop n*

mētoru メートル *meter n*

mezamashi tokei 目覚まし時計 *alarm clock n*

mibō jin 未亡人, yamome やもめ *widow, widower n*

mibun shōmei sho 身分証明書 *identification n*

michi 道 *street n*

kono michi no mukō gawa この道の向こう側 *across the street*

kono michi (no saki) この道(の先) *down the street* p6

dono michi. どの道? *Which street?*

ato nan bon no michi ga arimasuka? あと何本の道がありますか? *How many more streets?*

midiamu rea ミディアム レア *medium rare (meat) adj*

midiamu weru ミディアム ウェル *medium well (meat) adj*

midiamu ミディアム *medium (size) adj*

midori iro no 緑色の *green adj*

migi no 右の *right adj*

migi gawa ni arimasu. 右側にあります。*It is on the right.*

kado o migi ni magari masu. 角を右に曲がります。*Turn right at the corner.*

mijikai 短い *short adj*

mikon no 未婚の *maiden adj*

sore wa watashi no kyūsei desu. それは私の旧姓です。*That's my maiden name.*

mimi ga kikoenai 耳が聞こえない *deaf adj*

minato 港 *port (for ship) n*

minshu shugi 民主主義 *democracy n*

miri mētoru ミリメートル *millimeter n*

miri rittoru ミリリットル*milliliter n*

miru 見る *look, to look(to observe) v*

tada miteiru dake desu. ただ見ているだけです。*I'm just looking.*

koko o mite. ここを見て! *Look here!*

miru 見る *see, to see v*

misete itadake masu ka? 見せていただけますか? *May I see it?*

miryō sareta 魅了された *charmed adj*

mise 店 *shop n*

mise 店 *store n*

miseru 見せる *show, to show v*

misete itadake masen ka. 見せていただけませんか? *Would you show me?*

misuterī ミステリー *mystery (novel) n*

mīto bōru ミートボール *meatball n*

mitsukara nai 見つからない *missing adj*

mitsukeru 見つける *find v*

mizu 水 *water n*

kono mizu wa nome masu ka. この水は飲めますか? *Is the water potable?*

koko ni suidōsui wa arimasu ka. ここに水道水はありますか? *Is there running water?*

mizugi 水着 *swimsuit n*

mo ～も *～too (also) adv*

mochi kaeri yō no menyū 持帰り用のメニュー *takeout menu n*

modoru 戻る *return, to return (to a place) v*

mōfu 毛布 *blanket n*

moguru もぐる *dive v*

sukyūba daibu スキューバダイブ *scuba dive*

moku yō bi 木曜日 *Thursday n*
mondai 問題 *problem n*
mosuku モスク *mosque n*
motsu 持つ *have v*
motte imasu. 喘息を持っています。*I have asthma.* p167
motto sukunia もっと少ない *less adj*
mottomo chiisai, mottomo sukunai 最も小さい、最も少ない *least adj*
murasaki no 紫の *purple adj*
mushi yoke 虫除け *insect repellent n*
mushi 虫 *bug n*
mushiba 虫歯 *cavity (tooth cavity) n*

> mushiba ga aru yō nandesu. 虫歯があるようなんです。*I think I have a cavity.*

mushinron sha 無神論者 *atheist n*
mushiro むしろ *rather adv*
musuko 息子 / musuko san 息子さん *son* n
musume 娘/ojōsan お嬢さん *daughter n*
muttsu no 六つの *six adj*
muzukashii 難しい *hard adj (difficult)* / katai 堅い *(firm)*
myūjishan ミュージシャン *musician n*

N

nagai 長い *long adj*
nagaku 長く *long adv*

> dore kurai nagaku. どれくらい長く? *For how long?*

nagame 眺め *view n*

> bīchi no nagame ビーチの眺め *beach view*
> shigai no nagame 市街の眺め *city view*

nagareru, nagasu 流れる、流す *flush, to flush* v

> kono toire wa nagare masen. このトイレは流れません。*This toilet won't flush.*

naibu 内部 / naka 中 *inside*
naito kurabu ナイトクラブ *nightclub n*
nakusu 失くす *lose, to lose v*

> watashi wa pasupōto o nakushi mashita. 私はパスポートを失くしました。*I lost my passport.*
> watashi wa saifu o nakushi mashita. 私は財布を失くしました。*I lost my wallet.*
> watashi wa mayotte shimai mashita. 私は迷ってしまいました。*I'm lost.*

namae 名前 *name n*

> watashi wa ___ to mōshimasu. 私は___と申します。*My name is ___.*
> anata no namae wa nan desu ka. あなたの名前は何ですか? *What's your name?*

nan demo 何でも *anything n*
nan no 何の / 何 nani *what adv*

donna shurui no ____. どんな種類の____? *What sort of ____?*

_____ wa nan ji. _____は何時? *What time is _____?*

nana ban me no 七番目の *seventh adj*

nana jū no 七十の *seventy adj*

nanatsu no 七つの *seven adj*

nani ka 何か / nani 何 *something* n

nanika 何か /nanimo 何も / *any adj*

nanimo nai 何もない / sukoshi mo nai 少しもない、全くない mattaku nai *none n*

nanpa sen 難破船 *shipwreck n*

naosu 直す *correct v*

napukin ナプキン *napkin n*

nashi de ～なしで ～ *without prep*

natsu 夏 *summer n*

nebiki 値引き *discount n*

watashi wa nebiki no taishō ni narimasuka. 私は値引きの対象になりますか? *Do I qualify for a discount?*

neko ねこ *cat n*

nesshin na 熱心な *enthusiastic adj*

nettowāku ネットワーク *network n*

nezumi ねずみ *mouse n*

ni gatsu 二月 *February n*

ni kakoku go o hanasu 二ヶ国語を話す *bilingual adj*

niban me no 二番目の *second adj*

sekyuritī chekku pointo セキュリティ チェックポイント *security checkpoint*

sekyuritī gādo セキュリティガード / keibi in 警備員 *security guard*

nichi yō bi 日曜日 *Sunday n*

nihon no, nihon jin no 日本の、日本人の *Japanese adj*

nijū no 二十の *twenty adj*

nikaragua no, nikaragua jin no ニカラグアの、ニカラグア人の *Nicaraguan adj*

nikibi にきび *acne n*

niku 肉 *meat n*

nimotsu 荷物 / ryokō kaban 旅行カバン *luggage n*

ryokō kaban no funshitsu wa doko ni hōkoku shimasu ka. 旅行カバンの紛失はどこに報告しますか? *Where do I report lost luggage?*

funshitsu shita ryokō kaban o uketoru basho wa doko desu ka. 紛失した旅行カバンを受け取る場所はどこですか? *Where is the lost luggage claim?*

nin niku にんにく *garlic n*

ninki ga aru 人気がある *popular adj*

ninshin shita 妊娠した *pregnant adj*

nioi o kagu 匂いをかぐ *smell, to smell v*

no hō o konomu の方を好む *prefer, to prefer v*

no mukō gawa の向こう側 *across prep*

kono michi no mukō gawa この道の向こう側 *across the street*

no yō ni mieru のように見える *look, to look (to appear) v*

kore wa dō mie masu ka. これはどう見えますか? *How does this look?*

noboru 登る *climb, to climb v*

yama ni noboru 山に登る *to climb a mountain*

kaidan o noboru 階段を昇る *to climb stairs*

nomi komu 飲み込む *swallow, to swallow v*

nomi mono 飲み物 *drink n*

nomi mono o kudasai. 飲み物をください。*I'd like a drink.*

nomu 飲む *drink, to drink v*

nori sokonau 乗りそこなう *miss, to miss (a flight) v*

notte iku 乗っていく *ride, to ride v*

nozomu 望む, like, desire *v (to please)*

ga suki desu. ____が好きです。 ____ *I would like ____.*

nuno 布 *fabric n*

nuru 塗る *paint, to paint v*

nusumareta 盗まれた *stolen adj*

nusumu 盗む *steal, to steal v*

nuu 縫う / saihō o suru 裁縫をする *sew, to sew v*

nyūjīrando no, nyūjīrando jin no ニュージーランドの、ニュージーランド人の *New Zealander adj*

nyūjīrando ニュージーランド *New Zealand n*

nyūjōryō 入場料 *admission fee n*

nyūkō suru 入港する *board v*

O

oba おば / obasan おばさん *aunt n*

ōbāhīto suru オーバーヒートする *overheat, to overheat v*

kuruma ga ōbāhīto shimashita. 車がオーバーヒートしました。*The car overheated.*

ocha お茶 / cha 茶 *tea n*

ochido 落ち度 *fault n*

watashi ni ochido ga arimasu. 私に落ち度があります。*I'm at fault.*

sore wa kare ni ochido ga arimasu. それは彼に落ち度があります。*It was his fault.*

ochiru 落ちる *fall v*

odoru 踊る /dansu o suru ダンスをする *dance v*

ofuro ni hairu お風呂に入る *bathe, to bathe oneself v*

ofuro お風呂 *bath n*

ōgoe de yobu 大声で呼ぶ *shout v*

oi おい / oigo san 甥御さん *nephew n*

oji おじ / ojisan おじさん *uncle n*

okane お金 *money n*

okawari お替わり *refill (of beverage) n*

ōkii 大きい *big adj*

ōkii 大きい *large adj*

okkē オッケー *okay adv*

okotta 怒った *angry adj*

oku 置く *place, to place v*

oku 置く *put, to put v*

okure 遅れ *delay n*

> dono kurai okurere imasu ka. どのくらい遅れていますか? *How long is the delay?*

okuri mono 贈り物 *gift n*

okuru 送る *send, to send v*

okyaku お客 *guest n*

omocha おもちゃ *toy n*

> omocha ya おもちゃ屋 *toy store n*
>
> kodomo no omocha wa arimasu ka. 子供のおもちゃはありますか? *Do you have any toys for the children?*

omoi 重い *weigh v*

> watashi wa taijyū ga _____ arimasu. 私は体重が_____あります。*I weigh _____.*
>
> kore wa _____ no omosa ga arimasu. これは_____の重さがあります。*It weighs _____.* *See p7 for numbers.*

omosa 重さ *weights n*

omutsu おむつ *diaper n*

> omutsu wa doko de kaerare masu ka. おむつはどこで替えられますか? *Where can I change a diaper?*

ongaku 音楽 *music n*

> nama ensō 生演奏 *live music*

onna no ko 女の子 *girl n*

onsei no 音声の *audio adj*

opera オペラ *opera n*

operētā オペレーター *operator (phone) n*

ōpun kā オープンカー *convertible n*

orenji iro no オレンジ色の *orange (color) adj*

orenji jūsu オレンジジュース *orange juice n*

orību オリーブ *olive n*

oshaburi おしゃぶり *pacifier n*

osoi 遅い *late adj*

> dōka okure naide kudasai. どうか遅れないでください。*Please don't be late.*

osoi 遅い *slow adj*

osou 襲う *mug, to mug (someone) v*

> osowareta 襲われた *mugged adj*

osu 押す *push, to push v*

ōsutoraria no, ōsutoraria jin no オーストラリアの、オーストラリア人の *Australian adj*

ōsutoraria オーストラリア *Australia n*

oto ga urusai 音がうるさい *noisy adj*

otoko no ko 男の子 *boy n*

otoko 男 *man n*

otsuri おつり *change (money) n*

> otsuri o kudasai. おつりをください。*I'd like change, please.*

kono otsuri wa tadashiku arimasen. このおつりは正しくありません。*This isn't the correct change.*

otto 夫 / shujin 主人 / go shujin ご主人 *husband n*

oushi 雄牛 *bull n*

oya 親 *parent n*

oyogu 泳ぐ *swim, to swim v*

koko dewa oyoge masu ka. ここでは泳げますか? *Can one swim here?*

P

painto パイント *pint n*

pan パン *bread n*

panama no, panama jin no パナマの、パナマ人の *Panamanian adj*

paraguai no, paraguai jin no パラグアイの、パラグアイ人の *Paraguayan adj*

parēdo パレード *parade n*

pasu suru パスする *hold, to hold (gambling) v*

pasu suru パスする *pass, to pass v*

pasu shimasu. パスします。*I'll pass.*

pasupōto パスポート *passport n*

watashi wa pasupōto o nakushi mashita. 私はパスポートを失くしました。*I've lost my passport.*

pātī パーティー *party n*

seitō 政党 *political party*

pātonā パートナー *partner n*

perū no, perū jin no ペルーの、ペルー人の *Peruvian adj*

piano ピアノ *piano n*

pīnattsu ピーナッツ *peanut n*

pinku no ピンクの *pink adj*

pittari au ぴったり合う *fit (clothes) v*

pittari atte iru yō ni miemasu ka. ぴったり合っているように見えますか? *Does this look like it fits?*

piza ピザ *pizza n*

pondo ポンド *pound n*

ponpu ポンプ *pump n*

poppu myūjikku ポップ ミュージック *pop music n*

posuto kādo ポストカード *postcard n*

pōtā ポーター *porter n*

pōto wain ポートワイン *port (beverage) n*

puerutoriko no, puerutoriko jin no プエルトリコの、プエルトリコ人の *Puerto Rican adj*

purasuchikku プラスチック *plastic n*

purei suru プレイする *play, to play (a game) v*

purei プレイ *play n*

purofesshionaru na プロフェッショナルな *professional adj*

puroguramu プログラム *program n*

puroguramu o itadake masu ka. プログラムをいただけますか? *May I have a program?*

purotesutanto プロテスタント *Protestant n*

pūru プール *pool n*

R

rabendā iro no ラベンダー色の *lavender adj*

rajio ラジオ *radio n*

eisei rajio 衛星ラジオ *satellite radio*

ramu shu ラム酒 *rum n*

ranpu ランプ *light n (lamp)*

rappu toppu ラップトップ *laptop n*

raunji ラウンジ *lounge n*

rea no レアの *rare (meat) adj*

regē レゲー *reggae adj*

reibō 冷房 /eakon エアコン *air conditioning n*

reibō o sagete/agete itadake masen ka. 冷房を下げて/上げていただけませんか? *Would you lower / raise the air conditioning?*

rekishi teki na 歴史的な *historical adj*

rekishi 歴史 *history n*

remonēdo レモネード *lemonade n*

ren ai shōsetsu 恋愛小説 *romance (novel) n*

rentogen レントゲン *x-ray machine n*

reshīto レシート *receipt n*

ressha 列車 / densha 電車 *train n*

tokkyū ressha 特急列車 *express train*

futsū ressha 普通列車 *local train*

kono densha wa ______ e ikimasu ka. この電車は______へ行きますか? *Does the train go to ____?*

densha no jikokuhyō o itadake masu ka. 電車の時刻表をいただけますか? *May I have a train schedule?*

eki wa doko ni arimasuka. 駅はどこにありますか? *Where is the train station?*

ressun レッスン *lesson n*

resutoran レストラン *restaurant n*

yoi resutoran wa doko ni arimasu ka. よいレストランはどこにありますか? *Where can I find a good restaurant?*

rihatsu ten 理髪店 *barber n*

rikai suru 理解する *understand, to understand v*

wakari masen. わかりません。*I don't understand.*

wakari masu ka. わかりますか? *Do you understand?*

rikon shita 離婚した *divorced adj*

rimujin リムジン *limo n*

rippa na 立派な *great adj*

rittoru リットル *liter n*

riyōken 利用券 *voucher n*

roiyaru furasshu ロイヤル フラッシュ *royal flush n*

rōka 廊下 *hallway n*
rokkā ロッカー *locker n*
hokan rokkā 保管ロッカー *storage locker*
rokkā rūmu ロッカールーム *locker room*
rokku kuraimingu ロッククライミング *rock climbing n*
rokku ロック *rocks (ice) n*
rokku de onegai shimasu. ロックでお願いします。 *I'd like it on the rocks.*
rokkun rōru ロックンロール *rock and roll n*
roku gatsu 六月 *June n*
rokujū no 六十の *sixty adj*
romanchikku na ロマンチックな *romantic adj*
rōpu ロープ *rope n*
ryō 量 *amount n*
ryōgae 両替 *currency exchange n*
koko kara ichiban chikai ryōgae jo wa doko ni arimasu ka. ここから一番近い両替所はどこにありますか？ *Where is the nearest currency exchange?*
ryōkin puran 料金プラン *rate plan (cell phone) n*
ryōkin 料金 *fare n*
ryōkin 料金 *fee n*
ryōkin 料金 *rate (for car rental, hotel) n*
ichi nichi atari no ryōkin wa ikura desu ka. 一日当たりの料金はいくらですか？ *What's the rate per day?*
isshūkan atari no ryōkin wa ikura desu ka. 一週間当たりの料金はいくらですか？ *What's the rate per week?*
ryokō kaban 旅行カバン *(luggage)* **toranku** トランク *(in car) trunk n*
ryokō suru 旅行する *travel, to travel v*
ryokō 旅行 *trip n*
ryōri suru 料理する *cook, to cook v*
ryōri suru koto ga dekiru heya o onegai shimasu. 料理することができる部屋をお願いします。 *I'd like a room where I can cook.*
ryōri 料理 *dish n*

S

sābisu ryō サービス料 *service charge n*
sābisu サービス *service n*
kaisō 回送 *out of service*
sāfin suru サーフィンする *surf v*
sāfu bōdo サーフボード *surfboard n*
sagasu 探す *look for, to look for (to search) v*
pōtā o sagashite imasu. ポーターを探しています。 *I'm looking for a porter.*
sai aku 最悪 *worst*
saibā kafe サイバーカフェ *cybercafé n*

saibā kafe wa doko ni arimasu ka. サイバーカフェはどこにありますか? *Where can I find a cybercafé?*

saiban sho 裁判所 *court (legal) n*

saifu 財布 *purse n*

saifu 財布 *wallet n*

watashi wa saifu o nakushi mashita. 私は財布を失くしました。*I lost my wallet.*

dareka ni saifu o nusumare mashita. 誰かに財布を盗まれました。*Someone stole my wallet.*

saigo ni 最後に *last adv*

saikō no 最高の *best*

saisho no 最初の *first adj*

saishō 最小 *least n*

saizu サイズ *size (clothing, shoes) n*

sake 酒 *liquor n*

saki e 先へ / mae e 前へ *forward adj*

sakka 作家 *writer n*

samui 寒い *cold adj*

samui desu. 寒いです。*I'm cold.*

soto wa samui desu. 外は寒いです。*It's cold out.*

san bai no 3 倍の *triple adj*

san banme no 3番目の *third adj*

san gatsu 三月 *March (month) n*

san rūfu サンルーフ *sunroof n*

san 三 *three*

sango shō さんご礁 *reef n*

sangurasu サングラス *sunglasses n*

sanjū no 三十の *thirty adj*

sanka suru 参加する/shusseki suru 出席する *attend v*

sanso tanku 酸素タンク *oxygen tank n*

sarada サラダ *salad n*

sarubadoru no, sarubadoru jin no サルバドルの、サルバドル人の *Salvadorian adj*

sashi komu 差し込む *plug, to plug v*

sasu 指す *point, to point v*

____ no hōkō ni sashi shimeshite itadake masen ka. ____の方向に指し示していただけませんか? *Would you point me in the direction of____?*

sayōnara さようなら *goodbye n*

sedan セダン *sedan n* p46

see months of the year *month n*

seibetsu 性別 *sex (gender) n*

seigen sokudo 制限速度 *speed limit n*

seigen sokudo wa nan kiro desu ka. 制限速度は何キロですか? *What's the speed limit?*

seihin 製品 *product n*

seikatsu 生活 *living n*

nani o shite seikatsu shite imasu ka. 何をして生活していますか? *What do you do for a living?*

seiketsu na 清潔な *clean adj*
seikyū suru 請求する *bill v*
seikyū suru 請求する *charge, to charge (money) v*
seikyū 請求 *claim n*

baishō o seikyū shimasu. 賠償を請求します。*I'd like to file a claim.*

seki o suru 咳をする *cough v*
seki 咳 *cough n*
sekken 石鹸 *soap n*
sekyuritī gādo セキュリティガード / keibi in 警備員 *security guard*
semai 狭い *narrow adj*
sen 千 *thousand*
senaka o sasuru 背中をさする *back rub n*
senaka 背中 *back n*

senaka ga itami masu. 背中が痛みます。*My back hurts.*

senchi mētoru センチメートル *centimeter n*
senkyo 選挙 *election n*
senmen dai 洗面台 *sink n*
senmen yōhin 洗面用品 *toiletries n*
senpūki 扇風機 *fan n*
sensō 戦争 *war n*
sentaku / randorī 洗濯 *laundry n*
serufu sābisu no セルフサービスの *self-serve adj*
sētā セーター *sweater n*
setsudan sareta 切断された *disconnected adj*

opēretā san, denwa ga kirete shimai mashita. オペレータさん、電話が切れてしまいました。*Operator, I was disconnected.*

setsumei suru 説明する *explain v*
sewa o suru 世話をする *mother, to mother v*
shakō dansu 社交ダンス *ballroom dancing n*
sharin tsuki 車輪付き *wheeled (luggage) adj*
shatoru basu シャトル バス *shuttle bus n*
shatsu シャツ *shirt n*
shawā o abiru シャワーを浴びる *shower, to shower v*
shawā シャワー*shower n*

sore niwa shawā ga tsuite imasu ka? それにはシャワーが付いていますか? *Does it have a shower?*

shi gatsu 四月 *April n*
shi 市 / machi 街 *city n*
shiai 試合 *match (sport) n*
shiawase na 幸せな / ureshii 嬉しい *happy adj*
shichaku shitsu 試着室 *fitting room n*
shichaku suru 試着する *try, to try on (clothing) v*
shichi gatsu 七月 *July n*
shichimenchō 七面鳥 *turkey n*
shīfūdo シーフード / gyokai rui 魚介類 *seafood n*
shiharau 支払う *pay, to pay v*
shihei 紙幣 *bill (currency) n*

shikaku shōgai no 視覚障害の *visually-impaired adj*

shikke no aru 湿気のある *humid adj*

shima no 縞の *striped adj*

shimai 姉妹 / go shimai ご姉妹 *sister n*

shimatta しまった!/zan nen 残念! *Damn! expletive*

shinbun uriba 新聞売り場 *newsstand n*

shinbun 新聞 *newspaper n*

shindai 寝台 *berth n*

shindai 寝台 *sleeping berth n*

shinkoku suru 申告する *declare v*

> shinkoku suru mono wa arimasen. 申告するものはありません。*I have nothing to declare.*

shinpai na 心配な / shinpai shiteiru 心配している *anxious adj*

shinseki 親戚 *relative (family) n*

shinsen na 新鮮な *fresh adj*

shinzō hossa 心臓発作 heart *attack n*

shinzō 心臓 *heart n*

shio no nagare 潮の流れ *current (water) n*

shio 塩 *salt n*

> sore wa gen en desu ka. それは減塩ですか? *Is that low-salt?*

shiraberu 調べる *check, to check v*

shiraberu 調べる *search, to search v*

shiroi 白い *white adj*

shiruku シルク *silk n*

shiryoku 視力 *vision n*

shishoku suru 試食する *try, to try (food) v*

shita ni 下に *down adj*

shita no 下の *below adv*

shitagi 下着 *underwear n*

shitataru 滴る *drip v*

shitate ya 仕立て屋 *tailor n*

> yoi shitate ya o susumete itadake masen ka. よい仕立て屋を勧めていただけませんか? *Can you recommend a good tailor?*

shite yoi してよい *may v aux*

> ____ shitemo yoi desu ka. ____してもよいですか? *May I ____?*

shītsu シーツ *sheet (bed linen) n*

shitsumon suru 質問する *ask a question v*

shitsunai gaku 室内楽 *chamber music n*

shitte iru 知っている *know, to know (someone) v*

shitte iru 知っている *know, to know (something) v*

shiyō kanō na 使用可能な *available adj*

shiyōryō 使用料 *toll n*

shizuka na 静かな *quiet adj*

shō ショー *show (performance) n*

shō wa nanji desuka? ショーは何時ですか? *What time is the show?*

shōgai sha ni taiō shita 障害者に対応した *handicapped-accessible adj*

shōgai 障害 *disability n*

shōgo 正午 *noon n*

shohōsen 処方箋 / shohōyaku 処方薬 *prescription n* p40

shōka furyō 消化不良 *indigestion n*

shōkai suru 紹介する *introduce, to introduce v*

anata o ____ ni shōkai shimasu. あなたを____に紹介します。*I'd like to introduce you to ____.*

shoku nin 職人/kōgeika 工芸家 *craftsperson n*

shokuji 食事 *meal n*

shokuryō hin 食料品 *groceries n*

shomei 署名 *sign, to sign v*

doko ni shomei sureba ii desu ka? どこに署名すればいいですか? *Where do I sign?*

shōnika i 小児科医 *pediatrician n*

osusume no shōnika i wa imasu ka. お勧めの小児科医はいますか? *Can you recommend a pediatrician?*

shoppingu sentā ショッピングセンター *mall n*

shori suru 処理する *process, to process v*

shōsetsu 小説 *novel n*

shōyō de 商用で *business adj*

bijinesu sentā ビジネス センター *business center*

shōzō ga 肖像画 *portrait n*

shū 週 *week n*

konshū 今週 *this week*
senshū 先週 *last week*
raishū 来週 *next week*

shufu 主婦 *homemaker n*

shumi 趣味 *hobby n*

shuppansha 出版社 *publisher n*

shuppatsu suru 出発する *leave, to leave (depart) v*

shuppatsu 出発 *departure n*

shurui 種類 *kind (type) n*

sore wa donna shurui desu ka. それはどんな種類ですか? *What kind is it?*

sobakasu そばかす *freckle n*

sobo 祖母 / obāsan お祖母さん *grandmother n*

sōda sui ソーダ水 *seltzer n*

sōda ソーダ *soda n*

daietto sōda ダイエット ソーダ *diet soda*

sodatsu 育つ *grow, to grow (get larger) v*

doko de sodachi mashita ka. どこで育ちましたか? *Where did you grow up?*

soe mono 添え物 *side n*

yoko ni soete 横に添えて *on the side (e.g., salad dressing)*

sofu 祖父 / ojīsan お祖父さん *grandfather n*

sofubo 祖父母 *grandparent n*

sofuto uea ソフトウェア *software n*

sōji suru 掃除する *clean, to clean v*

> kyō, heya o sōji shite kudasai. 今日、部屋を掃除してください。*Please clean the room today.*

soko ni そこに *(nearby)* / asoko ni あそこに *(far) there (demonstrative) adv*

> arimasu ka. ありますか? *Is / Are there?*
> asoko ni あそこに *over there*

sokudo kei 速度計 *speedometer n*

sokudo o otosu 速度を落とす *slow, to slow v*

> sokudo o otoshite kudasai! 速度を落としてください! *Slow down!*

sono その *that (near) adj*

sonshō shita 損傷した *damaged adj*

sorerano それらの *those adj*

sōsu ソース *sauce n*

soto 外 *outside n*

subete no すべての *all adj*

> itsumo いつも *all of the time*
> ijō desu. dōmo arigatō. 以上です。どうもありがとう。*That's all, thank you.*

subete すべて *all n*

sugiru ～過ぎる ～ *too (excessively) adv*

sui yō bi 水曜日 *Wednesday n*

suiei pantsu 水泳パンツ *swim trunks n*

sūji 数字 / bangō 番号 *number n*

> heya wa nan ban. 部屋は何番? *Which room number?*
> anata no denwa bangō o oshiete itadake masu ka. あなたの電話番号を教えていただけますか? *May I have your phone number?*

sukejūru スケジュール *schedule n*

suki de aru 好きである *like, to like v (to please)*

> watashi wa koko ga suki desu. 私はここが好きです。*I like this place.*

sukoshi 少し *bit (small amount) n*

sukottorando no, sukottorando jin no スコットランドの、スコットランド人の *Scottish adj*

sukūtā スクーター *scooter n* p46

sukyan suru スキャンする *scan, to scan (document) v*

sukyūba daibingu o suru スキューバダイブをする *scuba dive, to scuba dive v*

sumi masen すみません *excuse (pardon) v*

> sumi masen すみません *Excuse me.*

sumi masen すみません *sorry adj*

> sumi masen. すみません。*I'm sorry.*

sumi 隅 *corner n*

sumi no 隅の *on the corner*

sumu 住む *live, to live v*

anata wa doko ni sunde imasu ka. あなたはどこに住んでいますか? *Where do you live?*

sunēku ai da! スネークアイだ! *Snake eyes! n*

sunōkeru スノーケル *snorkel n*

sūpā māketto スーパーマーケット *supermarket n*

supa スパ *spa n*

supaisu スパイス *spice n*

supea taiya スペア タイヤ *spare tire n*

supein no, supein jin no スペインの、スペイン人の *Spanish adj*

supein スペイン *Spain n*

supesharu スペシャル *special (featured meal) n*

supōtsu スポーツ *sports n*

sūpu スープ *soup n*

suramu gai スラム街 *slum n*

surōpu, kuruma isu スロープ、車椅子 *ramp, wheelchair n*

suru する *do, to do v*

susumeru 勧める *recommend, to recommend v*

sutaffu スタッフ *staff (employees) n*

sutajiamu スタジアム *stadium n*

sutēki hausu ステーキハウス *steakhouse n*

suteki na すてきな *nice adj*

sutoresu o kanjite iru ストレスを感じている *stressed adj*

sutorēto no ストレートの / chokumō 直毛 *straight (hair) adj*

koko o saki massugu ここをまっすぐ *straight ahead*

sutorēto de ストレートで *straight (drink)*

massugu ikimasu. まっすぐ行きます。 *Go straight. (giving directions)*

sutorēto ストレート *straight (gambling) n*

sūtsu kēsu スーツケース *suitcase n*

sūtsu スーツ *suite n*

suwaru 座る *sit, to sit v*

T

tabako o suu タバコを吸う *smoke, to smoke v*

tabako タバコ *cigarette n*

tabako hito hako タバコ 1 箱 *a pack of cigarettes*

tabe mono 食べ物 *food n*

taberu 食べる *eat v*

gaishoku suru 外食する *to eat out*

tadashii 正しい *correct adj*

watashi wa tadashii densha ni notte imasu ka. 私は正しい電車に乗っていますか? *Am I on the correct train?*

taishi kan 大使館 *embassy n*

taiya タイヤ *tire n*

taiya ga panku shima shita. タイヤがパンクしました。 *I have a flat tire.*

taiyō 太陽 *sun n*
takai 高い / se ga takai 背が高い *tall adj*
takai 高い *expensive adj*
takai 高い *high adj*
takaku nai 高くない *inexpensive adj*
takuji sho 託児所 *nursery n*
takuji sho wa arimasu ka. 託児所はありますか? *Do you have a nursery?*
takusan no 多い ōi / 沢山の *many adj*
takushī タクシー *taxi n*
takushī. タクシー! *Taxi!*
takushī o yonde itadake masen ka. タクシーを呼んでいただけませんか? *Would you call me a taxi?*
tamari ba 溜まり場 *hangout (hot spot) n*
tamesu 試す *try, to try (attempt) v*
tāminaru ターミナル *terminal (airport) n*
tamotsu 保つ *keep, to keep v*
tanomu 頼む *ask for (request) v*
tanomu 頼む *order, to order (request) v*
tanoshimu 楽しむ *enjoy, to enjoy v*
taoru タオル *towel n*
motto taoru o itadake masu ka. もっとタオルをいただけますか? *May we have more towels?*
taryō 多量 / takusan no 沢山の *much n*
tasukeru 助ける *help, to help v*
tasukete. 助けて! *Help! n*
tatsu 立つ *stand, to stand v*
tazuneru 訪ねる *visit, to visit v*
te 手 *hand n*
tebukuro 手袋 *glove n*
tēburu テーブル *table n*
futari yō no tēburu 2人用のテーブル *table for two*
tegoro na nedan no 手頃な値段の *moderately priced adj*
teikyō suru 提供する *offer, to offer v*
teinei na ていねいな/shinsetsuna親切な *courteous adj*
tekuno テクノ *techno n*
tenimotsu no 手荷物の *baggage adj*
tenimotsu hikiwatashi jo 手荷物引き渡し所 *baggage claim*
tenimotsu 手荷物 *baggage n*
tenisu テニス *tennis n*
tenisu kōto テニスコート *tennis court*
tenji 展示 *exhibit n*
tenji, amerika no 点字、アメリカの *braille, American n*
tenki yohō 天気予報 *weather forecast n*
tento テント *tent n*
terebi テレビ ***television*** *n*
tetsudai 手伝い /ashisutansu アシスタンス *assistance n*
tetsudau 手伝う *assist v*

to issho ni ～と一緒に～ *with prep*

tōchaku suru 到着する *arrive, to arrive v*

tōchaku 到着 *arrival(s) n*

tōgyū shi 闘牛士 *bullfighter n*

tōgyū 闘牛 *bullfight n*

toire トイレ *bathroom (restroom) n*

koko kara ichiban chikai kōshū toire wa doko ni arimasu ka. ここから一番近い公衆トイレはどこにありますか？ *Where is the nearest public bathroom?*

toire トイレ *restroom n*

kōshū toire wa arimasu ka. 公衆トイレはありますか？ *Do you have a public restroom?*

toire トイレ *toilet n*

toire no mizu ga afurete irun desu. トイレの水が溢れているんです。*The toilet is overflowing.*

toire ga tsumatte imasu. トイレがつまっています。*The toilet is backed up.*

toiretto pēpā トイレット ペーパー *toilet paper n*

toiretto pēpā ga naku nari mashita. トイレット ペーパーがなくなりました。*You're out of toilet paper.*

tojiru 閉じる *close, to close v*

tojita 閉じた *closed adj*

tōjō ken 搭乗券 *boarding pass n*

tōjō 搭乗 *board n*

tōjō shite 搭乗して *on board*

tōkei 闘鶏 *cockfight n*

tokkyū no 特急の *express adj*

tokubetsu yūsen chekku in 特別優先チェックイン *express check-in*

tokudai no 特大の extra-large *adj*

tōkuni 遠くに / tōi 遠い *far*

made wa doredake tōku hanarete imasu ka. ＿＿までではどれだけ遠く離れていますか？＿＿ *How far is it to* ＿＿*?*

tokuten 得点 *score n*

tomaru 停まる *stop, to stop v*

tomatte kudasai. 停まってください。*Please stop.*

tomare 止まれ *STOP (traffic sign)*

tomare, dorobō. 止まれ、泥棒! *Stop, thief!*

tomaru 泊る / taizai suru 滞在する *stay, to stay v*

＿＿nichi kan taizai suru yotei desu. ＿＿日間滞在する予定です。*We'll be staying for* ＿＿ *nights.* See p7 for numbers.

tōmei na 透明な *clear adj*

ton トン *ton n*

tōnyōbyō no 糖尿病の *diabetic adj*

toraberāzu chekku トラベラーズ チェック *travelers' check n*

toraberāzu chekku o genkin ni kōkan deki masu ka. トラベラーズチェックを現金に交換できますか? *Do you cash travelers' checks?*

tori kesu 取り消す *cancel, to cancel v*

watashi no furaito wa kyanseru saremashita. 私のフライトはキャンセルされました。*My flight was canceled.*

tori 鳥 *bird n*

torihiki 取引き *deal (bargain) n*

nante subarashii torihiki da. なんてすばらしい取引だ! *What a great deal!*

torinozoku 取り除く / nugu 脱ぐ *remove, to remove v*

toshi 歳 *age n*

nan sai desu ka. 何歳ですか? *What's your age?*

totemo とても *very*

tozan 登山 *climbing n*

tozan dō 登山道 / toreiru トレイル *trail n*

tozan dō wa arimasuka. 登山道はありますか? *Are there trails?*

tranpetto トランペット *trumpet n*

tsuā ツアー *tour n*

gaido tsuki tsuā wa arimasu ka. ガイド付きツアーはありますか? *Are guided tours available?*

onsei gaido tsuki tsuā wa arimasu ka. 音声ガイド付きツアーはありますか? *Are audio tours available?*

tsugi 次 *next prep*

no tsugi の次 *next to*

tsugi no eki 次の駅 *the next station*

tsukareta 疲れた / tsukarete iru 疲れている *tired adj*

tsukareta 疲れた *exhausted adj*

tsukau 使う *use, to use v*

tsukuru 作る *make, to make v*

tsuma 妻 / okusan 奥さん *wife n*

tsumatte iru つまっている *backed up (toilet) adj*

toire ga tsumatte imasu. トイレがつまっています。*The toilet is backed up.*

tsuno 角 *horn n*

tsureteiku 連れて行く *take, to take v*

eki made tsurete itte kudasai. 駅まで連れて行ってください。*Take me to the station.*

____ made iku niwa ikura kakari masu ka. ____まで行くにはいくらかかりますか? *How much to take me to ____?*

tsuri zao 釣竿 *fishing pole n*

tsūro 通路 *aisle n*

tsūyaku 通訳 *interpreter n*

tsūyaku ga hitsuyō desu. 通訳が必要です。*I need an interpreter.*

tsuzukeru 続ける *continue, to continue v*

tsuzuku 続く *last, to last v*

tsuzuru つづる *spell, to spell v*

tsuzuri o itte kudasai. つづりを言ってください。/ tsuzuri o itte morae masu ka. つづりを言ってもらえますか。*How do you spell that?*

U

ubau 奪う *rob, to rob v*

gōtō ni aimashita. 強盗に遭いました。*I've been robbed.*

ude 腕 *arm n*

ue ni 上に *up adv*

ue no 上の *above adj*

ueitā ウエイター *waiter n*

ueku appu kōru ウェークアップ コール *wake-up call n*

uesutan no ウェスタンの *western adj*

ugoku 動く *move, to move v*

uke ireru 受け入れる *accept, to accept v*

kurejitto kādo o tsukae masu ka. クレジットカードを使えますか? *Do you accept credit cards?*

uketoru 受け取る *receive, to receive v*

uma 馬 *horse n*

ume awase o suru 埋め合せをする *make up, to make up (apologize) v*

unten shu 運転手 *driver n*

unten suru 運転する *drive v*

uokka ウオッカ *vodka n*

ureshii 嬉しい *delighted adj*

urikire 売り切れ *sold out adj*

uru 売る *sell, to sell v*

uruguai no, uruguai jin no ウルグアイの、ウルグアイ人の *Uruguayan adj*

urusai うるさい *loud adj*

urusaku うるさく *loudly adv*

usagi うさぎ *rabbit n*

USB pōto USB ポート *USB port n*

ushi 牛 *cow n*

ushiro no 後ろの *behind adv*

usu chairo no 薄茶色の *hazel adj*

usui 薄い *thin adj*

uta 歌 *song n*

utau 歌う *sing, to sing v*

utsusu 移す *transfer, to transfer v*

okane o idō shitai no desuga. お金を移動したいのですが。*I need to transfer funds.*

uwagi 上着 *jacket n*

V

vendaje m, bando eido バンドエイド *band-aid n*

W

wai fai ワイファイ *wi-fi n*

wain ワイン *wine n*

waipā ワイパー *windshield wiper n*

waipā ワイパー *wiper n*

wakai 若い *young adj*

wakareta 別れた / bekkyo shite iru 別居している *separated (marital status) adj*

wakeru 分ける *split (gambling) n*
wakkusu ワックス *waxing n*
wāku auto ワークアウト*workout n*
ware yasui 割れやすい / waremono chūi」「割れ物注意」「*fragile adj*
watashi tachi (ni, o) 私達(に、を) *us pron*
watashi wa 私は *I pron*

Y

yaki (ni) sugita 焼き(煮)すぎた *overcooked adj*
yaku 焼く/yaki tsukeru 焼きつける *burn v*
koko de CD ni yakitsuke (kakikomi) deki masu ka. ここでCDに焼きつけ(書込み)できますか? *Can I burn a CD here?*
yakubutsu chiryō 薬物治療 *medication n*
yama 山 *mountain n*
tozan 登山 *mountain climbing*
yasai 野菜 *vegetable n*
yasui 安い *cheap adj*
yatoi nushi 雇い主 *employer n*
yawarakai 柔らかい *soft adj*
yoake 夜明け *dawn n*
yoake ni 夜明けに *at dawn*
yobidasu 呼び出す *page, to page (someone) v*
yobu 呼ぶ *(shout)* denwa o kakeru 電話をかける *(phone) call, to call v*
yobun no 余分の *extra (additional) adj*
yoi よい *good adj*
yōkoso ようこそ *welcome adv*
dō itashi mashite. どういたしまして。*You're welcome.*
yoku deiri suru よく出入りする *hang out (to relax) v*
yoku よく *well adv*
weru dan ウェル ダン *well done (meat)*
yoku yatta よくやった *well done (task)*
kibun ga yoku arimasen. 気分がよくありません。*I don't feel well.*
yokusō 浴槽 *bathtub n*
yomu 読む *read, to read v*
yon banme no 四番目の *fourth adj*
yon bun no ichi 四分の一 *one-fourth*
yonbun no ichi 四分の一 *quarter adj*
yon bun no ichi 四分の一 *one-quarter*
yonjū no 四十の *forty adj*
yori mo warui ～よりも悪い *～worse*
yori yoi より良い *better*
yorokobaseru 喜ばせる *please, to be pleasing to v*
yorokobi 喜び *pleasure n*
ureshii desu.嬉しいです。*It's a pleasure.*
yoru 夜 *night n*

yoru ni 夜に *at night*
ippaku atari 一泊当たり *per night*
yosan 予算 *budget n*
yottsu no 四つの *four adj*
yoyaku 予約 *appointment n*
yoyaku ga hitsuyō desu ka. 予約が必要ですか? *Do I need an appointment?*
yoyaku 予約 *reservation n*
____ no yoyaku o shitai no desuga. ____の予約をしたいのですが。*I'd like to make a reservation for ____.* See p7 for numbers.
yūbin de dasu 郵便で出す*mail v*
yūbin kyoku 郵便局 *post office n*
yūbin kyoku wa doko ni arimasu ka. 郵便局はどこにありますか? *Where is the post office?*
yūbin 郵便 / tegami 手紙 *mail n*
kōkūbin 航空便 *air mail*
kakitome 書留 *registered mail*
yudaya kyō no, yudaya jin no ユダヤ教の、ユダヤ人の *Jewish adj*
yūjin 友人 / tomodachi 友達 *friend n*
yūki no 有機の *organic adj*
yuki saki 行き先 *destination n*
yukkuri ゆっくり *slow(ly) adv*
motto yukkuri hanashite kudasai. もっとゆっくり話してください。*Speak more slowly.*
yurui ゆるい *loose adj*
yūsen hyōshiki 優先標識 *yield sign n*
yūshoku 夕食 *dinner n*

Z

zandaka 残高 *balance (on bank account) n*
zaseki 座席/seki 席 *seat n*
chairudo shiito チャイルドシート *child seat*
zasshi 雑誌 *magazine n*
zeikan 税関/kanzei関税 *customs n*
zeikin 税金 *tax n*
fuka kachi zei 付加価値税 *value-added tax (VAT)*
zenpō no 前方の *front adj*
furonto desuku フロント デスク *front desk*
furonto doa フロント ドア *front door*
zensoku 喘息 *asthma n*
zensoku ga arimasu. 喘息があります。/ zensoku o
zutsu 頭痛 *headache n*

JAPANESE—ENGLISH

NOTES

NOTES

NOTES

NOTES

NOTES

NOTES

NOTES